The College Panda
SAT Writing
Advanced Guide and Workbook
2nd Edition

ISBN: 978-0-9894964-9-0

For more information, visit thecollegepanda.com

Bulk order discounts available for teachers and companies. Please contact thecollegepanda@gmail.com for details.

To Oleg, Jimmy, and Azfar

Thank You!

Thank you for purchasing this book. If you enjoy it, I ask that you please leave a review on amazon. It really helps support my work.

If you haven't already, make sure to sign up for The College Panda newsletter at https://thecollegepanda.com

You'll also receive exclusive tips, updates, college admissions advice, inspirational stories, and resources that go far beyond the useless College Board information packets. This information is not found on the blog or anywhere else.

Don't miss out on tips that could make the difference on the SAT and in college admissions. Sign up now.

Table of Contents

Preparing for a Perfect Score

He who says he can and he who says he can't are both usually right. — Confucius

The SAT is just an exam. But because it can play such a big role in college admissions, a lot of parents and students worry. *What's the best way to prepare? How much should I do each week? Why am I not improving?*

Let's think back for a minute. You've taken plenty of exams already in high school. How did you pass all of them?

You studied.

Simple as that.

And if you did well, it means you studied the right things.

Your teacher told you what was going to be on the test and you reviewed and you practiced.

Well, despite all the concerns you might have, preparing for the SAT isn't that much different from taking a final at the end of the school semester.

Yes, the stakes are higher and the test is longer, but the way to success is the same. All your worries about study schedules and time limits are ones that you've already dealt with in school, and all the material you need to study is readily available. The College Board has released quite a few practice tests that will give you a good sense of not only the exam format but also the concepts that are tested. Resources like the book you are holding right now will walk you through every question type. Strategies and advice can be found on The College Panda blog and other online forums.

The concepts that are tested aren't anything new. You've been accumulating the knowledge needed to do well on the SAT throughout school, and while you may need to learn or relearn a few things, there won't be anything completely outside the scope of what you already know.

You just have to do your part—a lot of practice and a lot of review—and it will pay off.

For a complete understanding, this book is best read from beginning to end. That being said, each chapter was written to be independent of the others as much as possible. After all, you may already be proficient in some topics yet weak in others. If so, feel free to jump around, focusing on the chapters that are most relevant to your improvement.

Most chapters come with exercises. Do them. You won't master the material until you think through the questions yourself.

In addition to this book, which contains quite a bit of practice on its own, you should absolutely be doing the practice exams that The College Board has put out there. You can find all of them, along with answers and explanations, on The College Board's website.

The philosophy of this book is not to sell you a bag of tricks, but to actually teach you the concepts so that all the practice you do accelerates your understanding. It's my hope that after going through this book, you'll believe you can get a perfect score on the SAT.

IMPORTANT:

If you haven't already, make sure to sign up for The College Panda newsletter at https://thecollegepanda.com

You'll instantly gain access to a collection of all publicly released SAT past exams (the best preparation and practice).

You'll also receive exclusive tips, updates, college admissions advice, inspirational stories, and resources that go far beyond the useless College Board packets. This information is not found on the blog or anywhere else.

Don't miss out on tips that could make the difference on the SAT and in college admissions. Sign up now.

Test Breakdown & Test-taking Tips

The SAT Writing and Language section contains 44 questions to be completed in 35 minutes—that's about 48 seconds per question, a bit longer than the 36 seconds you would have on the corresponding ACT English section. Still, it's not a lot of time if you get bogged down on the tougher questions. Here's the recommended way to approach this section:

- Always take note of the title of each passage, which can help you make sense of the passage as well as main idea questions.

- Read the whole passage, skimming the areas with no questions and slowing down in the areas that do. Of course, pause to answer the questions as you go along. With practice, you'll find there is more than enough time to finish. If you find you're going too slow, start jumping from question to question without reading any parts of the passage in between.

- Because the SAT does not penalize you for wrong answers, NEVER leave any questions blank.

- When it comes to answering questions in context, make sure you read the sentences above and below the spot in question. For questions that ask you to place a sentence in the right place, you will need to revisit the entire paragraph. These are the questions you should bank up time for.

- Circle your answers in the test booklet first. Bubble them in later.

Constantly switching back and forth between the question and the answer sheet throws your mental concentration off balance. You lose momentum and focus. It's like trying to do homework while texting with a friend.

You want to transition to the next question without fumbling with papers on your tiny desk.

I recommend doing one passage at a time in your test booklet and then bubbling those answers in a batch (every ~11 questions). That way, you save time by focusing on one activity at a time. You're also less likely to bubble in the wrong answer because your concentration isn't diverted back and forth.

At the end, you'll have a record of your answers circled in your test booklet, which you can then go back to and cross check with your answer sheet if a discrepancy arises.

Furthermore, some perfectionist students are obsessive about how they fill in the answer bubble. They needlessly waste time darkening the bubble more than they need to and erasing stray marks. You might be one of them. By bubbling in many answers at once, you're at least keeping that OCD behavior to a minimum.

Here are the topics that are tested, ranked by the number of questions that test them:

Topic	# of Questions
Relevance & Purpose	4–10
Topic, Conclusion, & Transition Sentences	4–8
Word Choice	3–7
Commas, Dashes & Colons	4–9
Redundancy	2–4
Run-ons	2–3
Pronoun Reference	2–3
Placement	1–3
Combining Sentences	2
Transitions	1–5
Subject Verb Agreement	1–3
Awkward Phrasing	1–3
Apostrophes	1–2
Data Interpretation	1–3
Parallelism	1–3
Supporting Evidence & Examples	0–2
Tenses	0–2
Sentence Fragments	0–2
Idioms	0–2
Modifiers	0–2
Odds and Ends	0–2
Singular Plural Noun Inconsistency	0–1
Who vs. Whom	0–1

The topics in the table correspond to the chapters in this book. Some topics have been grouped together because they are commonly tested within the same question. If you're simply reviewing or you just picked up this book and don't have a lot of time, feel free to start with the most commonly tested topics. Otherwise, I recommend going through this book in order, as some topics will help you understand certain ones covered later.

Given the exam's relative ease and the curves that have been released so far, it's highly likely you will need to get every question correct to score the maximum scaled score of 800. Past curves and a Score Calculator can be found at thecollegepanda.com.

3
Relative Clauses

Many chapters in this book redefine or reexplain previous grammar terms so that those jumping from chapter to chapter still get a good sense of what's going on. But to get the full value out of this book, it's best that we learn a few basic things about sentences and their structures before moving on. We start by learning to identify the nonessential parts of a sentence, the ones that aren't needed for a sentence to be complete.

Take the following sentence:

The tiger ate my aunt earlier today.

Let's add something:

The tiger that was hungry ate my aunt earlier today.

By adding the underlined phrase to the sentence, we've described the tiger in more detail. These phrases are called **relative clauses** because they start with a relative pronoun—*who, whom, whose, which,* or *that.* While some relative clauses can be essential to the meaning of a sentence, they are never essential to the sentence being a complete sentence. In other words, they aren't important grammatically even though the resulting sentence can sound awkward when they are removed.

Let's add some more phrases:

After escaping, the tiger that was hungry ate my aunt, who was nice and juicy, earlier today.

Now these additional phrases are called **comma phrases** because they're set off by a pair of commas. Note that the second underlined phrase is also a relative clause. Some relative clauses require commas and some don't—we'll delve into those rules in a future chapter. Either way, comma phrases and relative clauses are not essential to the sentences they're in.

A crucial part of doing well on the SAT Writing section is knowing how to strip away all these secondary phrases to get back to the essence of the sentence:

The tiger ate my aunt earlier today.

None of the underlined phrases we added above can stand alone as complete sentences themselves. Yes, they add valuable details, but at the end of the day, what's left is the sentence that CAN stand alone by itself, the main idea. To trick you, the SAT will constantly throw long boring phrases at you left and right like a boxer jabbing at you with one hand to disguise the big punch he's planning with the other. Don't be fooled. Learn to strip away the unnecessary phrases and you'll get through questions more quickly and accurately. In future chapters, you'll learn to deconstruct other parts of sentences and develop a way of reading them that will help you get directly to the answer.

Exercise: Cross out all the comma phrases and relative clauses. What's left should still be a grammatically complete sentence (subject and a verb), even though the meaning may come off as incomplete. The first one is done for you. Answers for this chapter start on page 212.

1. ~~Although it may better mankind,~~ some critics of animal testing, ~~which is sometimes harmful to the animals,~~ claim it is cruel and inhumane.

2. After running the Boston marathon, Jack Kunis drank all the water that was left in his bottle and fell to his knees.

3. The lost ship and its treasure that had fallen to the bottom of the ocean were never found again.

4. Frank, in addition to his cousins, suffers from a condition known as hyperthymestic syndrome, which prevents one from ever forgetting anything.

5. Starting at the age of 10, Mrs. Smith kept a daily diary, which allowed her to recall the happy memories in life.

6. For years the chairman remained anonymous, referred to only by initials even within his inner circles.

7. Students whose grades are low will have to report to me, the principal of the school.

8. Every detail about every day since 1976, ranging from the time she got up to what she ate, has forever ingrained itself into her mind.

9. Ever since it allowed internet games, which were previously blocked, the library has been the place everybody wants to be nowadays.

10. With such sadness occupying her thoughts, Erika, a poor single mother of two, struggles to sleep at night, even when the babies themselves are fast asleep.

11. Farmers who want a good yield should use fertilizers that enrich the soil with nutrients.

12. Having worked so hard with blood, sweat, and tears, I long for the day I can finally say the SATs are over.

13. Culture shock, in some cases, can be severe enough to trigger mental breakdowns.

14. Mastery of martial arts requires a dedication that many do not have.

15. Mrs. Daughtry, a 74-year old married housewife recently discharged from a local hospital after her first psychiatric admission, came to our facility for a second opinion, one that she hoped would be different.

Prepositional Phrases

Most prepositions are direction/position words. Here's a list of common prepositions:

aboard	about	above	across	after	against	along	amid	among	around
as to	**at**	before	behind	below	beneath	beside	between	beyond	**by**
circa	despite	down	due to	during	except	**for**	**from**	**in**	**into**
like	near	**of**	off	**on**	onto	out	over	past	since
through	**to**	toward	under	until	up	upon	**with**	within	without

Now do you have to memorize these? Certainly not. Just familiarize yourself, especially with the bolded ones. Some words are prepositions in some cases and something else in others. Just remember that a preposition almost always has a noun following it. Take a look at these two sentences:

1. <u>Throughout the living room</u> was the scent <u>of fatty crabs that had expired weeks ago</u>.

2. I put my sister <u>on the diet</u> after it worked so well <u>for me</u>.

The preposition + noun combinations are underlined. These preposition and noun combinations are called **prepositional phrases**.

Prepositional Phrase	=	Preposition	+	Noun	+	Any Attached Describing Phrase
	=	*of*	+	*fatty crabs*	+	*that had expired weeks ago*

If you think a word is a preposition and there's a noun following it, chances are it's a preposition. Even if it's not, don't worry about being 100% on which words are prepositions; the SAT doesn't test you on them directly. For example, *after it* is not a prepositional phrase in the second sentence because it's part of a larger phrase—*after it worked so well*. If the sentence were *After school, I put my sister on a diet*, then *After* would act as a preposition. But again, as long as you get the general idea, you'll be fine. This just helps you later when you learn about subject verb agreement.

Here's the most important takeaway: prepositional phrases are **not essential** to the sentence they're in. While they may supply important details, sentences can stand alone grammatically without them (there will still be a subject and a verb).

Exercise: Cross out all prepositional phrases in the following sentences. Answers for this chapter start on page 213.

1. Hillary got into the boat for the short trip to Haiti.

2. If you do business with me, you'll never get the better end of the deal.

3. We'll need to see the receipts for the underwear you bought on Monday.

4. I drove by my house to check if the package from Amazon had arrived.

5. The eleven robbers broke into the casino vault with their perfectly executed plan.

6. Since the hypothesis of string theory, scientists have been back at the drawing board.

7. Everything that man creates carries within it the seeds of its own destruction.

8. Kelvin snuck out the door during the school assembly.

9. Within seconds of hearing about the trip to Antarctica, Charlotte packed shorts and sunglasses.

10. We found Teddy in a broken elevator at a rundown hotel in Thailand.

5
Idioms

Idioms are phrases that are correct just because that's the way we say them. On the SAT, idiom errors come in the form of an incorrect preposition.

Example 1

Wrong:	He is regarded **to be** an awesome speaker.
Correct:	He is regarded **as** an awesome speaker.

Example 2

Wrong:	That painting is similar **with** the red one.
Correct:	That painting is similar **to** the red one.

Example 3

Wrong:	She is suspicious **towards** me.
Correct:	She is suspicious **of** me.

Example 4

Wrong:	I have an interest **to** fishing.
Correct:	I have an interest **in** fishing.

Example 5

| Wrong: | The winner was awarded **of** a gold medal. |
| Correct: | The winner was awarded ~~of~~ a gold medal. |

Example 6

| Wrong: | The company was accused **to donate** millions of dollars to the President's campaign. |
| Correct: | The company was accused **of donating** millions of dollars to the President's campaign. |

There's no rhyme or reason behind these phrases and the right preposition can depend on the meaning of the sentence. Some are downright obvious because they sound so unnatural but some can be tough to spot, especially if you haven't encountered the idiom before. Practice will expose you to the most common ones, but sometimes, you'll have no choice but to rely on your instincts. Fortunately, the new SAT won't go out of its way to test you on obscure idioms.

Exercise 1: Correct the idiom errors below. Answers for this chapter start on page 213.

1. I don't care about your opinion ~~towards~~ *of* me.

2. Your ability ~~in getting~~ *to get* the perfect cards has caught the attention of casino surveillance.

3. The Olympic athlete was capable ~~in~~ *of* climbing Mt. Everest.

4. The public was opposed ~~against~~ *to* the war.

5. The children were prohibited ~~against~~ *from* playing outside at dark.

6. Unless you comply ~~to~~ *with* those food safety standards, we will shut you down.

7. Those who don't abide ~~with~~ *by* the rules are often the ones who successfully innovate.

8. China is becoming an economic hegemony ~~against~~ *over* foreign rivals who dare to compete.

9. By taking good care of pandas, zoos have succeeded ~~to save~~ *in saving* pandas from extinction.

10. I hope you are aware ~~about~~ *of* the raccoons that are mating in your basement.

11. She has lived ~~in~~ *on* Broome street for over fifty years.

12. She managed to get a position ~~in~~ *as* the director of the engineering department.

13. He was inclined ~~in accepting~~ *to accept* the new job offer, but wanted to wait.

14. The young graduate yearned ~~towards~~ *for* the days when he didn't have to worry about the bills.

15. Because she had many toxic relationships, Jane became accustomed ~~with~~ *to* yelling her way through arguments.

Exercise 2: Answers for this chapter start on page 213.

1. When I first started running as a child, I never thought that I'd ever get the chance <u>to be representative of</u> my local club at the Sydney regional finals.

   A) NO CHANGE
   B) in representing
   C) in representation of
   D) to represent

2. Unfortunately, injury has kept me bed-ridden <u>for</u> the rest of the season.

   A) NO CHANGE
   B) in
   C) at
   D) with

3. So I kept <u>towards</u> working at it, and ran the best times I had in years.

   A) NO CHANGE
   B) with
   C) on
   D) about

4. The weather took a turn for the worse, but as we made the first part of the ascent, hope <u>in success</u> was still strong.

   A) NO CHANGE
   B) of success
   C) to succeed
   D) to succeeding

5. Wearable technologies will make a huge impact <u>towards</u> the global smartphone marketplace in the coming years.

   A) NO CHANGE
   B) at
   C) on
   D) against

6. Dubai is home to one of the world's tallest buildings, which attracts its fair share <u>for</u> adrenaline junkie base-jumpers.

   A) NO CHANGE
   B) in
   C) with
   D) of

7. Spot welding relies <u>on</u> the heat caused by electrical resistance to fuse metal pieces together.

   A) NO CHANGE
   B) against
   C) by
   D) in

8. Spot welding is preferred <u>against</u> friction welding when fixing broken pipes.

    A) NO CHANGE
    B) over
    C) to
    D) more than

9. We more often observe loose allegiances between smaller gangs, <u>consisting in</u> various nationalities and ethnicities.

    A) NO CHANGE
    B) made up of
    C) made up in
    D) making up of

10. The President praised the initiative <u>in raising</u> funds from sources other than government grants.

    A) NO CHANGE
    B) for raising
    C) to raise
    D) on the raise of

11. To the avant-garde, innovation is a necessary component <u>about</u> greatness.

    A) NO CHANGE
    B) with
    C) of
    D) to

12. After speaking with our lawyers, we successfully petitioned <u>with</u> the patent office.

    A) NO CHANGE
    B) to
    C) towards
    D) OMIT the underlined portion.

13. Magnetic inductors are more efficient than wind power <u>by</u> a watt-by-watt basis.

    A) NO CHANGE
    B) on
    C) regarding
    D) as

14. The Mongols and the Chinese both tried to conquer Vietnam at various points <u>on</u> the second millennium.

    A) NO CHANGE
    B) upon
    C) in
    D) from

15. Irish dancing can trace its origins back to the time of the Druids, when it was believed that ritual processions should take place <u>in honoring</u> the sun spirit.

    A) NO CHANGE
    B) to honor
    C) of honoring
    D) for the honoring of

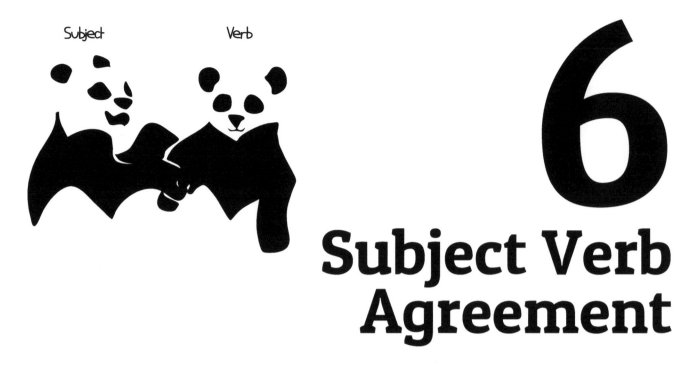

6
Subject Verb Agreement

You know how you have to conjugate the verb to match the subject in foreign languages? We have the same thing in English, and it can get tricky even though the simple cases seem so natural and obvious to us:

Example 1

Wrong:	You **is** smart.
Correct:	You **are** smart.

Example 2

Wrong:	Everyday the alarm clock goes off and we **wakes** up to confront our lives.
Correct:	Everyday the alarm clock goes off and we **wake** up to confront our lives.

The subject is a noun (person, place, or thing) that is the "doer" or "main feature" in the sentence. A verb is an action word. Think about the simple sentences above and how awkward it would be to have verbs that don't agree with the subject. You don't even have to know what the subject and verb of each sentence is to know that it's awkward. Now the SAT won't make it that easy on you; they'll intentionally try to trick your ear. Let's do an example:

> Investigations into the scandal (*shows/show*) a lot more than we want to know.

To pick the right verb, we must first find the subject. Let's start by applying what we learned in a previous chapter and cross out the prepositional phrases:

> Investigations ~~into the scandal~~ (*shows/show*) a lot more than we want to know.

What's left is the subject—investigations! Now the second step is to ask yourself whether *investigations* is singular or plural. Well, it's plural because of the *s*, meaning there's more than one. Therefore, we need the plural verb *show*. And that's the whole process! Cross out the prepositional phrases and you'll be able to pick the subject from the nouns that are left. It's usually the remaining noun closest to the verb.

If you're ever unsure of whether a verb such as *show* is singular or plural, test it by putting *he* and *they* in front and then asking yourself which sounds more correct:

He show... OR *They show...*

Hopefully, *They show...* sounds more correct to you, which means *show* is the plural form (since *they* is obviously plural).

Let's try some more difficult ones. Note that in the following example, we can cross out both a prepositional phrase and a comma phrase.

Example 3

Question:	Films by Miyazaki and Itami, including Miyazaki's *Spirited Away*, (*excites/excite*) the imagination.
Step 1:	Cross out the prepositional phrases/comma phrases/relative clauses: Films ~~by Miyazaki and Itami, including Miyazaki's *Spirited Away*~~, (*excites/excite*) the imagination.
Step 2:	What is the subject? *Films*
Step 3:	Is *Films* singular or plural? Plural.
Answer:	Films by Miyazaki and Itami, including Miyazaki's *Spirited Away*, **excite** the imagination.

Example 4

Question:	Her jewelry, in addition to her pokemon cards, (*was/were*) stolen by the robber.
Step 1:	Cross out the prepositional phrases/comma phrases/relative clauses: Her jewelry, ~~in addition to her pokemon cards~~, (*was/were*) stolen ~~by the robber~~.
Step 2:	What is the subject? *Her jewelry*
Step 3:	Is *Her jewelry* singular or plural? Singular.
Answer:	Her jewelry, in addition to her pokemon cards, **was** stolen by the robber.

You might think that the verb should be plural because the sentence mentions both jewelry and cards, but because of the comma phrase, the subject is just the jewelry.

Example 5

Question:	Beside the bins, where one could smell the stench of rotten eggs, (*was/were*) a pack of philosophy majors gathering cans for recycling.
Step 1:	Cross out the prepositional phrases/comma phrases/relative clauses: ~~Beside the bins, where one could smell the stench of rotten eggs~~, (*was/were*) a pack ~~of philosophy majors gathering cans for recycling~~.
Step 2:	What is the subject? *a pack*
Step 3:	Is *a pack* singular or plural? Singular.
Answer:	Beside the bins, where one could smell the stench of rotten eggs, **was** a pack of philosophy majors gathering cans for recycling.

Again, make sure you can identify that *was* is singular whereas *were* is plural. Everyone uses the correct form in simple conversation, but some students have trouble identifying the correct form in a grammar test setting.

Example 6

Question:	Inside heaven's kingdom (*rests/rest*) Charlie and his angels.
Step 1:	Cross out the prepositional phrases/comma phrases/relative clauses: ~~Inside heaven's kingdom~~ (*rests/rest*) Charlie and his angels.
Step 2:	What is the subject? *Charlie and his angels*
Step 3:	Is *Charlie and his angels* singular or plural? Plural.
Answer:	Inside heaven's kingdom **rest** Charlie and his angels.

Example 7

Question:	There (*is/are*) many other examples to support my point.
Step 1:	Cross out the prepositional phrases/comma phrases/relative clauses: There aren't any to cross out. Note that *to support* is not a prepositional phrase because it doesn't end in a noun. It's an infinitive.
Step 2:	What is the subject? *many other examples*
Step 3:	Is *many other examples* singular or plural? Plural.
Answer:	There **are** many other examples to support my point.

These last three examples show that the subject can appear after the verb, something the SAT loves to do to trip students up.

Another question variation you'll come across deals with helping verbs, which are necessary to form certain tenses. Examples of helping verbs are bolded below:

has seen
was forgotten
is watching
have been

When you see these verb forms, it is the helping verb that must agree with the subject.

Example 8

Question:	The few ideas that I've come up with last night (*has/have*) given my team enough to work with.
Step 1:	Cross out the prepositional phrases/comma phrases/relative clauses: The few ideas ~~that I've come up with last night~~ (*has/have*) given my team enough to work with.
Step 2:	What is the subject? *The few ideas*
Step 3:	Is *The few ideas* singular or plural? Plural.
Correct:	The few ideas that I've come up with last night **have** given my team enough to work with.

Example 9

Question:	The forks and knives are in the kitchen, and the jar with the thai peanut sauce (*has/have*) been sitting in the refrigerator.
Step 1:	Cross out the prepositional phrases/comma phrases/relative clauses: The forks and knives are in the kitchen, and the jar ~~with the thai peanut sauce~~ (*has/have*) been sitting in the refrigerator.
Step 2:	What is the subject? *the jar*
Step 3:	Is *the jar* singular or plural? Singular.
Answer:	The forks and knives are in the kitchen, and the jar with the thai peanut sauce **has** been sitting in the refrigerator.

Example 10

Question:	The players on our all-star tennis team (*is/are*) taken on luxury cruises every year.
Step 1:	Cross out the prepositional phrases/comma phrases/relative clauses: The players ~~on our all-star tennis team~~ (*is/are*) taken on luxury cruises every year.
Step 2:	What is the subject? *The players*
Step 3:	Is *The players* singular or plural? Plural.
Answer:	The players on our all-star tennis team **are** taken on luxury cruises every year.

Another question variation you might see is one in which the verb is in a phrase or clause you would normally cross out. For example,

I visited my aunt, who (is/are) a panda caretaker, earlier today.

Note that the underlined portion is a comma phrase. To find the subject if the verb is located in a phrase or clause like the one above, just ask yourself what it's describing. In this case, the phrase is obviously describing *my aunt*, which is singular. Therefore, we need the singular verb *is*.

I visited my aunt, who is a panda caretaker, earlier today.

Example 11

Question:	Where are the cookies that (*was/were*) in the cookie jar?
Answer:	Where are the cookies that **were** in the cookie jar?

In Example 11, we have a relative clause that describes *cookies*, which is plural.

Example 12

Question:	I have no interest in luxury products, which (*caters/cater*) only to the wealthy.
Answer:	I have no interest in luxury products, which **cater** only to the wealthy.

Now let's walk through a really tricky example that combines everything we've learned so far in this chapter:

> Mastery of magic tricks that truly (*surprises/surprise*) the audience (*requires/require*) lots of time.

Here, we have to figure out the subjects for two verbs. Cross out the prepositional phrases and relative clause:

> Mastery ~~of magic tricks that truly (*surprises/surprise*) the audience~~ (*requires/require*) lots ~~of time.~~

Now it's easy to see that *mastery* is the main subject of the sentence. *Mastery* is singular so we need the singular verb *requires*. After all, it's the *mastery* that *requires* a lot of time. But let's get back to the first verb, which is crossed out within the relative clause, and ask ourselves what that relative clause is describing. What is truly surprising the audience? Magic tricks! *Magic tricks* is plural so we need the plural verb *surprise*.

> Mastery of magic tricks that truly **surprise** the audience **requires** lots of time.

Now, a few more rules you should know:

Example 13

Question:	*The Simpsons* (*is/are*) the longest running American sitcom.
Answer:	*The Simpsons* **is** the longest running American sitcom.
Rule:	Names of books, TV shows, bands, and movies are all singular.

Example 14

Question:	Charles and Kate (*was/were*) at the ball last night.
Answer:	Charles and Kate **were** at the ball last night.
Rule:	Subjects joined by *and* are always plural.

Example 15

Question:	Everybody (*loves/love*) Raymond.
Answer:	Everybody **loves** Raymond.
Rule:	*Everybody, everything, every, anybody, anyone, no one* are all singular subjects.

Example 16

Questions:	Each of the candidates (*has/have*) two minutes to respond. Neither of the candidates (*wants/want*) to respond.
Answers:	Each of the candidates **has** two minutes to respond. Neither of the candidates **wants** to respond.
Rule:	*Each, neither,* and *either* are all singular subjects.

Before we go to the exercises, you probably have quite a few grammar rules swirling around in your head. Let's go over a few common errors that students make when they start thinking about subjects and verbs. Take a look at the following sentence:

He likes to sway to R&B music instead of rocking to AC/DC.

On the SAT, you must be able to identify which words are verbs before you can check for their subjects. Some students mistakenly think that *to sway* and *rocking* are verbs in that sentence. However, *to sway* is called an **infinitive** (*to be, to hate, to run,...*) and *rocking* is called a **gerund** (*running, cooking, exploding,...*). You've probably heard of infinitives in French or Spanish class, where it's the root form of a verb before you conjugate it. It's the same in English. Infinitives and gerunds are **not verbs so there's no need to check for subject-verb agreement**. The only actual verb in this example is *likes*. Again, gerunds and infinitives are **never verbs**. Don't waste time checking for their subjects.

Lastly, the SAT loves to throw in more than one verb in the same sentence. That way, one of the verbs can be buried deeper into the sentence to fool your ear. In these questions, split the sentence into two and make sure both verbs agree.

Example 17

Wrong:	John and Harry studied computer science and was recruited by Google to develop new services.
Sentence 1:	John and Harry studied computer science. *Correct.*
Sentence 2:	John and Harry was recruited by Google to develop new services. *Wrong.*
Correct:	John and Harry studied computer science and **were** recruited by Google to develop new services.

Example 18

Wrong:	Poisonous traps that attracts and then kills off rats are spread throughout this office.
Sentence 1:	Poisonous traps that attracts rats are spread throughout this office. *Wrong.*
Sentence 2:	Poisonous traps that then kills off rats are spread throughout this office. *Wrong.*
Correct:	Poisonous traps that **attract** and then **kill** off rats are spread throughout this office.

Example 19

Wrong:	I was walking down the street and were chatting with my friend about his day.
Sentence 1:	I was walking down the street. *Correct.*
Sentence 2:	I were chatting with my friend about his day. *Wrong.*
Correct:	I was walking down the street and **(was)** chatting with my friend about his day.

In Example 19, the second *was* is unnecessary because the first *was* serves as a helping verb for both *walking* and *chatting*. If we stripped out all the details of the sentence, it would read, *I was walking and chatting...*, which is a grammatically fine sentence.

Exercise 1: As a basic warm-up, fill in the right singular and plural verb forms for each of the following verbs. Answers for this chapter start on page 214.

		To Be	To Go	To Have	To Win	To Kiss
Present Tense	He					
	They					
Past Tense	He					
	They					

Exercise 2: Choose the correct verb. Answers for this chapter start on page 214.

1. Participants in the charity organization (*was*/*were*) angry when no one donated.

2. The habit of hugging your pillow while sleeping (*indicates*/*indicate*) that you miss someone.

3. Elderly criminals in Florida sometimes (*leads*/*lead*) the police on chases at speeds of 10 to 15 mph.

4. Bonnie and her boyfriend Clyde (*likes*/*like*) to jump into ponds to avoid the cops, often forgetting that they can't swim.

5. Every Bentley, Lamborghini, and Porsche (*is*/*are*) owned by Volkswagen.

6. Propaganda that's played off as the truth (*has*/*have*) been used throughout history to persuade the masses.

7. Forcing yourself to forget the pain someone else has caused you only (*hurts*/*hurt*) you more.

8. One of the skills I would like to learn (*is*/*are*) the ability to talk while inhaling through the nose.

9. Some of the superpowers I dream of having (*includes*/*include*) summoning jack o' lanterns on people's lawns during Halloween and making people burst into the Gangnam style dance.

10. Each iPhone 5 (*costs*/*cost*) Apple $168 and (*costs*/*cost*) us $699.

11. Each of the three little pigs (*was*/*were*) afraid of the big bad wolf.

12. According to the phonebook, the number of Americans named Herp Derp (*is*/*are*) four.

13. A good cook rinses the dishes and (*repeats*/*repeat*) the same recipes to perfection.

14. Please let me know if the group (*stumbles*/*stumble*) upon or (*manages*/*manage*) to find the train station.

15. A number of people (*has*/*have*) hyperthymesia, a condition that (*allows*/*allow*) them to remember every detail of their lives.

16. There (*was*/*were*) an awkward silence when Mike's date told him she was actually a man.

17. A flock of birds and a bear (*has*/*have*) been captured in the field.

18. There (*is*/*are*) three types of people in this world: those who can count and those who can't.

19. There (*is*/*are*) stashed below the frigid depths of the arctic a magnificent treasure that no one has ever been able to recover.

20. There (*is*/*are*) in the works of Emerson an underlying tone of quiet appreciation.

21. *Snow White and the Seven Dwarves* (*was*/*were*) purportedly based on cocaine; the seven dwarves were each side effects of the drug.

22. Harry, along with Ron and Hermione, (*attends*/*attend*) Hogwarts School of Wizardry.

23. Frodo, as well as Merry and Pippin, (*fights*/*fight*) to protect the one ring of power.

24. This picture book on the art of nudity in the modern age (*is*/*are*) a thought-provoking read.

25. The extent of our universe and those beyond constantly (*amazes*/*amaze*) me.

26. We found out that his mother, as well as his friends, (*was*/*were*) covering for Mike's crime.

27. Aliens from another planet (*has*/*have*) come here to kill us all.

28. The pigs you will be dissecting in this class (*is*/*are*) available as take-home dinners afterwards.

29. Human brain cells, the universe, and the internet all (*has*/*have*) similar structures.

30. Each team made up of one girl and one boy (*has*/*have*) to reenact a scene from Romeo and Juliet.

31. Speaking more than one language (*makes*/*make*) the brain more flexible and agile.

32. Getting to stuff my face silly with delicious food (*is*/*are*) the best part of being an obese food critic.

33. When (*was*/*were*) the cowboy and the Indians last here?

34. The class bully laughs at and then (*interferes*/*interfere*) with those trying to get work done.

35. Brendan and Brianna are out of money and (*has*/*have*) used up all possible guesses.

36. Paris and Nicole grew up rich and (*was*/*were*) sheltered all throughout life.

37. What (*does*/*do*) that fact have to do with anything we just talked about?

38. He sets his alarm but, when the morning comes, (*fails*/*fail*) to wake up.

39. Marcie and Michael exercise everyday and, in doing so, (*improves*/*improve*) their stamina.

40. Alice, in addition to a scarecrow, a tin man, and a lion, (*tries*/*try*) to find the Wizard of Oz.

41. A jar of hearts (*is*/*are*) on the counter.

42. Several trucks and an oil tanker near the highway exit (*was*/*were*) flipped on their sides.

43. Dreams within a dream that (*is*/*are*) spliced and diced up inside another dream (*confuses*/*confuse*) me.

44. A herd of cows and a slow moving tortoise (*is/are*) relaxing at the beach.

45. The lines for the elevator that normally (*carries/carry*) just five passengers (*was/were*) reinstated because the crowd of fat commuters (*was/were*) too heavy for it.

46. The diner near the dorms which (*houses/house*) the students (*serves/serve*) breakfast all day.

47. The widely recognized red coloring of stop signs everywhere (*alerts/alert*) people to stop.

Exercise 3: Answers for this chapter start on page 214.

The Writer's Life

On every author's bookshelf **1** (*is/are*) dusty and worn out reference books. In every desk drawer **2** (*sits/sit*) a stack of papers waiting to be edited. A wide variety of pens, most of which are blue, red, or black, **3** (*is/are*) scattered across the desk. The life of a writer is a lonely yet hectic existence.

The act of putting words on paper and editing them **4** (*is/are*) mentally draining. The notion that because words come naturally to us when we're speaking, they should also come easily when we're writing, **5** (*misrepresents/misrepresent*) the struggles that every author faces. Putting words together in a logical and coherent way is different from having a conversation, which has the benefit of context. If the reader does not understand something, the author does not have the luxury of explaining it another way.

In addition, writers do more than just write. Research and investigation into their subject matter **6** (*plays/play*) a crucial role in good writing. After all, perfect grammar and well-crafted sentences about a vague topic written off the top of one's head **7** (*does/do*) not make for a good read. Relevant books must be read and interviews must be conducted before an author feels informed enough to write something substantial.

Most writers learn their craft in school. A strong liberal arts education that **8** (*encompasses/encompass*) grammar, style, structure, and prose **9** (*fosters/foster*) great writing. Upon graduation, writers must develop and apply all those skills to the research, writing, and editing phases of any given project. Draft after draft, they have to rework and tweak what they've already done. This dedication to the craft and attention to detail that **10** (*rivals/rival*) that of a surgeon **11** (*requires/require*) discipline and work ethic. Authors such as James Joyce **12** (*has equated/have equated*) writing to torture. Only when all the pages in the book are written **13** (*does/do*) writers feel the true joy of writing.

Nevertheless, because many people think that writing is subjective and that there **14** (*is/are*) no right or wrong answers, the belief that writers have it easy, as well as all its underlying misconceptions, **15** (*persists/persist*).

Modifiers

Try to recognize what's funny about this sentence:

> After being beaten and deflated, the baker shaped and seasoned the dough.

The sentence is ridiculous because of the comma phrase at the start—it seems like the baker is being beaten before he goes off to work on the dough. *After being beaten and deflated* is called a **modifier** because it modifies or describes someone or something in the same sentence. Here, the modifier is misplaced. Instead, it should go right next to the thing it's supposed to modify:

> After being beaten and deflated, the dough was shaped and seasoned by the baker.

A modifier is like a describing phrase. How do you know if a phrase is a modifier? Usually it comes at the beginning of the sentence and is separated off by a comma (but not always). If all you read was *After being beaten and deflated*, your natural thought would be, "*Who or What is being beaten?*" Having that thought is how you know you're dealing with a modifier. Without the rest of the sentence, it leaves you wondering what's being talked about. When correcting sentences that have this error, you want to make sure there is a sensible noun that is right next to the modifier.

Let's do a couple examples so you can see how modifiers are tested.

Example 1

Wrong:	I bought a house from the local bakery made of gingerbread.
Correct:	I bought a house made of gingerbread from the local bakery.

Modifiers don't necessarily have to be at the start of the sentence. Here, *made of gingerbread* should be placed next to the *house* it's describing. Otherwise, it seems like the local bakery is the thing that's made of gingerbread.

Example 2

Wrong:	Watching the end of the world, our lives flashed before our eyes.
Correct:	While we were watching the end of the world, our lives flashed before our eyes.

In this example, the sentence makes no sense because *our lives* don't have eyes to watch the end of the world with. The modifier *Watching the end of the world* needs to modify *we* even though that word's not even in the sentence. Therefore, the correct version puts in the subject *we* and re-words the sentence.

The phrase *While we were watching the end of the world* is an example of a **dependent clause**, which contains a subject and a verb but can't stand alone as its own complete sentence. Dependent clauses are NOT modifiers. Note the difference between the wrong and correct versions. The wrong version uses a modifier whereas the correct version uses a dependent clause. Dependent clauses don't leave us wondering *who* or *what* like a modifier does. Reading just the first part of the correct version, we already know the subject is *we*. With dependent clauses, we don't have to worry about modifier errors, because again, they aren't modifiers.

Rule

Keep modifiers right next to the thing they're supposed to describe.

Example 3

Wrong:	Running fiercely to the bathroom, John's pants dropped.
Correct:	Running fiercely to the bathroom, John dropped his pants.

Understanding this example is SUPER IMPORTANT. On rare occasions, the SAT will try to trick you by putting the modifier *Running fiercely to the bathroom* right next to *John*. But here, it's not *John* but *John's pants* that's actually being modified. And of course, pants can't by themselves run to the bathroom. So be extremely careful when there's an apostrophe *s*.

Example 4

Wrong:	Spotted dealing cocaine, the police arrested the drug dealers.
Correct:	The police arrested the drug dealers, who were spotted dealing cocaine.

Example 5

Wrong:	Though cooked and seasoned to perfection, the taste of ketchup-covered octopus was revolting.
Correct:	Though cooked and seasoned to perfection, the ketchup-covered octopus had a revolting taste.
Correct:	The taste of ketchup-covered octopus, though cooked and seasoned to perfection, was revolting.

In this case, the modifier should modify the food itself, not the *taste* of it.

Note

English is a weird language. Don't be confused by constructions like the one below:

The magician walked across the stage, dazzling the crowd with card tricks.

This sentence is grammatically correct and does not contain a modifier error—it's understood that *dazzling the crowd with card tricks* applies to the subject, *the magician*, even though it's placed next to *the stage*. Modifier errors will typically occur when the describing phrase is at the start of the sentence, as in the examples above, so don't overanalyze these types of sentences. Note that the comma is important; without it, there WOULD be a modifier error.

Exercise 1: After seeing enough of these, you should be able to instinctively spot the ridiculousness (is that a word?) of sentences that have this error. There can be multiple ways of correcting them. By correcting these on your own, you'll learn to think for yourself and more quickly identify the correct answers on the SAT, rather than relying on the answer choices to "think" for you. Answers for this chapter start on page 217.

1. Hunting for deer, Julian's rifle misfired and burst into flames.

2. Having finished the SAT, the rest of life was easy.

3. Having had no water for five days, the steak and cheese sandwich was squeezed for the grease that we could drink.

4. Active in community service and local affairs, Obama's passion for politics is what would eventually lead him to the presidency.

5. By blasting music at home, the neighbors will start to acquire your musical taste.

6. By majoring in basket weaving, a lifetime of regret and despair awaits.

7. After catching a cold, my lung surgery was the perfect cure.

8. While on air at the radio station, the microphone of the talk show host exploded.

9. As a young child growing up in Massachusetts, Mitt's father gave him airplanes as gifts.

10. Hidden far from sunlight in the caves of Mars, scientists have uncovered an E.T. colony.

11. Chris saw the march of marines looking outside the window as crowds cheered on either side.

12. Overcooked and over-seasoned, Gordon Ramsay swore at the cook and dumped the fish into the garbage.

13. Dressed in a cute outfit and filled with cotton, Tiffany loved the soft feel of her teddy bear.

14. The magician dazzled and surprised the audience members wearing a cloak and top hat.

15. Decorated with colorful ornaments and stars, we took pictures by the Christmas tree.

16. After missing an easy goal, the crowd booed the soccer player.

17. Having forgotten about the homework assignment, his comments on the book in class were general statements that could apply to any book.

18. To get the best view of the movie, our seats were reserved in the front and center.

19. Prancing joyously from field to field, the scientist followed the deer.

20. Though skinny and awkward from the outset, Conan's sense of humor made him a television success.

21. Climbing from tree to tree, the explorers avidly watched the red pandas.

Exercise 2: Answers for this chapter start on page 217.

Tennis

Since the age of 10, [1] tennis has been my daughter Cayla's fascination. [2] Having watched them play live, Venus and Serena Williams became her idols and she tries to imitate their aggressive play style. [3] When other six year olds were watching cartoons, Cayla would be watching tennis. So, as encouraging parents, [4] lessons were the next step. At the ages of ten and eleven, the Williams sisters were enrolled at the Academy of Rick Macci to improve their game, so getting Cayla started with the game early seemed like a good idea.

1

A) NO CHANGE
B) tennis has been the fascination of my daughter Cayla.
C) my daughter Cayla has been fascinated with tennis.
D) my daughter Cayla's fascination has been tennis.

2

A) NO CHANGE
B) After Cayla watched them play live,
C) After watching live,
D) Watching them play live,

3

A) NO CHANGE
B) Having watched cartoons,
C) When watching cartoons,
D) Cartoons being watched by other six year olds,

4

A) NO CHANGE
B) lessons had to be
C) Cayla's lessons were
D) we decided lessons were

A simple sport, **5** the rules of tennis have not changed since 1890. The main idea is to hit the ball inside the opponent's side of the court with a racquet. Made and shaped from wood, **6** players found the first racquets difficult to play with, but by improving the underlying technology, **7** today's racquets are more powerful than ever before. Hitting the ball, **8** a player's grip must remain firm and balanced.

5

A) NO CHANGE
B) tennis has not had its rules changed
C) tennis's rules have not changed
D) no one has changed the rules of tennis

6

A) NO CHANGE
B) the game of tennis was
C) the first racquets were
D) the first racquets were found to be

7

A) NO CHANGE
B) they are
C) today's racquets have become
D) today's racquet creators have made them

8

A) NO CHANGE
B) the grip of the player must remain
C) the grip must be kept
D) a player must keep the grip

Because he thought of tennis as a serious sport, her coach was quite demanding. During one particular match, my daughter found it hard to see because of the sun. [9] She swung and missed the tennis ball squinting at the sky. Her coach got very angry.

Needless to say, we soon had to find her a new coach. Searching for one that was more patient, [10] it was time we asked our friends for recommendations. Playing tennis can be tough, but it should also be enjoyable. The new coach turned out to be great. [11] With spin and power, she taught Cayla a better way to serve the ball. The first time she spun the ball in, she jumped up and down excitedly like it was Christmas morning.

Growing in confidence, [12] her movements became more smooth. At one point, Cayla even challenged her coach to a friendly match. I can't wait to see how she evolves as a tennis player in the coming years.

9

A) NO CHANGE
B) She swung and missed the tennis ball by squinting at the sky.
C) She swung and missed, squinting at the sky, the tennis ball.
D) Squinting at the sky, she swung and missed the tennis ball.

10

A) NO CHANGE
B) we asked friends for
C) our friends gave us
D) our friends were asked for

11

A) NO CHANGE
B) She taught Cayla, with spin and power, a better way to serve the ball.
C) She taught Cayla a better way to serve, with spin and power, the ball.
D) She taught Cayla a better way to serve the ball with spin and power.

12

A) NO CHANGE
B) her movements were smoother.
C) she moved more smoothly.
D) the way she moved became smoother.

8
Run-ons

Most students think they know what a run-on is based on their 6th grade English class. So when I ask students whether the following is a run-on sentence, almost all students say yes:

I took the SATs, and I scored a 36, and I applied to MIT, and I got in!

Now this sentence may be long, wordy, and awkward, but the sentence is actually NOT a run-on sentence—it's grammatically correct. The reason it's correct is the use of the word *and*, which connects all the parts together.

I took the SATs, I scored a 36, I applied to MIT, I got in!

Now this IS a run-on sentence because several **complete sentences are being mashed together with just commas**.

The basic form of a run-on is this:

complete sentence	,	complete sentence

A run-on also occurs when there is nothing between the two complete sentences:

complete sentence	complete sentence

There are four main ways to fix a run-on. Let's go over them one by one with a simple run-on example:

He was hungry, he bought a Chipotle burrito.

Two complete sentences connected only by a comma—definitely a run-on that needs to be fixed.

1. Use periods:

complete sentence. complete sentence.

He was hungry. He bought a burrito.

2. Use a conjunction

> complete sentence, *conjunction* complete sentence.
>
> He was hungry, **so** he bought a burrito.

Note that a comma, if necessary, comes **before** the conjunction (we'll learn more about commas in a future chapter). Most students have learned the acronym FANBOYS to memorize the list of conjunctions:

For And Nor But Or Yet So

Memorize this list because it's super important.

Now here's a really important point: if two sentences are connected by a word that's not from the FANBOYS list, IT'S STILL A RUN-ON. This is how the SAT tricks you:

> He was hungry, **therefore**, he bought a Chipotle burrito.

This sentence is wrong because *therefore* is not a conjunction—it's not a member of FANBOYS. Instead, it's a transition word pretending to be a conjunction. Other words the SAT might use include *however, moreover, in addition to, nevertheless,* and *furthermore.* These words cannot be used as conjunctions.

3. Use the semicolon ;

> complete sentence; complete sentence.
>
> He was hungry; he bought a burrito.

Semicolons are the simplest way to edit run-ons, but in everyday speaking and writing, conjunctions are more common because they better express how two connected sentences are related. The SAT will test you on both ways. Note that this is also correct:

> He was hungry; therefore, he bought a Chipotle burrito.

But this one is INCORRECT:

> He was hungry; and he bought a Chipotle burrito.

Do not use both a conjunction and a semicolon. **Semicolons require complete sentences on either side.** By putting in a conjunction, the second part is no longer a complete sentence.

4. Change the wording so that you no longer have two complete sentences

This last method encompasses a number of run-on fixes. The best way will usually depend on the sentence we're working with. We'll go over the most common ways of revising the wording.

A. Dependent clause

> incomplete sentence, complete sentence.
>
> Because he was hungry, he bought a burrito.

By inserting *because* in front, the first half is no longer a complete sentence, and we're no longer mashing two complete sentences together. As a result, we don't need anything more than the comma. *Because he was hungry* is a **dependent clause—it doesn't make sense by itself**. An **independent clause** is just another term for a complete sentence or thought like *he bought a Chipotle burrito*. **It makes sense by itself.** A dependent clause with an independent clause is not a run-on and therefore does not require a conjunction or a semicolon.

When it comes to rewording the burrito example, using a dependent clause turns out to be the best solution, but let's take a look at some examples where other solutions work better.

B. Relative clause (*who, which, that*)

Example 1

Wrong:	The teacher yelled at Alicia, she had left her homework at home.
Correct:	The teacher yelled at Alicia, who had left her homework at home.

Example 2

Wrong:	The hackers copied the company's central databases, these contain sensitive data on customers.
Correct:	The hackers copied the company's central databases, which contain sensitive data on customers.

C. A noun phrase set off by commas

Example 3

Wrong:	Yesterday, Russia deployed troops on the border, this is a clear violation of the peace agreement.
Correct:	Yesterday, Russia deployed troops on the border, a clear violation of the peace agreement.

Example 4

Wrong:	The Burj Khalifa is the tallest building in the world, it attracts thousands of tourists each year.
Correct:	The Burj Khalifa is the tallest building in the world, attracting thousands of tourists each year.

D. Modifier

Example 5

Wrong:	People named it after inventor Nikola Tesla, the tesla coil is used in radio transmitters and electrotherapy.
Correct:	Named after inventor Nikola Tesla, the tesla coil is used in radio transmitters and electrotherapy.

Example 6

Wrong:	He is reflecting on the meaning of life, Henry tried to find philosophical answers to life's problems.
Correct:	Reflecting on the meaning of life, Henry tried to find philosophical answers to life's problems.

E. Use *and* to join verbs

Example 7

Wrong:	James turned up the music, he danced like there was no tomorrow.
Correct:	James turned up the music and danced like there was no tomorrow.

Let's recap what we've learned so far with some examples that are revised in several different ways.

Example 8

Wrong:	You should memorize the list of conjunctions, it will help immensely on the SAT.
Correct:	You should memorize the list of conjunctions, for it will help immensely on the SAT.
Correct:	You should memorize the list of conjunctions; it will help immensely on the SAT.
Correct:	You should memorize the list of conjunctions because it will help immensely on the SAT.

As a side note, the conjunction *for* is rarely used in conversation.

Example 9

Wrong:	I love the game of basketball, however, I don't play it myself.
Correct:	I love the game of basketball, but I don't play it myself.
Correct:	I love the game of basketball; however, I don't play it myself.
Correct:	I love the game of basketball, even though I don't play it myself.

After reading the third correct version, you might be wondering why *even though* is correct and *however* is incorrect. What's the difference? Well, with *however*, you still have two independent clauses on either side of the comma. With *even though*, you have an independent clause with a dependent clause, which is not a run-on:

Wrong:	I love the game of basketball, however, I don't play it myself.
	<u>Independent clause</u> <u>Independent clause</u>
Fine:	I love the game of basketball, even though I don't play it myself.
	<u>Independent clause</u> <u>Dependent clause</u>

Example 10

Wrong:	Nightmares keep me awake at night; yet I oddly feel energized in the morning.
Correct:	Nightmares keep me awake at night; however, I oddly feel energized in the morning.
Correct:	Nightmares keep me awake at night, yet I oddly feel energized in the morning.
Correct:	Although nightmares keep me awake at night, I oddly feel energized in the morning.

Again, don't use semicolons and conjunctions (like *yet* in this example) together. Semicolons require two complete sentences on either side.

Example 11

Wrong:	One of my idols is Michael Jackson, he was one of the best performers of his time.
Correct:	One of my idols is Michael Jackson, who was one of the best performers of his time.
Correct:	One of my idols is Michael Jackson, one of the best performers of his time.

The first correct version uses a relative clause. The second uses a noun phrase.

Example 12

Wrong:	When I try to go to sleep, nightmares keep me awake at night, after brushing my teeth, I oddly feel energized in the morning.
Correct:	When I try to go to sleep, nightmares keep me awake at night, yet after brushing my teeth, I oddly feel energized in the morning.
Correct:	When I try to go to sleep, nightmares keep me awake at night; after brushing my teeth, however, I oddly feel energized in the morning.

Despite all the clauses in example 12, we have two complete thoughts being mashed together:

1. When I try to go to sleep, nightmares keep me awake at night.

2. After brushing my teeth, I oddly feel energized in the morning.

The SAT will try to trick you in this way by putting in a lot of relative clauses and comma phrases to keep you from realizing something's a run-on. When that happens, read carefully and look for where a complete thought ends and where another one begins.

Reminder 1

If there's already a conjunction or if we're not connecting two complete sentences in the first place, then there's NO error. For example:

Although the plan was perfect, the clumsy criminals, who by now would have been millionaires, are locked in jail cells, slowly waiting out their sentences.

Looking at where the commas are, at no point are we trying to combine two complete sentences on either side, so the sentence is perfectly fine.

Reminder 2

Never use more than one way of correcting a run-on within the same sentence. Don't use a semicolon with a conjunction. Don't use a conjunction with a dependent clause, etc. The following examples are all incorrect:

- Jerry ran away last summer; and I haven't seen him since.
- Even though the coffee in Rome is amazing, but I still like Starbucks coffee more.
- Every year my brother visits New York City; which he considers the greatest city in the world.
- Henry tripped over the rock, and falling head first into the water.
- Running through the finish line, and Donna leaped for joy.

Exercise 1: Identify whether the sentence is a run-on (some may be correct) and if so, where it occurs. The first one is done for you. Answers for this chapter start on page 219.

1. A caller from Memorial Park reported a man beating his head against a wall, he was heading to work.
   ⇑

2. A completely naked long-haired brunette in her 20s was pumping gas into a Hummer on the corner of Beachmont, no one got a good look at the vehicle's license plate.

3. In New York, the train system is difficult to learn, however, the food is fantastic and diverse.

4. When a man became so upset with the lack of parking enforcement in his town, he reported his own parking violation, and the police showed up to subdue him with a stun gun, apparently he became combative and screamed at the officers that they weren't doing their job.

5. There's a big chance that if you're 16 or older, you've already met the person you'll marry.

6. Wanting to be sure that what he had been sold was real weed, Phillip Donahue approached two officers and asked them to test his pipe, as a result, he was arrested and charged with drug possession.

7. Jimmy hid in the dumpster when Mr. Trump, his boss, walked by, unfortunately, Mr. Trump had to throw something away and saw him crouching there, forcing Jimmy to confess that he actually lived there.

8. Zoe likes to ace her tests but resents it when her classmates ask her how much she studied, sometimes Zoe will just say that she didn't study at all when in fact she had stayed up all night.

9. At the time, discovering quantum physics looked like a waste of time and money, but it is now the foundation of all modern technology, thus, when people claim that math and science are of no relevance, it drives Dr. Tyson into a deep rage.

10. Playing them day and night, Shawn and his video games were inseparable, however, once he got a girlfriend, everything changed.

11. Despite his friends' tearful pleas for forgiveness, Jonathan maintained a deep grudge against everyone who had ever asked for a pencil and never returned it, an act he considered a crime against humanity.

12. Suddenly realizing the movie was too scary for her, Maya panicked and looked at her watch, there was still 20 minutes left, enough time to still make her uneasy about what was to come.

13. The salesman, aware that he was going to lose a sale if he didn't make something up, claimed that the laptop could not be customizable and that the only options were in the store.

14. As a young girl, Lindsay was praised as a talented and burgeoning actress, as an adult, she fell into the dark world of sex, drugs, and alcohol and would never reclaim her former glory.

15. Omega-3 fish oil provides essential fatty acids for your nutritional health, furthermore, it soothes back pain and muscle aches.

16. Last Saturday, Peter Parker was bit by a spider, after that incident, he would never be the same again.

Exercise 2: Answers for this chapter start on page 219.

1. Despite the cracks in the kitchen wall and the leaky <u>faucet;</u> the apartment sold for over double what it was worth.

   A) NO CHANGE
   B) faucet
   C) faucet,
   D) faucet, but

2. The waiter tried to sell the most expensive bottle of wine to the young diners, all <u>of them</u> decided that it wasn't worth it.

   A) NO CHANGE
   B) the diners
   C) of whom
   D) DELETE the underlined portion.

3. The letter, which declared a revolution in Cuba, was drafted by the leader of the <u>rebels, it was</u> typed up by his brother.

   A) NO CHANGE
   B) rebels,
   C) rebels and
   D) rebels; and it was

4. Because malaria, a disease transmitted by mosquitoes, can be fatal, <u>so</u> we made sure to take vaccinations before our trip to Africa.

    A) NO CHANGE
    B) and
    C) but
    D) DELETE the underlined portion.

5. When the school board wanted to cut spending in <u>half, which</u> the teachers complained that they already didn't have enough textbooks to go around.

    A) NO CHANGE
    B) half;
    C) half,
    D) half:

6. Jack bought the used car knowing that he would have to fix it <u>up; it</u> was the only one he liked.

    A) NO CHANGE
    B) up; for
    C) up, it
    D) up, which

7. Fans stood in a long line that stretched down and around the <u>block, they were</u> waiting for the box office to open.

    A) NO CHANGE
    B) block and
    C) block; while
    D) block,

8. Doctors must adhere to best practices and obey certain hospital guidelines, <u>they</u> limit the amount of medication that can be prescribed to patients.

    A) NO CHANGE
    B) which
    C) and
    D) DELETE the underlined portion.

9. The managers debated the issue with the employees to get their <u>feedback; even though</u> they had already made their decision.

    A) NO CHANGE
    B) feedback,
    C) feedback; but
    D) feedback even though

10. Most mixed martial arts fighters today practice brazilian <u>jiu-jitsu, this is</u> a brutal form of martial arts that focuses on grappling.

    A) NO CHANGE
    B) jiu-jitsu, being
    C) jiu-jitsu;
    D) jiu-jitsu,

11. SAT scores are extremely important. They are only one part of the <u>application, however, grades</u> and teacher recommendations are other factors that colleges take into account.

    A) NO CHANGE
    B) application however grades
    C) application. However, grades
    D) application, however. Grades

12. Although buyers are aware of their decisions and the marketing that plays into <u>them, however, some</u> persuasive forces that affect purchasing behavior go unnoticed.

    A) NO CHANGE
    B) them, some
    C) them, but some
    D) them: some

13. <u>It is praised as</u> Tarantino's greatest accomplishment, the movie *Pulp Fiction* interlaces several stories of seemingly unrelated incidents.

    A) NO CHANGE
    B) Praised as
    C) People praise it as
    D) It is

14. Environmentalists have worked hard to rid the river of toxic <u>chemicals, but</u> the population of fish still hasn't recovered to previous levels.

    A) NO CHANGE
    B) chemicals; but
    C) chemicals,
    D) chemicals, however,

15. The movie theater provided large leather seats with slots for popcorn and <u>drinks, furthermore,</u> the screen was crystal clear to make for a great 3-D viewing experience.

    A) NO CHANGE
    B) drinks; furthermore,
    C) drinks; and
    D) drinks, in addition,

16. As a doctor, Billy consults with patients about their <u>conditions, he</u> recommends a course of action to correct them.

    A) NO CHANGE
    B) conditions and
    C) conditions; and then
    D) conditions, which he

Exercise 3: Answers for this chapter start on page 219.

Sir John Alexander Macdonald

Sir John Alexander Macdonald, the first Prime Minister of Canada, is widely praised as a great Canadian hero. **1** We didn't have his determination and tenacity, our great country would not be the same as it is today.

2 Born in Scotland on January 11, 1815, John immigrated to the New Country with his parents at a very young age. The exact year of his arrival is unknown. He soon began working under a local lawyer in **3** Kingston, his mentor died before he could complete his apprenticeship. Young Macdonald was not quite old enough to take over the **4** practice, however, this didn't stop the ambitious lad. He immediately opened his own practice.

5 He had several high profile cases, John quickly became a prominent figure in legal venues. This notoriety prompted the young man to run for a legislative seat in the House of **6** Commons, he won in 1844.

1
A) NO CHANGE
B) Without
C) We lacked
D) Because

2
A) NO CHANGE
B) He was born;
C) He was born
D) Born,

3
A) NO CHANGE
B) Kingston, however, his mentor
C) Kingston; but his mentor
D) Kingston, but his mentor

4
A) NO CHANGE
B) practice, so
C) practice; however,
D) practice,

5
A) NO CHANGE
B) After,
C) After
D) He was in

6
A) NO CHANGE
B) Commons,
C) Commons; which he
D) Commons, which he

Just like John, the country was struggling to make a mark on the [7] world, in 1877, Mr. Macdonald was awarded the position of Premier of the United Province of Canada. However, at this point Canada was far from being [8] united, much less a real province.

The political state was in shambles. The efforts of the King of England to populate the country was a dismal [9] failure the people in the west had no interest at all in joining what politicians were calling "Canada." None of this deterred John's ambition of creating the country of his dreams. He developed the Canadian Pacific Railway and created the Northwest Mounted [10] Police; convincing British Columbia, Manitoba, and Prince Edward Island to join the confederation.

Even at the age of 60, Macdonald did not slow down [11] one bit, in 1885, he engineered the first National Park in Alberta. Believing that he could attract the attention of tourists to [12] Canada, so he gathered the country's best architects and construction workers to design one of the world's most beautiful destinations.

Sir John A. Macdonald served as the Prime Minister of Canada from 1867 to 1873 and then again from 1878 to 1891. He was given the honor of knighthood for his dedication to crown and [13] country, people today still travel on the Macdonald-Cartier highway every day!

7
A) NO CHANGE
B) world. In 1877,
C) world, however, in 1877,
D) world, moreover, in 1877,

8
A) NO CHANGE
B) united, and much less
C) united; much less
D) united, though much less

9
A) NO CHANGE
B) failure. The people
C) failure; and the people
D) failure, the people

10
A) NO CHANGE
B) Police convincing
C) Police by convincing
D) Police, he convinced

11
A) NO CHANGE
B) one bit, therefore, in 1885,
C) one bit; in 1885,
D) one bit; and in 1885,

12
A) NO CHANGE
B) Canada,
C) Canada;
D) Canada, and

13
A) NO CHANGE
B) country, with people
C) country, so people
D) country. People

9 Fragments

A sentence fragment is a piece or part of a sentence. It's an incomplete sentence, one that's missing a subject or a verb. For example:

Floating on the river.

Of course, that one's easy to spot. The SAT will give you sentence fragments so long that by the time you've read to the end of them, you'll have forgotten where you started. You'll commonly see fragments in which the entire sentence is a relative clause (e.g. *who, which, that, where*), a dependent clause (e.g *although, while, when*), or a gerund phrase (e.g. *being, walking, singing*). If you read a sentence out loud and it lacks a sense of completion or the whole thing just sounds weird by the end, chances are it's a sentence fragment.

Example 1

Wrong:	People who have a sense of entitlement and feel absolutely no sympathy for those less fortunate even when they take advantage of their services.
Correct:	People who have a sense of entitlement and feel absolutely no sympathy for those less fortunate even when they take advantage of their services **make me sick**.

Example 1 is a relative clause sentence fragment.

Example 2

Wrong:	Because my broken heart, which you have left hardly beating in my chest, is the reason for my endless suffering.
Correct:	**My broken heart**, which you have left hardly beating in my chest, is the reason for my endless suffering.

Example 2 is a dependent clause sentence fragment.

Example 3

Wrong:	Russell Brand, the English comedian, being one of the funniest celebrities alive.
Correct:	Russell Brand, the English comedian, **is** one of the funniest celebrities alive.

Example 3 is a gerund phrase sentence fragment.

There is no one absolute way to fix a sentence fragment. On the SAT, the simpler ones are easy to spot and fix. Often times, the trickier ones will involve removing words like *who, which, although, because, since,* and *despite* as in Example 2.

Exercise 1: Turn the following sentence fragments into complete sentences. Answers are flexible. Answers for this chapter start on page 221.

1. Tony's toys, which were hidden in the cupboard so that nobody could get to them.

2. When I was given the opportunity to speak in front of the graduating class as if I were some celebrity or movie star.

3. Dumping him on the first date because he smelled so bad even though she knew he had just returned from a wrestling match.

4. It is very convenient that the grocery store I live next to. And the surrounding malls and restaurants are open late at night.

5. In the middle of the night, when most people are sleeping while I sneak to the kitchen to eat.

6. Like the moment you realize your cereal is soggy because you left it in the milk too long.

7. The butler who served the Wright family for several years and later became a successful businessman.

8. The tennis champion waving his racquet up towards a roaring crowd with his right hand and lifting the trophy with his left.

9. Even though Aaron fully believed that his actions, now the cause of much public controversy, were morally and ethically right, but the prosecutors would hear none of it.

10. The negative thoughts that were constantly on Floyd's mind as he got into the ring.

11. Disgusted by the lack of cleanliness in the men's bathroom yet curious about the sanitation in the ladies' room.

12. I wore the pants you bought me. And the purple tie that the saleswoman picked out.

13. As they walk down the street, check out the stores, and talk about life.

14. Although pandas are one of the most likable mammals but are one of the most rare.

Exercise 2: Answers for this chapter start on page 221.

Dining with the Kids

For centuries, eating in a restaurant [1] being considered a social event. Business meetings, family gatherings, special events, and many other occasions [2] celebrating in restaurants. This is not necessarily because serving a large crowd at home is a lot of work, but more because the food and drinks are served by [3] others, allowing everyone in the group to relax and socialize without worrying about empty plates or glasses.

Some restaurants [4] that cater specifically to families and children, though they are the exception rather than the rule. Unfortunately, eating a meal in a restaurant with three children under the age of ten is anything but [5] relaxing. Especially for the waiters and waitresses who serve them. The Continental Diner in my town, which has a special section just for [6] children so that they are isolated from the customers who want a nice and quiet conversation over dinner.

1

A) NO CHANGE
B) was being
C) has been
D) that is

2

A) NO CHANGE
B) are celebrating
C) are celebrated
D) celebrated

3

A) NO CHANGE
B) others. Allowing
C) others; allowing
D) DELETE the underlined portion.

4

A) NO CHANGE
B) catering
C) are catering
D) cater

5

A) NO CHANGE
B) relaxing, especially
C) relaxing;
D) relaxing, and especially

6

A) NO CHANGE
B) children to keep them
C) children, keeps them
D) children, keeping them

During one particular night on a **7** weekday. We took our three kids to their classmate Kate's birthday party. **8** Held at a pizza place that combined bowling with the dining experience. While the kids had fun **9** bowling and the parents could chat with each other without too much interruption. Of course, most of the parents **10** being concerned with their children's behavior and kept a watchful eye on them. **11** Tommy and Lilly were, the siblings of the birthday girl, entertained themselves by rolling multiple bowling balls down the lane at the same time.

7
A) NO CHANGE
B) weekday, we took
C) weekday, when we took
D) weekday, having taken

8
A) NO CHANGE
B) It was held
C) Being held
D) Having been held

9
A) NO CHANGE
B) bowling, the parents
C) bowling. The parents
D) bowling, and the parents

10
A) NO CHANGE
B) concerned
C) were concerning
D) were concerned

11
A) NO CHANGE
B) Tommy and Lilly
C) While Tommy and Lilly were
D) As Tommy and Lilly

To ensure that the kids were busy and [12] engaged. The restaurant had many activities besides bowling. [13] One, air hockey, which involves two players with pushers and one puck. Another was arcade basketball, my favorite game. As the clock ticks down, players [14] shooting basketballs as fast as they can into the basket. When the night was over, my three [15] kids, who finding it difficult to leave the party behind.

12

A) NO CHANGE
B) engaged since the restaurant
C) engaged at the restaurant,
D) engaged, the restaurant

13

A) NO CHANGE
B) One was
C) One being
D) One of these,

14

A) NO CHANGE
B) who are shooting
C) who shoot
D) shoot

15

A) NO CHANGE
B) kids, finding
C) kids found
D) kids, who found

10
Redundancy

Redundancy questions involve removing unnecessary words. On the SAT, you'll encounter two types of redundancy:

- Words that essentially repeat or unnecessarily define previous words (Examples 1 and 2)
- Inflated and useless phrases that could be omitted or condensed into fewer words (Example 3 and 4)

Example 1

Wrong:	Our problem is that we're too self-aware of ourselves.
Correct:	Our problem is that we're too self-aware.

Self-aware already implies *ourselves*, so we don't need *of ourselves* in the sentence.

Example 2

Wrong:	I once believed and had faith in the power of love.
Correct:	I once believed in the power of love.

The phrase *had faith in* repeats the same meaning as *believed*.

Example 3

Wrong:	Joey bought a super-sized hamburger due to the fact that he was really hungry.
Correct:	Joey bought a super-sized hamburger **because** he was really hungry.

Example 4

Wrong:	The legal documents were reviewed in a way that was deemed thorough.
Correct:	The legal documents were reviewed **thoroughly**.

Inflated phrases like *due to the fact that* and *in a way that was deemed* must be made concise.

Example 5

Wrong:	The reason why red pandas have ringed tails is because they are relatives of both the giant panda and the raccoon.
Correct:	Red pandas have ringed tails **because** they are relatives of both the giant panda and the raccoon.
Correct:	**The reason** red pandas have ringed tails is that they are relatives of both the giant panda and the raccoon.

This specific redundancy error is very common. It has three words that essentially mean the same thing—*reason, why,* and *because,* all of which point to the cause of something. You only need one of those words.

Example 6

Wrong:	After hearing the spy's information, the general knew that an attack was imminent in the future.
Correct:	After hearing the spy's information, the general knew that an attack was imminent.

Imminent by definition means *in the future.*

Example 7

Wrong:	It's only on the night before the test that I wish my notes had been more clearer.
Correct:	It's only on the night before the test that I wish my notes had been **more clear**.

It's unnecessary to use both *more* and the *-er* ending because they convey the same thing.

Example 8

Wrong:	The last to sing, Jason and Jesse made sure to amaze the crowd with a full range of vocals at the end of the performance.
Correct:	**The last to sing**, Jason and Jesse made sure to amaze the crowd with a full range of vocals.
Correct:	Jason and Jesse made sure to amaze the crowd with a full range of vocals **at the end of the performance**.

Example 9

Wrong:	We should evacuate the building immediately in the hypothetical event that a fire occurs.
Correct:	We should evacuate the building immediately **if a fire occurs**.

The phrase *in the hypothetical event that a fire occurs* is too wordy and awkward. How much a certain phrase can be shortened can be a matter of style. Luckily for you, the answer choices will be very clear-cut on the SAT. You'll definitely know from the answer choices when they're testing wordiness.

Example 10

Wrong:	The Black Friday deals attracted hordes of shoppers. These shoppers rampaged through the doors as the stores opened.
Correct:	The Black Friday deals attracted hordes of shoppers, **who** rampaged through the doors as the stores opened.

Example 11

Wrong:	The commander's charge into the opposing army was fearless, an act of bravery.
Correct:	The commander's charge into the opposing army was fearless, an act of bravery.

Example 12

Wrong:	Generic drugs are usually cheaper than when buying name-brand ones.
Correct:	Generic drugs are usually cheaper than when buying name-brand ones.

Exercise 1: Correct the redundancy errors (repeated meaning) in the following sentences. Answers are somewhat flexible. Answers for this chapter start on page 222.

1. In her biography about her life, she writes about overcoming poverty and fear.

2. During high school, I sung in a trio that consisted of three people.

3. Scratching the rash made it more worse than before.

4. The reason why most people give up on New Year's resolutions is because they're too accustomed to old habits.

5. The plagiarist who copied the works of others was banned indefinitely from the journalism industry.

6. There's a good chance that an earthquake has the possibility of happening within the next week.

7. After her graduation speech, Zoe was thirsty and needed to drink something.

8. Because James was an optimist with a positive outlook on life, he faced his struggles with a smile on his face.

9. Seafood restaurants are becoming less and less expensive due to the abundance and oversupply of fish.

10. Her verbal statements in her conversation with me led me to believe that she was holding something from me.

11. The sisters reunited at the house where they grew up as siblings upon their father's death.

12. Building his own motorcycle, which would belong to him, Quentin looked forward to the day when he would be old enough to drive it.

13. My aunt is a beginner who just started learning about photography.

14. The president gave a strong message that was quite powerful to the world in his speech yesterday.

15. This year, the volcano came alive as if it were angry and the eruption lasted for days, which numbered quite a few.

16. In 1472, Christopher Columbus set sail and thereby rigged a boat and charted a course towards India.

17. Since he quit his job, his savings have suffered, decreasing the balance in his bank account quite a bit.

18. When she walked into the room, he lost his concentration and couldn't focus on the task at hand.

Exercise 2: Correct the redundancy errors (inflated/useless phrases) in the following sentences. Answers for this chapter start on page 222.

1. The plane that had crash-landed was found at the location of New Hampshire.

2. On the occasion of July 4th, the residents of Lynn waited along the beach to see the massive fireworks display.

3. Linzy completed the 100 mile trail by means of bike.

4. Marine biologists estimated that the beached whale weighed in the rough neighborhood of about 200 tons.

5. The director decided to give the aspiring journalist a job by virtue of the fact that he was so persistent.

6. The child continued to ask his mother for chocolate chip cookies in spite of the nature of her initial rejection.

7. When it comes to college applications, all decisions made are on a final basis.

8. If it can be determined to be feasible, a flexible work arrangement allows employees the freedom to work on a schedule suited to them.

9. As police officers, we express our desire to have a commitment to public safety.

10. If Michelle answers the last question correctly, she stands to win in the excess of a million dollars.

11. With a booming agricultural sector, China exports rice, wheat, potatoes, tea, and other crops in addition to them.

12. Do not lift the pressure valve in the lead up to the time the astronaut has landed safely.

13. As shown by the one particular case of the Black Plague, one disease can kill millions of people.

14. Weightlifting is more physically demanding and harder on the bones than the people who would rather go swimming.

15. The case was solved when several eyewitnesses decided to participate in cooperation with the police.

Exercise 3: Answers for this chapter start on page 222.

King Henry VIII's Divorce

King Henry VIII is famous for his large size and his many wives, **1** for which he is popularly known. His most enduring legacy, however, was **2** his separation and division of the Church of England from the Roman Catholic Church.

Henry was never expected to be king. His older brother Arthur was **3** the heir and next in line to the throne, but when Henry was 11 years old, Arthur **4** perished fatally. Arthur had recently married Catherine of Aragon, the daughter of King Ferdinand of **5** Spain, a short time ago. Eager to protect diplomatic relations with Spain, Henry's father betrothed **6** his son Henry to marry Catherine when he came of age.

1
- A) NO CHANGE
- B) for which he is most known.
- C) which he is known for.
- D) DELETE the underlined portion and end the sentence with a period.

2
- A) NO CHANGE
- B) his separation
- C) the separateness
- D) his splitting division

3
- A) NO CHANGE
- B) the successive heir
- C) the heir
- D) the successive next in line

4
- A) NO CHANGE
- B) died.
- C) fatally died.
- D) perished and died.

5
- A) NO CHANGE
- B) Spain, shortly before.
- C) Spain.
- D) Spain, not long ago.

6
- A) NO CHANGE
- B) his son, Henry,
- C) Henry, his son,
- D) Henry

Henry became **7** king, ascending to the throne in 1509 at the young age of 17 upon his father's death. Over the years, Catherine bore him six children **8** throughout their time together, but only one survived infancy, a daughter. Henry needed a male heir to ensure a peaceful succession of the throne after his death. As time passed, the absence of a son increasingly **9** worried and troubled Henry more and more, to the point that he began to fear that God was punishing him for marrying his brother's wife.

At this time, **10** the Catholic Church had the sole authority to end a marriage, and even then only by **11** declaring in an announcement that the marriage had never truly existed in God's sight. Henry sought such an annulment from the Pope. Unswayed by Henry's arguments from the biblical book of Leviticus and pressured by Catherine's nephew, King Charles V of Spain, the Pope **12** was unconvinced and refused the annulment.

7
A) NO CHANGE
B) king
C) king, on the throne
D) king to the throne

8
A) NO CHANGE
B) as time passed
C) one by one
D) DELETE the underlined portion

9
A) NO CHANGE
B) worried Henry more and more,
C) worried Henry,
D) troubled Henry more and more,

10
A) NO CHANGE
B) only the Catholic Church
C) the Catholic Church was the only one that
D) it was only the Catholic Church that

11
A) NO CHANGE
B) declaring
C) proclaiming and declaring
D) proclaiming under a declaration

12
A) NO CHANGE
B) refused
C) unconvincingly refused
D) decided to refuse

And so Henry took matters into his own hands to obtain the divorce he wanted [13] on his own. Having already begun an affair with a woman named Anne Boleyn, all he needed was a church that would marry him to [14] Anne and that would be sufficient. He maneuvered to get his own man appointed Archbishop of Canterbury in 1532, and then he got Parliament to declare him the Supreme Head of the Church of England [15] after that in 1534.

Henry's actions opened the door for the Protestant Reformation in [16] England, which led the way to forever altering the future of his country. Anne, however, did not bear him a son. In fact, only one of his six wives bore him a son, and this son, Edward, reigned for only [17] a few years, six as a matter of fact.

13
A) NO CHANGE
B) himself.
C) by himself.
D) DELETE the underlined portion and end the sentence with a period.

14
A) NO CHANGE
B) Anne, which would be adequate.
C) Anne.
D) Anne, being enough to nullify the divorce.

15
A) NO CHANGE
B) subsequently in 1534.
C) in 1534.
D) DELETE the underlined portion and end the sentence with a period.

16
A) NO CHANGE
B) England to
C) England, which
D) England,

17
A) NO CHANGE
B) six years.
C) six years, in fact.
D) six short years.

Parallelism I - Lists

You probably know from math that parallel lines are two lines that go in the same direction. The concept is similar in English in the way we structure certain things together.

> I like flying planes, riding trains, and driving automobiles.

Notice the same format for each of the things in the list: gerund (word ending in *ing*)-noun, gerund-noun, gerund-noun. It sounds nice and fluid when the sentence is put together that way. It would be awkward and incorrect to say:

> I like flying planes, riding trains, and to drive automobiles.

Here's another correct version:

> I like to fly planes, to ride trains, and to drive automobiles. (infinitive-noun pattern)

It's also correct to leave out the *to*'s because they're implied to carry over to all three items in the list:

> I like to fly planes, ride trains, and drive automobiles.

But again, you must be consistent—it would be incorrect to write:

> I like to fly planes, ride trains, and to drive automobiles.

The *to* is used again after being left out in the second item. Let's walk through some examples so you see what sentences need to be parallel on the SAT:

Example 1

Wrong:	In chess, remember these three goals: get your pieces to the center, capture the opposing pieces, and attacking the opposing king.
Correct:	In chess, remember these three goals: get your pieces to the center, capture the opposing pieces, and **attack** the opposing king.

Example 2

Wrong:	Fans of Teresa admire her ability to sing, her passion for performance, and she has good looks.
Correct:	Fans of Teresa admire her ability to sing, her passion for performance, and **her good looks**.

Example 3

Wrong:	The baby crawled quickly, sleeps softly, and cried loudly.
Correct:	The baby crawled quickly, **slept** softly, and cried loudly.

Parallelism requires the verb tenses to be the same.

Example 4

Wrong:	The fashion designer was praised for her creative, comfortable, and her having innovative clothing.
Correct:	The fashion designer was praised for her creative, comfortable, and ~~her having~~ innovative clothing.

Parallelism most often shows up in a series or a list of things as in the examples above, but it can also come up when pairing two phrases together, especially with *and* or *or*:

Example 5

Wrong:	I respect his eloquence and that he is brave.
Correct:	I respect his eloquence and **his bravery**.

Example 6

Wrong:	Hunting under the moonlight and to howl on top of the mountains were instinctual when the full moon appeared above the werewolves.
Correct:	Hunting under the moonlight and **howling** on top of the mountains were instinctual when the full moon appeared above the werewolves.

Example 7

Wrong:	I like singing more than dance.
Correct:	I like singing more than **dancing**.

Example 8

Wrong:	To learn what it means to love someone is accepting the flaws of others.
Correct:	To learn what it means to love someone is **to accept** the flaws of others.

Example 9

Wrong:	The school was designed to be a place where creativity would be celebrated and hard work was rewarded there.
Correct:	The school was designed to be a place where creativity would be celebrated and **hard work (would be) rewarded**.

Note that *would be* can be left out because it's implied to carry over.

Example 10

Wrong:	The principal planned to improve teacher training and clearer rules for student conduct should be established.
Correct:	The principal planned to improve teacher training and **(to) establish clearer rules for student conduct**.

Example 11

Wrong:	The people who ride the bus or have taken the train can't afford to drive to work.
Correct:	The people who ride the bus or **take** the train can't afford to drive to work.

Example 12

Wrong:	Traveling the world has given me the pleasure of meeting new people, to explore different ways of life.
Correct:	Traveling the world has given me the pleasure of meeting new people, **of exploring** different ways of life.

Exercise 1: Make the following sentences parallel. Answers for this chapter start on page 224.

1. That she looks beautiful and her charm help her get out of speeding tickets.

2. Visitors to my hometown in the middle of nowhere can experience rides on the bus, drinks at the tavern, and eating at the McDonald's.

3. Because of their amazing sense of smell, quick agility, and they have fierceness when protecting themselves, lions are the kings of the savannah.

4. My tasks today are to file for divorce, burn my house down, and to start all over.

5. By investing in nuclear energy, we can save the environment, jobs, and it costs us less.

6. In his free time, Wild Bill likes smoking Cuban cigars and to drink the finest red wine Martha's Vineyard has to offer.

7. Quickly and being silent, Jesse and Walt snuck by the sleeping police officers and made off with a barrel of methylamine.

8. Inspired by the hard work of his immigrant father, Jeremy wanted to pay for college, find a job, and a new house.

9. According to Apple, Samsung's directors need to admit they violated Apple's patent, pay the fines, and also needed is to recall all their products.

10. Samsung's executives responded by completely rejecting Apple's ultimatum in court and they countersued Apple back for patent infringement.

11. The 300 men trained diligently, screamed fiercely into battle, and valiantly fights.

12. At the yard sale, Jimmy found dusty writings of Einstein, containers of fossils, and Chinese opium boxes.

13. American immigrants took huge risks to leave their homelands and searching for a better life elsewhere.

14. Come to the next party prepared to eat a lot, to dance a lot, and with a thirst for drinks.

15. As soon as he graduated from high school, he packed all his belongings, rushed to the college campus, and leaves his parents behind.

Exercise 2: Answers for this chapter start on page 224.

Trip to Paris

The last year of high school was filled with optimism and **1** emotions that were nostalgic. It was like standing on a bridge that must be crossed, leaving behind the carefree days of youth and **2** stepped into a life of responsibilities, business meetings, and **3** paying bills. My friends and I decided to have one last trip together before heading off in our own directions.

My friends had decided to go to college on the other side of the country, **4** join an environmental group to save the rainforest, or work for their parents in the family business, which was what I was doing in the same town I'd lived in all my life. Out of the three of us, I needed this vacation the most. I had never left the state, let alone **5** departing from the country. So when Tom suggested we spend the summer in Europe, I was thrilled. After all, travel is a great way to bond with others and **6** to learn about the world.

1
A) NO CHANGE
B) nostalgia.
C) nostalgic emotions.
D) emotions of nostalgia.

2
A) NO CHANGE
B) to step
C) stepping
D) we stepped

3
A) NO CHANGE
B) bills that have to be paid.
C) having to pay bills.
D) bills.

4
A) NO CHANGE
B) to join
C) joining
D) they will join

5
A) NO CHANGE
B) the country.
C) from the country.
D) depart from the country.

6
A) NO CHANGE
B) the world can be learned about.
C) for learning about the world.
D) we can learn about the world.

We landed at Heathrow Airport at about 4pm, **7** would sleep in the terminal for a few hours, and took a connecting flight to Paris. We almost missed our flight because of the loud, pushy, and **8** large size of the crowd. On the flight, we **9** were reading books, watched movies, and listened to music. When we arrived, it finally dawned on us that we were all alone in a foreign country. As students and **10** we were clueless tourists, we walked aimlessly through the streets with giant backpacks.

7
A) NO CHANGE
B) we slept
C) slept
D) sleeping

8
A) NO CHANGE
B) large crowd.
C) crowd that was large.
D) having a large crowd.

9
A) NO CHANGE
B) read books,
C) decided to read books,
D) had books to read,

10
A) NO CHANGE
B) as well
C) being
D) as

We found a car rental place and chose a Volkswagen Beetle that was inexpensive to rent and [11] easily driven. It was perfect for taking us through the streets of Paris and [12] to show us the popular tourist sites. The history of Paris dates back to the third century. Today, the city is known for its coffee culture and [13] for its fashion boutiques. It didn't take long for us to realize there was no way we could see everything in just a few hours, so we just toured the usual tourist attractions like the Louvre, the Eiffel tower, and [14] we went to the Arc de Triomphe. By having a budget and [15] we stuck to it, we had enough money to try a three star Michelin restaurant afterwards!

11
A) NO CHANGE
B) easy to drive.
C) driven easily.
D) was easily driven.

12
A) NO CHANGE
B) showed us
C) showing us
D) the showing of

13
A) NO CHANGE
B) having fashion boutiques.
C) with its fashion boutiques.
D) it has fashion boutiques.

14
A) NO CHANGE
B) the landmark called the Arc de Triomphe.
C) such as the Arc de Triomphe.
D) the Arc de Triomphe.

15
A) NO CHANGE
B) stuck to it,
C) having it stick,
D) sticking to it,

Parallelism II - Pairs

Here's a little test I do with students. Of the following, which sounds the most natural to you?

A. Pandas prefer Japanese food over German food.
B. Pandas prefer Japanese food to German food.
C. Pandas prefer Japanese food more than German food.

Most students choose A or C in conversation but only B is correct. When you pair two things up with prefer, you must use the prefer ... to ... form. Here are the following pair forms you MUST memorize. The first four are by far the most commonly tested.

Pair	Example Sentence
Neither ... nor ...	I will give up **neither** my money **nor** my integrity.
Either ... or ...	If you had to save **either** your mother **or** your dad, who would it be?
Between ... and ...	It's getting to the point where we can pick **between** reality **and** fantasy.
Not only ... but also ...	He was **not only** late for school **but also** rude to the teacher.
Not so (much) ... as ...	The Porsche is **not so (much)** luxurious **as** (it is) expensive.
Both ... and ...	Barry sold **both** the dehumidifier **and** the TV.
As ... as ...	His brain was **as** fried **as** a sizzled hot dog.
Prefer ... to ...	Most people **prefer** California weather **to** New York weather.
Just as ... so (too) ...	**Just as** the physicist muses about the universe, **so (too)** the marine biologist ponders over the depths of the seas.
So ... that ...	He is **so** handsome **that** girls fall in love with him at first sight.
From ... to ...	She is involved with activities ranging **from** beekeeping **to** volleyball.
More/Less ... than ...	He has eaten **more** donuts **than** everyone else has combined.

Rule

The words in each pair in the previous table always go together when used in a paired construction (i.e. *prefer* always goes with *to*, *between* always goes with *and*, . . .).

Example 1

Wrong:	It's so hard to decide between the cheaper priced meal or the higher quality one.
Correct:	It's so hard to decide **between** the cheaper priced meal **and** the higher quality one.

Example 2

Wrong:	The college experience is not only an exciting time to meet new people and also a stressful one because of the level of independence required.
Correct:	The college experience is **not only** an exciting time to meet new people **but also** a stressful one because of the level of independence required.

Pair errors like the ones above are like freebies as long as you remember to check for them. There is, however, one additional thing you have to be aware of.

Rule

In a paired construction, the two things being paired up should be as parallel as possible.

To give a simple sentence illustration:

I want to not only   X   but also   Y   .

X and Y have to be as parallel as possible, much like items in a list from the last chapter. Let's look at an example.

Example 3

Wrong:	Today, I want to not only go jogging but also dive.
Correct:	Today, I want to not only **go jogging** but also **go diving**.

Example 4

Wrong:	Today, I not only want to go jogging but also dive.
Correct:	Today, I not only **want to go jogging** but also **want to go diving**.

Note the subtle difference—the placement of the *not only . . . but also . . .* affects the parallelism.

Example 5

Wrong:	The candidate ran for office not only because he was power-hungry but also his belief that he could do a better job.
Correct:	The candidate ran for office not only **because he was power-hungry** but also **because he believed that he could do a better job**.

Example 6

Wrong:	My favorite sound at the beach is either the crash of the waves or seagulls.
Correct:	My favorite sound at the beach is either **the crash of the waves** or **the chirping of the seagulls**.

Example 7

Wrong:	Neither the fierce yelling nor the screams that were loud could wake Travis from his midday nap.
Correct:	Neither **the fierce yelling** nor **the loud screaming** could wake Travis from his midday nap.

Example 8

Wrong:	I prefer the music of The Beatles to Justin Bieber.
Correct:	I prefer **the music of *The Beatles*** to **the music of Justin Bieber**.

Example 9

Wrong:	The enjoyment of owning a dog lies not so much in cleaning up after it as the relationship that is formed with it.
Correct:	The enjoyment of owning a dog lies not so much **in cleaning up after it** as **in forming a relationship with it**.

Of course, this type of parallelism doesn't apply to *as ... as ...* , *so ... that ...* , or *more/less ... than ...* —these pairs are instead used for comparisons:

He was **as** sneaky **as** a ninja.

Just make sure you **do** use the proper forms:

Example 10

Wrong:	Golf is not so great as some people say it is.
Correct:	Golf is not **as** great **as** some people say it is.

Example 11

Wrong:	I have more bananas compared with you.
Wrong:	I have more bananas then you (do).
Correct:	I have more bananas **than** you (do).

Exercise: Fix the paired constructions in the following sentences. Answers for this chapter start on page 226.

1. The college experience is not only an exciting time to meet new people ~~and~~ also a stressful one because of the level of independence required.

    but

2. Oleg works out daily not only to improve his physique but also his cardiovascular strength.

    to improve

3. The massive data breach reminded us not only of the need for better digital security but also data retention policies.

    of the need for

4. Critics have to rate both the food at the restaurant itself and other competing restaurants with the same cuisine.

    the food at

5. Though a horror fan, she preferred happy children's books ~~over~~ Stephen King.

    to Stephen King's books

6. She wasn't a fan of either the pizza at Domino's ~~nor~~ Reggie's.

    or the pizza at

7. I hope you suffer neither the pain of breaking up nor ~~lost love's regret.~~

    the regret of lost love

8. Winston Churchill is known not only for his eloquence but also for ~~having~~ charisma.

    his

9. Fruits aren't actually ~~so~~ necessary to one's diet as most doctors would have you believe.

    as

10. Just as most politicians come from a law background, ~~biology is the background of most doctors.~~

    most doctors come from a biology background

11. Apple products are not so much a statement of technological performance as style and status.

    a statement of

12. Having a GPS system is not only convenient but also ~~of necessity~~ when driving to new places.

    necessary

13. There is no comparison between China's economic power and ~~Japan.~~

    Japan's

14. My new book is not only comprehensive but also ~~has conciseness.~~

    concise

15. Not only were the books the most widely read, they ~~influenced much of the philosophical thought during that time.~~ *were also the most influencial to philosophical thought during that time*

Parallelism III - Faulty Comparisons

Much like the paired constructions in the last chapter, some comparisons also require parallelism. If you think about it, comparing two things is simply another way of pairing them up. For certain comparisons, you need to make sure you're comparing things of the same TYPE. Here's the basic idea:

Example 1

Wrong:	Characters in Chekhov's plays have always been crazier than Vogel's plays.
Correct:	Characters in Chekhov's plays have always been crazier than **characters in Vogel's plays**.

Example 2

Wrong:	Like the underwear made by Hanes and Armani, Calvin Klein makes you feel comfortable.
Correct:	Like the underwear made by Hanes and Armani, **underwear made by Calvin Klein** makes you feel comfortable.

Example 3

Wrong:	Hitler's world view, like Italy's dictator Mussolini, was so warped that injustice became justice.
Correct:	Hitler's world view, like Italy's dictator **Mussolini's view of the world**, was so warped that injustice became justice.
Correct:	Hitler's world view, like Italy's dictator **Mussolini's**, was so warped that injustice became justice.

By using the apostrophe *s*, we don't need to repeat *view of the world*—it's implied.

A common question students ask me is whether a sentence like the following is actually parallel given what we just learned.

The lion growls louder than the tiger.

The answer is yes because the verb *growls* (or *does*) is implied:

The lion growls louder than the tiger **(growls)**.
The lion growls louder than the tiger **(does)**.

Example 4

Wrong:	Winters in Boston are way colder than Los Angeles.
Correct:	Winters in Boston are way colder than **winters in Los Angeles**.
Correct:	Winters in Boston are way colder than **those in Los Angeles**.

Example 5

Wrong:	The competition among recreational chess players is much more intense than recreational bingo players.
Correct:	The competition among recreational chess players is much more intense than **the competition among recreational bingo players**.
Correct:	The competition among recreational chess players is much more intense than **that among recreational bingo players**.

In Examples 4 and 5, notice how we can use pronouns like *those* and *that* as substitutes to avoid repetition yet maintain parallelism.

Example 6

Wrong:	I like singing more than dance.
Correct:	I like singing more than **dancing**.

Example 7

Wrong:	During the holidays, purchases of shoes outnumbered computers, toys, and jewelry combined.
Correct:	During the holidays, purchases of shoes outnumbered **purchases of computers, toys, and jewelry combined**.

Notice how tricky Example 7 is—you cannot compare *purchases of stuff* with *stuff* itself.

Example 8

Wrong:	To love someone deeply is truly understanding how another person feels.
Correct:	To love someone deeply is **to (truly) understand** how another person feels.
Correct:	**Loving** someone deeply is truly understanding how another person feels.

Exercise: Correct the following faulty comparisons by making them parallel. There may be multiple ways of doing so. Answers for this chapter start on page 226.

1. When the tour guide brought up how similar Edison's inventions were to the inventor Nikola Tesla, Jimmy suggested that Edison might have just taken the idea from Tesla.

   those of

2. No personality is as weird as the physics teacher at my school, Mr. Greenman.

   that of

3. Gina's skill in archery pales in comparison to her rifle-shooting.

   skill in

4. At the festival, Abraham rocked out to Cannibal Corpse's death metal music, which he thought was less stale than the other groups.

   the music

5. Clothes worn by young adults in the 80's were much wilder than the teenage crowd now.

   clothes worn by

6. For some people, giving gifts is far easier than to receive them.

   receiving

7. With the popularity of iPhones and iPads, Steve Jobs's legacy may surpass Microsoft founder Bill Gates.

8. Efforts made by activists to curb global warming have been less effective than environmentally-conscious consumers.

   those made by

9. Geographers have shown that the area of Australia is more than 20 times Japan.

   the area of

10. In France, public supply of water is run more efficiently than electricity and heating.

    public supply of

11. The gummy bears that Syed ordered off of Amazon turned out to be cheaper and of higher quality than eBay.

    the ones he ordered off

12. The molecular structure of Carbon is considered superior in terms of reactivity compared to most other elements.

    the molecular structure of

13. The percentage of the U.S. budget devoted to health care far exceeds the budget for education.

    devoted to

14. It's far more entertaining to watch a football game than actually playing in one.

    to actually play

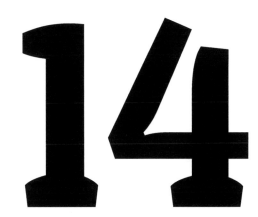

Pronoun Reference

Take a look at this sentence:

> To avoid a ticket, Alice told the police that Alice didn't realize Alice was pressing harder on the accelerator pedal because Alice had gained 40 pounds in two months.

Hopefully, reading that shows you why we need pronouns, which are words that represent other nouns. If we didn't have pronouns, everything would sound repetitive and confusing.

Here's the better version:

> To avoid a ticket, Alice told the police that **she** didn't realize **she** was pressing harder on the accelerator pedal because **she** had gained 40 pounds in two months.

Here are some examples of pronouns:

	Singular	Plural
Subject Pronouns	*He, She, It*	*They*
Object Pronouns	*Her, Him, It*	*Them*
Possessive Pronouns	*Hers, His, Its*	*Theirs*
Possessive Adj. Pronouns	*Her, His, Its*	*Their*
Relative Pronouns	*This, That, Which*	*These, Those*
Reflexive Pronouns	*Himself, Herself, Itself*	*Themselves*

Don't worry about memorizing the names or types—just familiarize yourself with the words so that you can tell whether something's a pronoun or not.

You need to know only two rules for pronouns, but they're really important:

Rule 1

A pronoun must clearly stand for ONE and ONLY ONE other NOUN.

Rule 2

A singular noun must be referred to by a singular pronoun. Likewise, a plural pronoun must be referred to by a plural pronoun.

Example 1

Wrong:	Whenever Jason and Alexander sit down at a buffet, **he** eats way more food.
Correct:	Whenever Jason and Alexander sit down at a buffet, **Jason** eats way more food.

This example violates rule 1 because we don't know who eats more. *He* could refer to either Jason or Alexander.

In conversation, we might say something like *"He eats way more food,"* and that's grammatically fine because we know from the context of our conversation who *he* is. But on the SAT, a pronoun with no clear reference is an error.

Example 2

Wrong:	Even if a student gets in early, **they** still have to maintain good grades during senior year.
Correct:	Even if a student gets in early, **he or she** still **has** to maintain good grades during senior year.

In this example, rule 2 is being violated. We know that *they* obviously refers to *student*, but *they* is a plural pronoun while *student* is a singular noun. *He or she* is the singular pronoun we must use (yes, it's singular). Again, we must use singular pronouns for singular nouns and plural pronouns for plural nouns.

Example 3

Wrong:	At the police station, **they** found a pile of cash stashed in her bra.
Correct:	At the police station, **the inspectors** found a pile of cash stashed in her bra.

Who's *they*? Here, *they* doesn't even have a reference—it doesn't represent any noun that we can see in front of us. Sure, we could assume that *they* refers to the police, but *police* is not a noun in this sentence—it's an adjective. Remember that a pronoun MUST stand for an existing noun somewhere.

Example 4

Wrong:	My teammate deleted my part of the essay. The next day, I confronted him about **this**.
Correct:	My teammate deleted my part of the essay. The next day, I confronted him about **this deletion**.
Correct:	My teammate deleted my part of the essay. The next day, I confronted him about **his reasons for doing so**.

In this example, it's not explicit what *this* stands for. The easiest way to fix reference errors involving *this, that, these,* or *those* is to either add the noun right after or replace the pronoun altogether with something else. By inserting the word *deletion* into the sentence, we essentially define what *this* is.

Think of pronouns as shortcuts or aliases for other files on your computer. The original file must exist for there to be a shortcut. Furthermore, the shortcut must match the file it represents. You wouldn't want to click on a shortcut only to open something other than what you were expecting.

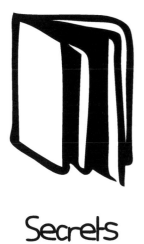

Note

The pronoun *it* can be used in the following way:
- It was a dark and stormy night.
- It took 10,000 years for the star's rays to reach us.

These are completely fine sentences where you shouldn't worry at all about pronoun errors.

Here are a few more questions and answers so you get the hang of it:

Example 5

Wrong:	Drunk with beer bottles in both hands, Michael slid and dropped **it** on the rug.
Correct:	Drunk with beer bottles in both hands, Michael slid and dropped **them** on the rug.

Example 6

Wrong:	The senior class has organized **their** school trip to the Antarctic.
Correct:	The senior class has organized **its** school trip to the Antarctic.

Example 7

Wrong:	Because the restaurant was amazingly successful, **they** hired more employees to run it.
Correct:	Because the restaurant was amazingly successful, **it** hired more employees to run it.

Example 8

Wrong:	I got so much in the mail today. I've been opening all **those** since noon.
Correct:	I got so much in the mail today. I've been opening all **those letters** since noon.

Example 9

Wrong:	Everyone wished that **they** had cheaper textbooks rather than the rip-offs that were required.
Correct:	Everyone wished that **he or she** had cheaper textbooks rather than the rip-offs that were required.

Example 10

Wrong:	A good chef always takes good care of **their** equipment.
Correct:	A good chef always takes good care of **his or her** equipment.

Example 11

Wrong:	Because the blankets got torn in the wash, we must replace **it** before the customer gets back.
Correct:	Because the blankets got torn in the wash, we must replace **them** before the customer gets back.

Example 12

Wrong:	The lion and the tortoise were about to get into a fight when **it** fell down a ditch.
Correct:	The lion and the tortoise were about to get into a fight when **the tortoise** fell down a ditch.

Example 13

Wrong:	Few chairs are as comfortable as **that** made by the Herman-Miller company.
Correct:	Few chairs are as comfortable as **those** made by the Herman-Miller company.

In this last example, *those* refers to *chairs*. Because *chairs* is plural, we need *those* instead of *that*, which is singular. It's easy to remember because you would always say *that car, that jet, that book* and *those cars, those jets, those books* rather than the other way around.

Exercise 1: Fix the pronoun error in the following sentences. The pronoun you need to fix is bolded. Some of them have flexible answers and some require you to also change the verb. Answers for this chapter start on page 227.

1. When I looked up at the stars, I couldn't believe **it was** so many light-years away.

2. Although many people believe the tiger is fierce and ferocious, **they are** actually quite peaceful.

3. Anyone who misses **their** parents can just go home.

4. The toxic level of water bottles isn't apparent to most people because they assume **its** plastic content is harmless.

5. After searching the whole day for my brother's shoes, I told him I wasn't able to find **it**.

6. Birds must migrate south during the winter season because **it manages** to survive only in warmer climates.

7. Until technological advances enable **it** to consume less fuel for thrust and power, the possibility of space rockets to Mars will remain remote.

8. By the time **it** can be fixed up, cleaned, and upgraded, old cell phones will be completely irrelevant compared to newer ones.

9. The food that **they** serve at the restaurant is absolutely delicious.

10. The secretary unplugged the keyboard from the computer and cleaned **it**.

11. Joey was required to go to a meeting but **it** never stated the location.

12. Before the state university could open up a new program in astrophysics, **they** needed funding from alumni.

13. The government is so arrogant in **their** ability to solve problems that **they have** silenced the voice of the people.

14. The show *American Idol* has as **their** premiere judge a man who can't sing himself.

15. Elle told the teacher that **she** had made a mistake.

16. My iPhone fell onto the glass plate, but thankfully **it** didn't break.

17. Some spiders can inject **itself** with poison to enact revenge on their predators.

18. Anthony used to hang out all the time with Albert until **he** got the big promotion at work.

19. When a person dies, **their** sense of hearing is the last to go whereas touch and sight are the first.

20. The city of Boston, which weathered the American Revolution, regularly offers tours that honor **their** local heroes.

21. One of the unique features of the red panda, an exotic creature that lives in the eastern Himalayas, is **their** ringed tail, which is used as a blanket in the cold.

22. The health department should be able to handle the paperwork by **themselves**.

23. My mom cooked some traditional Russian dishes, but I hate eating **that**.

24. I took my old computer to the store and luckily **they** were able to fix it.

Exercise 2: Answers for this chapter start on page 227.

True Crime Writer

Like most authors, Ann Rule didn't dive into the world of writing right after college. Although she did major in creative writing, her real passion was in unraveling the mysteries of the criminal mind. **1** They didn't have majors related to forensics and crime, so she took many courses related to science and psychology.

Ann began her adult life as a police officer for the Seattle Police Department, which was known across the country for **2** their high profile cases. Even though she liked **3** it more, she also wrote regularly for the *True Detective* magazine and volunteered at an abuse hot line.

When writing for the magazine, Ann used a fake name, Andy Stark. She also published several books under **4** that. While many say that the writing style of her works is similar to that of Edward Stratemeyer, creator of the Nancy Drew series, she maintains that **5** they aren't. Her stories' characters, who are quite eccentric, by **6** itself are enough to distinguish her work from others.

1
- A) NO CHANGE
- B) It
- C) Those
- D) Her college

2
- A) NO CHANGE
- B) its
- C) these
- D) her

3
- A) NO CHANGE
- B) them
- C) the police work
- D) that

4
- A) NO CHANGE
- B) this.
- C) that name.
- D) them.

5
- A) NO CHANGE
- B) it isn't.
- C) they aren't them.
- D) they don't.

6
- A) NO CHANGE
- B) its own
- C) their own
- D) themselves

Ms. Rule's first book was titled *The Stranger Beside Me*, which, like many of her other books, was turned into a movie. Ann played a large part in **7** its making. In fact, she wrote the script for the movie and distributed **8** them to everyone involved. She also worked as a consultant and even helped choose the actors for the different roles. Ann liked to choose actors that resembled the characters that **9** he or she was playing.

Ann Rule loves her fan base. After the release of each book, she makes a special point of answering **10** their emails and attending as many book signings as possible even though **11** they have caused her serious problems with her wrist. Halfway through, she had to start using a rubber stamp instead of signing **12** them personally. Ann had to cancel appearances after the release of her latest book because of a broken hip, but any reader can still get **13** his or her favorite book autographed by mailing it in.

7
A) NO CHANGE
B) their makings.
C) those.
D) them.

8
A) NO CHANGE
B) it
C) this
D) those

9
A) NO CHANGE
B) it was
C) they were
D) were

10
A) NO CHANGE
B) these
C) her fans'
D) its

11
A) NO CHANGE
B) it has caused
C) this has caused
D) this is of the cause of

12
A) NO CHANGE
B) the books
C) it
D) those

13
A) NO CHANGE
B) their
C) them
D) its

15 Tenses

There are a lot of different tenses but here are some of the ones you'll encounter:

Tense	Verb		
	To Hug	To Swim	To Be
Present	*He hugs...*	*He swims...*	*He is...*
Past	*He hugged...*	*He swam...*	*He was...*
Future	*He will hug...*	*He will swim...*	*He will be...*
Present Perfect	*He has hugged...*	*He has swum...*	*He has been...*
Past Perfect	*He had hugged...*	*He had swum...*	*He had been...*

The present perfect and the past perfect are rarely tested on the SAT, but we'll touch on them later in this chapter so you'll know how to evaluate the cases where they might be correct.

The most common verb-related error you'll see on the SAT is tense inconsistency. You need to ensure that the tenses in a sentence make sense. **Most of the time, that means changing everything to either past tense or present tense.**

Example 1

Wrong:	Whenever we stopped by the market, my mom always tries to negotiate the prices.
Correct:	Whenever we **stop** by the market, my mom always **tries** to negotiate the prices.
Correct:	Whenever we **stopped** by the market, my mom always **tried** to negotiate the prices.

Example 2

Wrong:	After winning Wimbledon in 2012, Federer regained the top ranking and declares himself the best in the world.
Correct:	After winning Wimbledon in 2012, Federer **regained** the top ranking and **declared** himself the best in the world.

Example 3

Wrong:	The end of World War II came when German forces surrender in Berlin and Italy.
Correct:	The end of World War II came when German forces **surrendered** in Berlin and Italy.
Rule:	Often times, dates or historical events in the question tell you the past tense is needed.

Example 4

Wrong:	Although the cheetah holds the record for fastest land animal, many other mammals outlasted it.
Correct:	Although the cheetah holds the record for fastest land animal, many other mammals **outlast** it.
Rule:	Statements of fact or of the way things are (things that are always true and will continue to be true) must be in present tense.

There are some cases where verbs don't have to be consistent because of the meaning of the sentence. Sometimes we DO want to talk about two actions that happened in different time periods.

Example 5

Correct:	When I **was** young, I hated vegetables, but now I **love** them.
Correct:	Because he **was** late for the anniversary dinner, she **is** thinking about leaving him.

Both of the sentences above are correct because the meaning **intends** for the verb tenses to be inconsistent. As you're checking for tenses on the SAT, make sure you take the meaning of the sentence into consideration. Don't be too robotic.

As a side note, answer choices with *would* or *would have* are typically correct only when dealing with hypotheticals:

- If I were rich, I **would** buy a Ferrari.
- If she had done her homework, she **would have** gotten an "A" this semester.

Before we dive into perfect tenses, let me first say that **answer choices containing the present perfect or past perfect tenses are almost always wrong.**

So if you see the following answer choices:

A) NO CHANGE (connects)
B) connected
C) had connected
D) has been connected

You can be pretty certain the answer won't be C or D. That's because on the SAT, the answers to tense-related questions tend to be the shortest and simplest ones.

Having said that, the SAT will mix it up on rare occasions to prevent the test from being gamed. Fortunately, a basic understanding of the present perfect and past perfect tenses is all you need to handle these edge cases effectively.

Present Perfect

The present perfect (*has/have + past participle*) is used to show that an action started in the past and continues into or has some effect on the present.

Past   Present

- He **has stared** at the computer for four hours. (*He may still be staring right now.*)
- They **have finished** their homework for today. (*They don't have any more work to do now.*)
- Mrs. Parker **has taught** fifth grade ever since I can remember. (*She still teaches fifth grade.*)

Tip

Sentences that require the present perfect usually have the words *since, for,* or *from* in them.

Example 6

Wrong:	Ever since she saw how pandas were gruesomely hunted, Kristie devotes her life to panda conservation.
Correct:	Ever since she saw how pandas were gruesomely hunted, Kristie **has devoted** her life to panda conservation.

Example 7

Wrong:	For over fifty years, New York City was the capital of fine dining on the East Coast.
Correct:	For over fifty years, New York City **has been** the capital of fine dining on the East Coast.

Past Perfect

The past perfect (*had + past participle*) is used to specify the order in which two past events happened. The first event is denoted by the past perfect while the second event is left in simple past. For example,

I **had danced** the night away by the time I fell asleep.

1st event   2nd event

Dancing   Falling asleep   Past

The *dancing* happened before the *falling asleep*.

Example 8

Wrong:	All of a sudden, Jimmy vividly remembered where he has hidden the jewelry.
Correct:	All of a sudden, Jimmy vividly remembered where he **had hidden** the jewelry.
Correct:	All of a sudden, Jimmy vividly remembered where he **hid** the jewelry.

As you can see from Example 8, the past perfect is often optional (simple past being the default). This is a good thing to be aware of, but don't go worrying about whether you need the past perfect or not in every situation. This topic is rarely tested and the SAT will never make it that complicated; there will always be only one right answer choice.

Because verb tenses is a complex topic full of subtleties, students often ask me about various sentences that illustrate concepts beyond the scope of this chapter. My response is always the same: *Don't overthink tenses on the SAT. You do not need to know every little rule and exception. The questions you encounter will have clear-cut answers.*

Exercise 1: Make the tenses consistent in the following sentences. Answers for this chapter start on page 229.

1. When Columbus and his crew discovered America in 1492, many Indian tribes <u>welcome</u> them graciously.

2. The United States is considered the melting pot because its inhabitants <u>included</u> immigrants from all over the world.

3. Although the giant panda's diet consists primarily of bamboo, most other bears <u>hunted</u> for their food.

4. The door was decorated with ornate imprints of animals and <u>has</u> a stained glass window in the middle.

5. Every Sunday, Jane cleans the house and does the laundry at the same time her dad <u>could have mowed</u> the lawn.

6. She bought her dress at Wal-Mart yet it <u>impresses</u> everyone at the party.

7. Every year he wishes for an end to world hunger and <u>prayed</u> for a cure for cancer.

8. Whereas astronomers focus on the stars to advance the frontier of science, astrologists <u>studied</u> the constellations to predict whether bad things will happen today.

9. To create the bracelet, Jane carefully slipped beads onto the band and then <u>had twisted</u> it into a circular shape.

10. It's easy to tell when the teacher is being boring because some students start to fidget with their pens while others <u>have yawned</u>.

11. Admissions officers <u>had looked</u> at several factors when determining whether to admit an applicant.

12. In today's fast-paced world, news sometimes spreads on social media faster than it <u>could have traveled</u> through traditional media.

Exercise 2: Answers for this chapter start on page 229.

1. The electric violinist put the speakers on full blast and <u>shaken</u> up the house.

    A) NO CHANGE
    B) shook
    C) had shook
    D) begun to shake

2. The incredible salary <u>had been</u> one of the reasons I am staying at my boring job.

    A) NO CHANGE
    B) will have been
    C) was
    D) is

3. When Rick finally reached the train station across from the bus stop, the last train <u>has already left.</u>

    A) NO CHANGE
    B) already leaves.
    C) is leaving already.
    D) had already left.

4. I like to shop at the used bookstore because the people there are so friendly. It <u>was</u> a popular place to discover great books that can't be found elsewhere.

    A) NO CHANGE
    B) is
    C) had been
    D) was considered

5. The host presented the awards on the show and the winners <u>are</u> honored to receive them.

    A) NO CHANGE
    B) had been
    C) would have been
    D) were

6. It's unlikely the property developer will be able to convince him to move out; James <u>lived</u> in that house for 30 years.

    A) NO CHANGE
    B) lives
    C) has lived
    D) had lived

7. When my uncle <u>has gone</u> to buy a new computer, the salesman told him that he couldn't get a discount.

    A) NO CHANGE
    B) had gone
    C) went
    D) goes

8. Jay wasn't promoted to colonel until he <u>has proven</u> himself as a sergeant.

    A) NO CHANGE
    B) proves
    C) had proven
    D) will prove

9. Showing us that his car has a GPS, the driver <u>claims</u> that he always knows the fastest route.

    A) NO CHANGE
    B) claiming
    C) having claimed
    D) has claimed

10. There <u>have been</u> mysterious ghost sightings at the old mansion ever since the owner abandoned it years ago.

    A) NO CHANGE
    B) are
    C) will be
    D) had been

11. In 1869, Watson and Crick discovered something that <u>surprised</u> many scientists at that time – DNA.

    A) NO CHANGE
    B) had been surprised
    C) will have surprised
    D) surprises

12. Richard Branson has invested in many successful startups, built a global empire worth billions, and <u>traveling</u> all across the world.

    A) NO CHANGE
    B) travel
    C) traveled
    D) had traveled

13. Since I graduated last Tuesday with a degree in Floral Management, I <u>was looking</u> for a job and a place to stay.

    A) NO CHANGE
    B) had looked
    C) looked
    D) have been looking

14. While online tutorials make learning convenient and accessible, teachers <u>hold</u> students accountable in a way that promotes action and retention.

    A) NO CHANGE
    B) held
    C) had held
    D) holding

15. At the zoo, monkeys play on the handlebars and exotic birds <u>had chirped</u> in their elaborate cages.

    A) NO CHANGE
    B) chirp
    C) chirped
    D) could have chirped

Exercise 3: Answers for this chapter start on page 229.

1. Acupuncture starts with needles being inserted at the right locations. After that initial stage, the needles <u>had been</u> heated to strategically stimulate certain areas of the body.

    A) NO CHANGE
    B) have been
    C) were
    D) are

2. Pluto <u>had long been</u> considered a planet until scientists deemed it too small.

    A) NO CHANGE
    B) has long been
    C) is long
    D) was long being

3. Last year, the teacher <u>had chosen</u> the most difficult textbook, and the class average dropped steadily throughout the semester.

    A) NO CHANGE
    B) chose
    C) chooses
    D) choosing

4. While we were on vacation, my brother and I <u>will quietly creep</u> out of our hotel room to go swimming with the sharks in the ocean.

    A) NO CHANGE
    B) quietly creep
    C) are quietly creeping
    D) quietly crept

5. Performing on the streets, I sing popular pop songs at the same time my partner <u>can play</u> the guitar in the back.

    A) NO CHANGE
    B) played
    C) had played
    D) plays

6. Scientists <u>had explored</u> the possibility of alien life on other planets for centuries, but only now has space technology become advanced enough to collect firsthand data from faraway planets.

    A) NO CHANGE
    B) have explored
    C) explored
    D) explore

7. When I went to Texas for my cousin's wedding, I drive over 200 miles to see the sites and avoid flying on a plane.

   A) NO CHANGE
   B) have driven
   C) drove
   D) will drive

8. The residents of Colorado celebrated when their state would become the first to legalize marijuana.

   A) NO CHANGE
   B) has become
   C) becoming
   D) became

9. Once he noticed the new symptoms, the doctor took Mark off the medication that he prescribes six weeks before.

   A) NO CHANGE
   B) had prescribed
   C) has prescribed
   D) will prescribe

10. By 1999, the internet would have already drastically changed the way people around the world communicate.

   A) NO CHANGE
   B) had already drastically changed
   C) already drastically changes
   D) has already drastically changed

11. From its start as an online bookstore, the internet retailer Amazon will expand into markets such as groceries that many thought were outside its reach.

   A) NO CHANGE
   B) expands
   C) has expanded
   D) had expanded

12. Martin Luther King Jr. fought for racial equality and led the Civil Rights Movement. He called the American people to stand up for freedom, equality, and justice.

   A) NO CHANGE
   B) called on
   C) calls on
   D) calls

13. After what he said, it will be hard for him to recover in the polls, let alone won the election.

   A) NO CHANGE
   B) winning
   C) win
   D) will win

14. By the time we got a seat at Peter Luger's Steakhouse, most of the waiters went to go home.

   A) NO CHANGE
   B) have gone
   C) had gone
   D) are going

15. During the Renaissance, the painters have experimented with different styles that combined the classics with new scientific knowledge.

   A) NO CHANGE
   B) have been experimenting
   C) experiment
   D) experimented

16

Commas, Dashes, & Colons

In this chapter, we'll go over all the rules you need to know for each punctuation mark and give you examples and exercises that cover the full range of ways they can be tested. Just so we're on the same page, we'll first review the semicolon (covered in the *Run-ons* chapter).

The Semicolon

A semicolon is used to join two independent clauses.

Examples:

- I love the game of basketball; however, I don't play it myself.
- The tribe was left without food for weeks; the members had no choice but to resort to cannibalism.
- Bats are nocturnal creatures; they come out only during the night.

Anytime a semicolon isn't being used for this purpose, it's incorrect. The SAT loves to use semicolons to do dirty things they're not supposed to:

Example 1

Wrong:	The platter was filled with berries, crackers; and cheese.
Correct:	The platter was filled with berries, crackers, and cheese.

Example 2

Wrong:	Ready for the journey of a lifetime; the boy hopped on the spaceship.
Correct:	Ready for the journey of a lifetime, the boy hopped on the spaceship.

The Comma

Of all the punctuation marks, the comma has the most uses. Here are the ones that are most frequently tested.

1. Use a comma after an introductory clause, phrase, or modifier.

Example 3

Wrong:	Although he is lactose intolerant he likes to eat pizza for lunch.
Correct:	Although he is lactose intolerant, he likes to eat pizza for lunch.

Example 4

Wrong:	Trapped in a mine the victims found it hard to see and breathe.
Wrong:	Trapped in a mine, the victims found it hard to see and breathe.

Example 5

Wrong:	At the end of the rainbow we saw a bowl of Lucky Charms cereal.
Correct:	At the end of the rainbow, we saw a bowl of Lucky Charms cereal.

Example 6

Wrong:	When I turn 16 I'm going to buy a car.
Correct:	When I turn 16, I'm going to buy a car.

Example 7

Wrong:	Because she's been so busy I haven't seen her in a month.
Correct:	Because she's been so busy, I haven't seen her in a month.

2. Use commas to separate three or more items in a series.

Example 8

Wrong:	His hobbies included jumping off planes, crashing helicopters and eating jellyfish.
Correct:	His hobbies included jumping off planes, crashing helicopters, and eating jellyfish.

Example 9

Wrong:	After college, James had three options: get a job, apply to graduate school or become a criminal.
Correct:	After college, James had three options: get a job, apply to graduate school, or become a criminal.

The comma between the last two items is sometimes called the serial or Oxford comma. Although some style guides make it optional, most require it. On the SAT, the Oxford comma is required.

3. Use commas to set off nonrestrictive/nonessential elements.

I will elaborate on the terms *nonrestrictive* and *nonessential* after a few examples, but just keep in mind they mean the same thing.

Example 10

Wrong:	Great white sharks the most fearsome creatures of the sea are actually less dangerous than they appear.
Correct:	Great white sharks , the most fearsome creatures of the sea , are actually less dangerous than they appear.

The phrase *the most fearsome creatures of the sea* is **nonessential** because it just adds additional description to the sentence. **If we take it out, what's left is still a sentence that makes sense grammatically.** This is the first part to understanding nonessential elements. The following examples illustrate the second part.

Example 11

Wrong:	The guy, cleaning the room, is the janitor.
Correct:	The guy/ cleaning the room/ is the janitor.

The phrase *cleaning the room* is an **essential** element because it specifies which guy. In other words, there are multiple guys in the room, and we need a restrictive phrase to limit the scope of who or what we're talking about.

The best method of determining whether something is restrictive or non-restrictive is to ask yourself this question: *Does the phrase narrow down what we're talking about?*

If yes, the phrase is essential and SHOULD NOT be set off by commas. If no, the phrase is not essential and SHOULD be set off by commas. Take, for instance, the following two examples:

Example 12

Wrong:	Students, who work hard, will ace the SATs.
Correct:	Students/ who work hard/ will ace the SATs.

Example 13

Wrong:	Jonathan who works hard will ace the SATs.
Correct:	Jonathan , who works hard , will ace the SATs.

In Example 12, the phrase *who work hard* narrows down the scope of who we're talking about. Otherwise, the sentence would be talking about ALL students. It's only the *students who work hard* who will ace the SATs.

In Example 13, the phrase *who works hard* does NOT narrow down who we're talking about. We already know it's just one person—Jonathan—and he happens to work hard.

Example 14

Wrong:	Stephen King's first novel *Carrie* was a surprise success.
Correct:	Stephen King's first novel , *Carrie* , was a surprise success.

Example 15

| Wrong: | The poem, *The Road Not Taken*, is one of Robert Frost's most famous works. |
| Correct: | The poem/ *The Road Not Taken*/ is one of Robert Frost's most famous works. |

In Example 15, the title of the poem is an essential element because it narrows down which poem is being referred to. If you took out the title, the sentence would lose its meaning. In Example 14, *Carrie* is nonessential because *Stephen King's first novel* already designates which book it is and doesn't narrow anything down further. In other words, *Stephen King's first novel* was already enough to get us down to one book. Yes, *Carrie* is an important piece of information, but that's not relevant when deciding what is essential vs. nonessential.

The SAT loves to test this concept with people's occupations:

Example 16

| Wrong: | Crowds stood in line to see author, J.K. Rowling, at the bookstore in London. |
| Correct: | Crowds stood in line to see author/ J.K. Rowling/ at the bookstore in London. |

J.K. Rowling narrows down what author we're talking about.

Example 17

| Wrong: | The man at the front of the line scientist, John Willard, wouldn't stop complaining about the rain. |
| Correct: | The man at the front of the line, scientist/ John Willard, wouldn't stop complaining about the rain. |

John Willard is essential to *scientist*, so there shouldn't be a comma between them. However, the phrase *scientist John Williard* is nonessential to *man at the front of the line* because it doesn't narrow down who we're talking about any further. Therefore, the phrase as a whole should be set off by commas.

If that was a lot to take in, take a deep breath and review this section until you truly understand essential vs. nonessential elements. Because if you do, you'll fly through questions that most other students get stuck on.

Moving on, when the word *that* is used, it's always for restrictive/essential elements (commas are unnecessary) whereas *which* is usually used for nonrestrictive/nonessential elements (commas are necessary).

Example 18

| Wrong: | Runners around the world participate in the Boston Marathon which is 26 miles long. |
| Correct: | Runners around the world participate in the Boston Marathon, which is 26 miles long. |

Example 19

| Wrong: | The path, that we took yesterday, is 15 miles long. |
| Correct: | The path/ that we took yesterday/ is 15 miles long. |

Example 20

Wrong:	Next to the Japanese restaurant, I like, is the ice cream place.
Correct:	Next to the Japanese restaurant I like is the ice cream place.

The essential phrase *I like* is just the shortened version of *that I like*. The word *that* is sometimes omitted.

Example 21

Wrong:	Lions are carnivorous or meat-eating mammals.
Correct:	Lions are carnivorous, or meat-eating, mammals.

Phrases that help define a previous term in this manner are nonessential.

4. Use commas to set off transitions and intervening phrases.

This rule piggybacks off the previous one since most transitions and intervening phrases are nonessential to the sentences they're in, but more examples never hurt anyone.

Example 22

Wrong:	Some animals are nocturnal; for example the coyote hunts during the night.
Correct:	Some animals are nocturnal; for example, the coyote hunts during the night.

Example 23

Wrong:	When I told my parents I was pregnant, they were to my relief supportive and understanding.
Correct:	When I told my parents I was pregnant, they were, to my relief, supportive and understanding.

Example 24

Wrong:	Penguins unlike most other birds cannot fly.
Correct:	Penguins, unlike most other birds, cannot fly.

Example 25

Wrong:	Most bats are blind. Their sense of hearing however is amazing.
Correct:	Most bats are blind. Their sense of hearing, however, is amazing.

CHAPTER 16   COMMAS, DASHES & COLONS

The Colon

Colons are used after an independent clause to direct attention to a list, a noun phrase, quotation, or another independent clause that provides a summary or clarification. Here are some examples:

- A classic eggs benedict breakfast should include the following ingredients: poached eggs, english muffins, bacon, and hollandaise sauce.

- Tokyo is one of the cleanest cities in Asia: the street cleaners sometimes have no work to do.

- Cambridge is home to two of the best universities in the world: MIT and Harvard.

- I had no choice but to utter the truth in front of the judge: my brother was guilty.

- The speaker had a few last words of wisdom for the students: "Always do what you are afraid to do."

Rule

A colon can only come after an independent clause. Therefore, all of the following are incorrect, even though they may seem like correct uses of the colon:

- The dangerous animals you have to watch out for are: lions, tigers, and pythons.
- The evidence consists of: emails, text messages, and phone calls.
- The local bakery sells many delicious desserts such as: cheesecake, lemon tarts, and brownies.

None of the examples above need the colon.

The Dash

Dashes (—) are used to separate interrupting thoughts and phrases from the rest of the sentence, often for dramatic effect. The interrupting thought will typically be a list, a restatement, or an additional detail.

1. When the interrupting thought is at the end of the sentence, use a single dash.

Examples:

- The city is full of people you would never meet in my hometown—bums, actors, models, the crazy, and the oddly dressed.

- Life is like a puzzle—half the fun is in trying to work it out.

- There are only two vegetables I will ever eat—eggplant and corn.

- Everywhere we traveled in Kyoto there were vending machines—some served green tea while others carried only juice.

But wait a second! Doesn't a colon do the same thing? Yes, when a single dash is used in this way, it can be swapped out for a colon. However, a dash can be used in a few more cases than a colon can. For example, the dash can be used for a dramatic pause, something you wouldn't use a colon for.

- Frank took the goldfish from the bowl, carried it to the bathroom, put it in the toilet—and dropped it.

- Cecilia is ready to tell the truth—or so she says.

Dashes can also be paired up (see next point), but colons can't be. So while a dash can almost always take the place of a colon, a colon cannot always take the place of a dash. The SAT will never give you both a colon and a dash as answer choices when they are interchangeable.

2. When the interrupting thought is in the middle of the sentence, use a pair of dashes.

Examples:

- All our kitchen equipment—from the steel pans used for sauces to the premium-grade oven—had to be sold to cover our losses.

- The Loch Ness Monster—a sea creature that is rumored to exist but has never been found—supposedly comes out only during the winter.

- When my teacher found the cookies I was hiding—all 154 of them—she ate them all herself.

- My cousin was a world-class wrestler—he still is—but now he focuses on coaching others.

A pair of dashes is very often (but not always) interchangeable with a pair of commas or a pair of parentheses. After all, they're all ways of setting off a nonessential phrase in the middle of a sentence. This brings us to the following rules:

Rule 1

A sentence should still make sense on its own if the interrupting phrase between the dashes is removed. If it doesn't, the dashes are not being used correctly. Take a look at this example:

The homerun ball smashed through—the neighbor's window—and rolled into the living room.

This sentence is incorrect because it doesn't make sense if *the neighbor's window* is removed. *Smashed through what?* The correct version would not use dashes at all:

The homerun ball smashed through the neighbor's window and rolled into the living room.

Rule 2

A dash can only pair up with another dash. A comma can only pair up with another comma. A parenthesis can only pair up with another parenthesis. You cannot mix and match.

Example 26

Wrong:	All our kitchen equipment—from the steel pans used for sauces to the premium-grade oven, had to be sold to cover our losses.
Wrong:	All our kitchen equipment (from the steel pans used for sauces to the premium-grade oven—had to be sold to cover our losses.
Correct:	All our kitchen equipment, from the steel pans used for sauces to the premium-grade oven, had to be sold to cover our losses.
Correct:	All our kitchen equipment—from the steel pans used for sauces to the premium-grade oven—had to be sold to cover our losses.
Correct:	All our kitchen equipment (from the steel pans used for sauces to the premium-grade oven) had to be sold to cover our losses.

Don't worry about which of the correct versions is best. The SAT will never ask you to choose between answer choices that are interchangeable.

Now here's how the SAT will try to trick you. They'll give you a sentence like the following:

I like to walk everyday—not for exercise, but for alone time.

Based on what we learned earlier, your immediate reaction might be that the sentence is wrong because the dash and the comma should not be paired up together. Either the comma should be replaced with a dash or the dash should be replaced with a comma.

However, that would be an incorrect reading of the sentence. The sentence is not trying to set off *not for exercise* as an interrupting thought. How do we know? Rule 1. If it were an interrupting thought, the sentence would still make sense without it, but removing the phrase from the sentence leaves us with

I like to walk everyday but for alone time.

which doesn't make sense on its own. Instead, the entire second half of the sentence, *not for exercise, but for alone time*, is the interrupting thought. And since it comes at the end, only a single dash is needed. Therefore, the original sentence is grammatically correct and should be read as two parts with a dash in between. Note that the comma before "but" is simply a pause. It's optional and has nothing to do with the dash.

Example 27

Wrong:	His missed catch was one of the most epic failures, there is no other way to describe it—in sports history—one we won't be able to forget for a long time.
Correct:	His missed catch was one of the most epic failures—there is no other way to describe it—in sports history, one we won't be able to forget for a long time.

Notice the run-on in the wrong version.

Common Punctuation Misuses

Before we get to some exercises, it'll be helpful to review some frequently tested punctuation misuses.

1. Don't use punctuation before prepositional phrases (e.g. *at, for, in, of, on, to, with*).

There are definitely exceptions, so don't be too automatic with this rule, but on the SAT, **punctuation before a preposition is almost always wrong**. This rule especially holds when the preposition is one that usually goes with its preceding words (e.g. the *of* in *consists of*). Some examples will clarify:

Example 28

Wrong:	She was waiting, at the train station.
Correct:	She was waiting/ at the train station.

Example 29

Wrong:	The police investigation, of the crime scene, didn't turn up any clues.
Correct:	The police investigation/ of the crime scene/ didn't turn up any clues.

Example 30

Wrong:	Robert wants to make changes; to the essay before we submit it.
Correct:	Robert wants to make changes/ to the essay before we submit it.

Example 31

Wrong:	Rolex watches are designed: with elegance, style, and luxury in mind.
Correct:	Rolex watches are designed/ with elegance, style, and luxury in mind.

Example 32

Wrong:	Andy Murray, of Great Britain, competed intensely, for the gold medal in tennis.
Correct:	Andy Murray/ of Great Britain/ competed intensely/ for the gold medal in tennis.

Example 33

Wrong:	The runner was surprised— by the number of people who showed up to cheer him on.
Correct:	The runner was surprised—/ by the number of people who showed up to cheer him on.

2. Don't use any punctuation after *such as*, *like*, or *including*

Example 34

Wrong:	The Thai restaurant serves noodle dishes such as: pad thai, pad see ew, and kua gai.
Correct:	The Thai restaurant serves noodle dishes such as/ pad thai, pad see ew, and kua gai.

Example 35

Wrong:	When I tried frog legs for the first time, I thought it tasted like: chicken.
Correct:	When I tried frog legs for the first time, I thought it tasted like/ chicken.

3. Don't use any punctuation before *that*

Example 36

Wrong:	The report indicates, that the pollution above Beijing has reached an all-time high.
Correct:	The report indicates/ that the pollution above Beijing has reached an all-time high.

There are exceptions, but this rule will serve you well much more often than not, especially on the SAT.

4. Don't put semicolons, dashes, or colons where commas should be used

Example 37

Wrong:	The patient lifted up his sleeve; revealing a deep scar on his forearm.
Correct:	The patient lifted up his sleeve, revealing a deep scar on his forearm.

Exercise 1: Answers for this chapter start on page 231.

1. The Rolex Daytona, the most luxurious watch ever <u>released,</u> sells for a staggering half a million dollars.

   A) NO CHANGE
   B) released
   C) released:
   D) released—

2. My brother is a decent tennis <u>player, he serves well:</u> but his forehand could be hit with a bit more accuracy.

   A) NO CHANGE
   B) player—he serves well—
   C) player, he serves well—
   D) player, he serves well;

3. I practice scales on the piano <u>everyday—not because I want to,</u> but because I have to.

   A) NO CHANGE
   B) everyday; not because I want to
   C) everyday not because I want to;
   D) everyday, not because I want to;

4. As the country becomes increasingly health conscious, fast food chains are removing a number of artificial ingredients from their <u>offerings:</u> sodium nitrite, aluminum silicate, canthaxanthin, and monosodium glutamate.

   A) NO CHANGE
   B) offerings;
   C) offerings
   D) offerings,

5. Google's search engine is not only effective but also <u>easy to use,</u> the home page is nothing more than a search field.

   A) NO CHANGE
   B) easy to use:
   C) easy to use
   D) used easily:

6. These strange rainbow <u>lights, a phenomenon only recently discovered in photographs of the town</u> remain one of science's unsolved mysteries.

   A) NO CHANGE
   B) lights a phenomenon only recently discovered in photographs of the town,
   C) lights, a phenomenon only recently discovered, in photographs of the town
   D) lights, a phenomenon only recently discovered in photographs of the town,

7. The handbook lays out the most common mistakes when it comes to <u>writing;</u> lack of structure, having nothing to say, and repetitiveness.

   A) NO CHANGE
   B) writing,
   C) writing
   D) writing:

8. While I was on my trip to Thailand, Claire went on a shopping spree to <u>buy</u> a new car and a new wardrobe without my permission.

    A) NO CHANGE
    B) buy:
    C) buy;
    D) buy,

9. There are more stars in space than there are grains of <u>sand,</u> on all of Earth's beaches.

    A) NO CHANGE
    B) sand;
    C) sand—
    D) sand

10. Environmentalists have marched into the streets to protest the country's lax attitude towards deforestation, which has proven to be devastating to the local deer <u>population: only</u> twenty sightings in the past year.

    A) NO CHANGE
    B) population, and only
    C) population; only
    D) population. Only

11. What you should remember from this whole ordeal <u>is: that there</u> can be no progress without sacrifice.

    A) NO CHANGE
    B) is that there
    C) is, that there
    D) is that there,

12. The greatest accomplishment in professional tennis is winning all four grand slam tournaments in a single <u>year, the Australian Open, Roland Garros</u> (held in France), Wimbledon (held in Britain), and the U.S. Open.

    A) NO CHANGE
    B) year, the Australian Open, Roland Garros,
    C) year: the Australian Open, Roland Garros
    D) year: the Australian Open, Roland Garros,

13. Raised in a family that had toiled day after day on a <u>farm.</u> Andrew Blomfeld liked to hire people that were hard workers, even if they lacked talent.

    A) NO CHANGE
    B) farm,
    C) farm:
    D) farm;

14. Benjamin Franklin was introduced to democratic ideals when he read one of the most influential works of his <u>time;</u> John Locke's *Two Treatises of Government*.

    A) NO CHANGE
    B) time, about
    C) time:
    D) time

15. The kitchen was <u>renovated: with</u> new marble tiles, extra cabinets and cupboards, and a stainless steel sink.

    A) NO CHANGE
    B) renovated, with
    C) renovated with
    D) renovated with:

16. Of all the things the President could have done to improve the economy, he chose to shift his attention to the one thing that was considered <u>irrelevant; and it was</u> health care.

    A) NO CHANGE
    B) irrelevant: being
    C) irrelevant:
    D) irrelevant to

17. Even though he killed hundreds of innocent people, the fighter pilot was portrayed <u>as</u> a hero back at home.

    A) NO CHANGE
    B) as,
    C) as:
    D) as;

18. Designed with the user in <u>mind. The</u> new phone features a slick interface for accessing all your important notes, emails, and contacts.

    A) NO CHANGE
    B) mind, the
    C) mind: the
    D) mind the

19. While most students at MIT use their intellect to better the <u>world, for example, creating vaccines for deadly viruses,</u> some are using their exceptional math skills to beat the card games in Vegas.

    A) NO CHANGE
    B) world; for example, creating vaccines for deadly viruses,
    C) world, for example, creating vaccines for deadly viruses
    D) world—for example, creating vaccines for deadly viruses—

20. Sleep is essential for a healthy <u>lifestyle; an analysis funded by the National Institute of Health,</u> shows that ongoing sleep deficiency increases the risk of heart disease, high blood pressure, and diabetes.

    A) NO CHANGE
    B) lifestyle—an analysis funded by the National Institute of Health,
    C) lifestyle, an analysis funded by the National Institute of Health,
    D) lifestyle: an analysis funded by the National Institute of Health

21. Designed for young professionals seeking convenience, the apartment complex is close to public <u>transportation; it's</u> 5 minutes away from the train station—and includes amenities such as private parking spaces and in-unit laundry machines.

    A) NO CHANGE
    B) transportation. It's
    C) transportation—it's
    D) transportation, it's

Exercise 2: Answers for this chapter start on page 231.

1. The rapid pace of technological <u>development however</u> has enabled more people to survive on less.

    A) NO CHANGE
    B) development; however,
    C) development however,
    D) development, however,

2. Drinking coffee, scientists <u>have discovered</u> may help prevent heart disease.

    A) NO CHANGE
    B) have discovered,
    C) have discovered. It
    D) have discovered; it

3. I've decked out my laptop with a keyboard cover, pokemon <u>stickers</u> and a transparent case.

    A) NO CHANGE
    B) stickers—
    C) stickers;
    D) stickers,

4. Novak Djokovic, one of the best tennis <u>players, of the modern era,</u> is worshipped as a god in Serbia.

    A) NO CHANGE
    B) players of the modern era
    C) players of the modern era,
    D) players of the modern era—

5. The koala <u>bear—known for</u> its pouch, lives in eastern Australia, where they play in the eucalyptus trees.

    A) NO CHANGE
    B) bear, known for,
    C) bear, known for
    D) bear, known, for

6. Due to budget constraints, the chairman could not acquiesce, <u>or give in to,</u> the organization's demand for more funding.

    A) NO CHANGE
    B) or, give in to,
    C) or give in, to
    D) or give in; to

7. Mario dodged blazing <u>fireballs, turtles, with hammers,</u> and venus fly traps to rescue Princess Peach.

    A) NO CHANGE
    B) fireballs, turtles with hammers,
    C) fireballs; turtles with hammers,
    D) fireball, turtles with hammers

8. Ron had <u>mentioned, that</u> the place on the corner had really good strawberry ice cream.

   A) NO CHANGE
   B) mentioned; that
   C) mentioned that
   D) mentioned—that

9. A senior at the big accounting firm PWC pleaded not guilty to forging the <u>books,</u> claiming that it was his coworkers who did it.

   A) NO CHANGE
   B) books;
   C) books; and he was
   D) books

10. New York University professor and <u>researcher, Joshua Grossman,</u> claims that his research is definitive and trustworthy.

    A) NO CHANGE
    B) researcher Joshua Grossman
    C) researcher Joshua Grossman,
    D) researcher, Joshua Grossman

11. Known for its noodle dishes, the restaurant down the street always has <u>customers,</u> most of whom are Asian.

    A) NO CHANGE
    B) customers, and
    C) customers;
    D) customers; and

12. In 2004, no one could have predicted that Facebook—started by just a few college <u>drop-outs</u> would become the tech-giant it is today.

    A) NO CHANGE
    B) drop-outs;
    C) drop-outs,
    D) drop-outs—

13. Although the fire chief didn't mention it explicitly, everyone listening knew exactly what he was <u>referring to the fire</u> that wiped out the block—and almost the entire town—in a week.

    A) NO CHANGE
    B) referring—to the fire
    C) referring to: the fire
    D) referring to; the fire

14. John Landry apprenticed under Dutch <u>architect Thomas Johannsen</u> while he completed his studies.

    A) NO CHANGE
    B) architect, Thomas Johannsen,
    C) architect; Thomas Johannsen,
    D) architect, Thomas Johannsen

15. It's hard to find time for lunch because I have to juggle so many <u>responsibilities,</u> filing taxes, taking phone calls, printing spreadsheets, and writing emails.

    A) NO CHANGE
    B) responsibilities:
    C) responsibilities
    D) responsibilities;

16. Growing up in poverty, I often <u>dreamed, of the luxury,</u> that I was working towards.

    A) NO CHANGE
    B) dreamed of the luxury
    C) dreamed, of the luxury
    D) dreamed of the luxury,

17. Because he embraced failure instead of avoiding <u>it, and Chris</u> quickly learned how to play the piano, speak Spanish, and solve the Rubik's Cube.

    A) NO CHANGE
    B) it; Chris
    C) it, Chris
    D) it, Chris,

18. The safari guides warned us of getting too close to dangerous <u>animals such as:</u> unicorns, vampires, and werewolves.

    A) NO CHANGE
    B) animals, such as:
    C) animals, such as
    D) animals, such as,

19. Makeshift tables and a large collection of desks, piled on top of one <u>another forced</u> co-workers to collaborate with each other.

    A) NO CHANGE
    B) another: forced
    C) another; it forced
    D) another, forced

20. Jared Klein, a researcher at KIP Labs, was skeptical about the <u>results—'We</u> cannot draw any meaningful conclusions from the experiment since the subjects in the control group were not randomly selected."

    A) NO CHANGE
    B) results: "We
    C) results, we
    D) results; we

21. The annual company gala will feature a dinner buffet with oysters, steak, and <u>lobster if</u> the sales target is met (at least $500,000 by the next quarter), bonuses will be distributed to all employees.

    A) NO CHANGE
    B) lobster, if
    C) lobster, and if
    D) lobster if:

Exercise 3: Answers for this chapter start on page 231.

Origami

Origami originated in Japan, but today it is practiced all over the world. Literally, the word means "folding paper" and refers to the creation of decorative shapes and figures from paper. Example creations [1] include animals, lanterns, and boats. Most bookstores stock the most common way people discover and start [2] origami, being a kit. Kits generally have lines and [3] arrows; and they're often dotted to show you where to make the fold and how to manipulate the paper into the desired shape.

The most basic design, the one most people are taught [4] first: is the Japanese crane. Like most [5] designs, it starts with a square piece of paper and eventually turns into an intricate design that is tough to reverse engineer.

1

A) NO CHANGE
B) include:
C) include—
D) include,

2

A) NO CHANGE
B) origami:
C) origami;
D) origami

3

A) NO CHANGE
B) arrows, often dotted,
C) arrows, often dotted—
D) arrows often dotted,

4

A) NO CHANGE
B) first—
C) first,
D) first

5

A) NO CHANGE
B) designs; it
C) designs: it
D) designs, and it

Although special origami paper can be bought at craft 6 stores; any paper that can hold a fold can be used. You can even glue colored tissue paper or aluminum foil to regular paper for an interesting look. Normal copy paper suffices for simple folds, but it's a bit too 7 heavy, for more delicate designs. Very heavy paper is ideal for wet-folding, a technique developed by 8 artist, Akira Yoshizawa in the early 1900s. Wet-folding allows you to manipulate the paper into 9 curves: impossible with dry paper—to create sculpture-like designs that look more realistic.

The paper traditionally used in Japan is called *washi*, which refers to hand made paper but translates literally to "Japanese paper." It is much tougher than paper made from wood pulp. Washi is most commonly made from the bark of the gampi tree, but bamboo, wheat, 10 rice, and hemp are often used as well. Miyao 11 Hayaki, a famous origami practitioner in Tokyo continues to develop different materials as the craft evolves.

6
A) NO CHANGE
B) stores,
C) stores, which
D) stores—

7
A) NO CHANGE
B) heavy for:
C) heavy for
D) heavy, for,

8
A) NO CHANGE
B) artist, Akira Yoshizawa,
C) artist Akira Yoshizawa
D) artist Akira Yoshizawa,

9
A) NO CHANGE
B) curves; impossible with dry paper;
C) curves: impossible with dry paper,
D) curves—impossible with dry paper—

10
A) NO CHANGE
B) rice; and
C) rice: and
D) rice, and,

11
A) NO CHANGE
B) Hayaki, a famous origami practitioner in Tokyo,
C) Hayaki, a famous origami practitioner, in Tokyo
D) Hayaki a famous origami practitioner in Tokyo,

17
Apostrophes

Apostrophes serve two purposes—possession and contraction.

Possession

To show possession, always add an **'s** unless the noun is plural and ends in *s*, in which case add only the apostrophe.

Example 1

Wrong:	The cats hat is on the floor.
Correct:	The **cat's** hat is on the floor.

Example 2

Wrong:	Louis' scarf is 3 feet long.
Correct:	**Louis's** scarf is 3 feet long.

Example 3

Wrong:	A giraffes' neck is quite long.
Correct:	A **giraffe's** neck is quite long.

Example 4

Wrong:	Both players's jerseys were soaked with sweat.
Correct:	Both **players'** jerseys were soaked with sweat.

Example 5

Wrong:	Because he was hungry, the babysitter ate all the childrens' ice cream.
Correct:	Because he was hungry, the babysitter ate all the **children's** ice cream.

Example 4 is plural and ends in *s*. Example 5 is also plural but *children* doesn't end in *s*. Note the difference in how the possessive is formed.

The SAT loves to test apostrophes by unnecessarily attaching them to plural nouns, as in the following examples.

Example 6

Wrong:	The couple ordered several dishes' to satiate their appetite for the chef's food.
Correct:	The couple ordered several **dishes** to satiate their appetite for the chef's food.

Example 7

Wrong:	The restaurant owner's target high-class diners who can appreciate the subtlety of their dishes.
Correct:	The restaurant **owners** target high-class diners who can appreciate the subtlety of their dishes.

Contraction

Apostrophes can also be used to take the place of missing words or letters. For example, *it's* is short for *it is* and *can't* is short for *cannot*. The following is a table of common contractions:

Contraction	stands for...
it's	it is
they're	they are
who's	who is
could've	could have
he's	he is
I've	I have
you're	you are
that's	that is

As you probably know, there are quite a few words that get commonly confused with possessives and contractions that sound the same. Here are the ones you need to know for the SAT:

it's vs. its

it's (contraction for *it is*) – He told me that **it's** an alien from outer space.
its (possessive) – The poster fell from **its** spot on the wall.

they're vs. their vs. there

they're (contraction for *they are*) – **They're** going to meet us at the restaurant.
their (possessive) – The students passed in **their** homework late.
there (location) – Jacob put the water bottle over **there**.

who's vs. whose

who's (contraction for *who is*) – **Who's** that person sitting by himself?
whose (possessive) – I have a friend **whose** mother is an accountant.

Whenever you're on a question that deals with contractions, ALWAYS read the sentence with the uncontracted version to see if it makes sense.

Example 8

Wrong:	The book has a cool picture on it's cover.
Correct:	The book has a cool picture on **its** cover.

Would the uncontracted phrase *it is cover* make sense in Example 8? Nope. We need the possessive *its*.

Example 9

Wrong:	He is the actor whose most known for his role in *Batman*.
Correct:	He is the actor **who's** most known for his role in *Batman*.

In Example 9, we mean to say *who is* and can do so using the contracted version, *who's*.

Exercise: Answers for this chapter start on page 232.

1. Praised by critics for <u>it's having</u> innovative plot and cinematography, the director's first movie was a huge hit at the box office.

   A) NO CHANGE
   B) its
   C) it's
   D) their

2. After the funeral was held for the brave soldiers, the general scattered their <u>bodies</u> ashes into the sea.

   A) NO CHANGE
   B) body's
   C) bodys
   D) bodies'

3. Writing code for applications and websites requires a lot of deep thinking that can place quite the burden on the <u>programmers mind.</u>

   A) NO CHANGE
   B) programmer's mind.
   C) programmers' mind.
   D) programmers's mind.

4. Because they live in affluent areas that are hot year-round, each of my <u>friends' houses</u> has a swimming pool.

   A) NO CHANGE
   B) friend's houses
   C) friends's houses
   D) friends houses

5. I go to a school <u>who's</u> parking lot can accommodate only 10 cars.

   A) NO CHANGE
   B) whose
   C) that the
   D) where

6. The teacher told us that the <u>semester's grades</u> will be released a week from now.

   A) NO CHANGE
   B) semesters grades
   C) semesters' grades
   D) grade's for the semester

7. Every day, I look at the <u>weeks</u> deadlines and make sure I'm on track to meet them.

   A) NO CHANGE
   B) weeks'
   C) week's
   D) weeks's

8. After their meeting with the principal, <u>the teachers'</u> gossiped amongst themselves about who would be fired.

   A) NO CHANGE
   B) the teachers
   C) the teacher's
   D) the teachers's

9. Examining the mountain in front of them, the hikers were confident in <u>they're ability to climb its</u> rocky terrain.

   A) NO CHANGE
   B) they're ability to climb it's
   C) their ability to climb its
   D) their ability to climb it's

10. Known for his powerful hooks, Mike Tyson was once <u>one of boxings</u> most fearsome competitors.

    A) NO CHANGE
    B) boxings
    C) boxing's
    D) one of boxing's

11. Before the dancers could finish, a loud noise in the audience disrupted <u>their</u> rhythm and ruined the entire performance.

    A) NO CHANGE
    B) they're
    C) it's
    D) there

12. Taylor took the frame down, added a fresh coat of paint on each of <u>it's</u> sides, and inserted a new picture.

    A) NO CHANGE
    B) they're
    C) its
    D) their

13. My friends love to eat. Inside they're refrigerator, there's always a full stock of snacks and
drinks.

   A) NO CHANGE
   B) they're refrigerator, theirs
   C) their refrigerator, theirs
   D) their refrigerator, there's

14. One end of the cable goes through the top
opening of the wooden pole and the other end
wraps around it's foundation.

   A) NO CHANGE
   B) they're
   C) its
   D) their

15. The deck of Emily's parents's yacht had been
completely destroyed by the hurricane.

   A) NO CHANGE
   B) Emily's parents'
   C) Emily's parents
   D) Emilys parents'

16. The novel's protagonist, who's telekinetic
powers are capable of mass destruction, is a
seemingly quiet and shy girl.

   A) NO CHANGE
   B) whose
   C) who has
   D) with her

17. The water dripped down from the ceiling, hit
the cabinet, and dripped onto the rooms floor.

   A) NO CHANGE
   B) room's
   C) rooms'
   D) rooms's

18. We will host a casino night where the players
donate their winnings to charity.

   A) NO CHANGE
   B) there
   C) they're
   D) its

19. Because she was late to work, Joanne had to
report to the factorys' director.

   A) NO CHANGE
   B) factory's
   C) factories'
   D) factories

20. After doctors found her lying unconscious on
the floor, they rushed her to the infirmary's
emergency room.

   A) NO CHANGE
   B) infirmaries
   C) infirmaries'
   D) infirmarys

21. The judge critiqued the womens' fashion
choice's during the beauty pageant.

   A) NO CHANGE
   B) womens's fashion choices
   C) womens fashion choices'
   D) women's fashion choices

22. After a long day, the workers' reward themselves with pizza and a few beers.

   A) NO CHANGE
   B) workers
   C) worker's
   D) workers's

18 Word Choice

One of the most commonly tested concepts is word choice, choosing the most appropriate word in context. Unfortunately, it's impossible to cover the infinite number of ways this concept can show up. After all, there are hundreds of thousands of words and no formulaic rules for why one word should be chosen over the other. Although you'll have to rely on your fluency in English for a lot of them, the SAT does not make these questions difficult. In fact, the answer must be clear enough so that it's not up to opinion.

Example 1

Mark worked on a farm for many years to <u>sponsor</u> his wife and kids, who stayed at home.

A) NO CHANGE
B) compensate
C) fund
D) provide for

The answer choice that best fits is D. The other choices might make sense in a business context, but not in a family context.

Sometimes, the SAT will throw you a word choice question with tougher vocabulary:

Example 2

The immigration office could not handle the <u>amalgamation</u> of applicants trying to escape tyranny in their home country.

A) NO CHANGE
B) diffusion
C) prevalence
D) influx

Amalgamation means a combination or mixture of something. *Diffusion* means a spreading out or distribution. *Prevalence* means being widespread or common. *Influx* means the arrival or entry of large numbers of people or things. The answer is D, *influx.*

On some questions like the ones above, you just have to "know it." On others, a few general guidelines will help.

1. Avoid exaggerated, overly dramatic, or high-sounding language

Don't choose overly complicated words when simple words are enough to express the intended meaning. But don't think that an answer choice is high-sounding just because you don't know what it means.

Example 3

The startup didn't become <u>financially beneficial</u> until it reached a critical mass of customers using the app on a daily basis.

A) NO CHANGE
B) profitable
C) commercially rewarding
D) worthy of great compensation

The answer is B, the simplest choice. All the other choices are high-sounding ways of saying *profitable*.

Example 4

The employees put forth a plan to cut spending by fifty percent but their boss rejected their <u>audacious scheme.</u>

A) NO CHANGE
B) brash industrial action.
C) bold proposal.
D) spirited counsel.

The answer is C. All the other choices are overly dramatic and exaggerated.

2. Avoid casual or informal language

Example 5

Tired from the 20 mile hike, Yasmine retired to her tent and <u>snoozed.</u>

A) NO CHANGE
B) hit the sack.
C) slept.
D) dozed off.

The answer is C. The other answers are too informal.

Example 6

A recently passed law requires that public transportation meet new safety standards, forcing state governments <u>to foot the bill</u> for the construction of new railroads.

A) NO CHANGE
B) pick up the tab
C) pay
D) shell out

The answer is C. Again, the other answers are too conversational.

3. Avoid vague and wordy language

Vague words to look out for include *people, things, something, stuff, matters, aspects, tons of*.

Example 7

In anticipation of Black Friday, store owners are making sure they have a wide variety of <u>products</u> in stock.

A) NO CHANGE
B) items for customers
C) stuff to sell
D) things that can be purchased

The answer is A. The other answers are unnecessarily vague and wordy.

4. Be aware of commonly confused words

Example 8

Ketchup is a better <u>compliment to french fries then</u> mustard.

A) NO CHANGE
B) compliment to french fries than
C) complement to french fries then
D) complement to french fries than

The answer is D. A *complement* is something that goes well with something else, whereas a *compliment* is something nice you say to someone. *Than* is used for comparisons; *then* is used to mean *at that time* or *next*.

Remember:

- more/less than (NOT more/less then)
- could have/could've (NOT could of)

Here's a list of other commonly confused words you should know:

- accept vs. except
- affect vs. effect
- allusion vs. illusion
- ascent vs. assent
- cite vs. sight vs. site
- ensure vs. insure
- advice vs. advise
- council vs. counsel
- elicit vs. illicit
- altar vs. alter

- eminent vs. imminent
- precede vs. proceed
- access vs. excess
- fair vs. fare
- allude vs. elude
- waive vs. wave
- respectfully vs. respectively
- discreet vs. discrete
- adverse vs. averse
- disinterested vs. uninterested

Keep in mind that the guidelines above are just guidelines. Every question is different and not all of them will apply to every one. Your own judgment will be your best weapon once you've done enough practice.

Exercise 1: Answers for this chapter start on page 233.

Campbell's Thousand-Faced Hero

Joseph Campbell's 1949 comparative study of mythology, *The Hero with a Thousand Faces*, presents a fascinating concept that can be applied to many of the great stories of modern times.   He found that many hero stories ▮1 among time and cultures ▮2 clone a similar pattern, a 17-stage journey, in fact.   The three major ▮3 boundaries of this jour-ney are the hero's departure, his initiation, and his return.

▮4 In agreement with Campbell's schema, ev-ery hero receives ▮5 a plea to adventure into the unknown, usually inspired by a ▮6 vision that changes the hero's understanding of himself and his purpose in life.

1

A) NO CHANGE
B) across
C) on
D) over

2

A) NO CHANGE
B) recap
C) follow
D) redo

3

A) NO CHANGE
B) separate things
C) discrete partitions
D) stages

4

A) NO CHANGE
B) Pertaining to
C) According to
D) In relation to

5

A) NO CHANGE
B) a ring
C) a call
D) an invitation

6

At this point, the writer wants to indicate that the hero has gone through a dramatic transforma-tion. Which choice best accomplishes this goal?

A) NO CHANGE
B) revelation
C) goal
D) dream

In *Star Wars*, Luke [7] reasons out that his father was a Jedi knight and receives his father's lightsaber from Obi-Wan Kenobi.

After his foster parents are killed, Luke chooses to [8] jump head-first into an adventure with Obi-Wan through distant galaxies. Similarly, in *The Matrix*, Neo is presented with the truth that he has not been living in the real world, which is actually a barren wasteland. He chooses to take "the red pill," unplugs from the [9] earthly affairs he has known for his entire life, and enters a [10] discontented reality.

7

A) NO CHANGE
B) discerns
C) detects
D) discovers

8

A) NO CHANGE
B) hop on
C) board
D) embark on

9

A) NO CHANGE
B) civilized world
C) global matters
D) cultured domain

10

A) NO CHANGE
B) down in the dumps
C) desolate
D) disagreeable

The initiation stage involves many trials, temptations, and failures. Luke Skywalker **11** endures dangerous battles, undergoes difficult training with Yoda, and eventually faces the evil Darth Vader, **12** as well as the truth that Vader is his father. In the process, he loses his hand and is nearly killed. Neo submits to intense training and self-questioning under **13** adverse conditions', which culminates in a fight with Agent Smith.

After **14** hammering away through great suffering and adversity, the hero returns as a new person with greater power and self-understanding, in possession of some knowledge, ability, or token that **15** achieves his newfound mastery. Luke successfully faces Darth Vader and wins him back to the good side. Batman returns, and Neo rises from the dead with greater powers than before.

11

At this point, the writer would like to suggest that Luke was <u>successful</u> in battle. Which choice best accomplishes this goal?

A) NO CHANGE
B) triumphs through
C) suffers through
D) goes through

12

A) NO CHANGE
B) furthermore
C) also plus
D) with

13

A) NO CHANGE
B) adverse conditions
C) averse conditions
D) averse condition's

14

A) NO CHANGE
B) hanging tough
C) sticking it out
D) persevering

15

A) NO CHANGE
B) reports
C) reflects
D) describes

Exercise 2: Answers for this chapter start on page 233.

Chivalry

In modern times, the word "chivalry" is generally assumed to refer to men treating women with respect and courtesy, opening doors for them, pulling out chairs for them, and giving up their seats on buses and in crowded rooms. In medieval times, however, the term 1 transported a much richer meaning that underlay the expectations placed on aristocratic men. The word comes from the French word *chevalier*, which means "horseman." In general, it referred to any man who could 2 spare enough change to arm himself and ride his own horse into battle—3 in other words, a knight. In those days very few men were able to do so, hence the 4 association between chivalry and the aristocracy.

1
A) NO CHANGE
B) moved
C) carried
D) displayed

2
A) NO CHANGE
B) afford
C) accumulate the assets
D) bear the expenses

3
A) NO CHANGE
B) in which case,
C) therefore,
D) in summary,

4
A) NO CHANGE
B) attachment
C) organization
D) union

Over time, what began as an idealization of knightly conduct during the Crusades of the 11th and 12th centuries [5] developed into a complex system of ethics governing a knight's behavior toward God, his lord, both his allies and his enemies, and women and children. The literature of the late middle ages, particularly the Arthurian legends, [6] electrified the imaginations of [7] quite a few peasants to love and believe in the ideal of the courtly knight. In *Sir Gawain and the Green Knight*, written in the late 1300s, Sir Gawain displays an almost obsessive desire to [8] participate in the chivalric code. Other characters constantly reference his reputation as a knight known for both his [9] fantastic mind in battle and his excellent manners.

5

A) NO CHANGE
B) persisted
C) transmogrified
D) substituted

6

A) NO CHANGE
B) exploded
C) inspired
D) amped up

7

A) NO CHANGE
B) a giant number of
C) thousands of
D) tons of

8

A) NO CHANGE
B) achieve
C) attain the heights of
D) adhere to

9

A) NO CHANGE
B) know-how
C) smarts
D) prowess

Raymond Lull's 13th-century manual on chivalry specified the ethical expectations, rules, and instructions a knight should follow. He was to be a man of able body, good lineage, and wealth. He was to be in control of his abilities and his wealth, giving aid to those in need and protecting women and children. He was to be loyal to his lord, courageous in his defense, and a **10** savvy person. **11** Basically, he was to be a man of honor, who would stay true to his Christian faith and keep his word at all costs. These standards **12** effected the behavior of eminent medieval lords but don't seem to have as much of an influence today.

This old notion of chivalry should not be a relic of the past. After all, honor, loyalty, humility, courage, and generosity are **13** relevant in all aspects of our increasingly global society. Perhaps the modern definition of chivalry should be **14** refreshed to incorporate its original meaning.

10
A) NO CHANGE
B) perspicacious sage.
C) wise advisor.
D) master mind.

11
At this point, the writer wants to emphasize that honor was the highest priority for a knight. Which choice best accomplishes this goal?
A) NO CHANGE
B) First,
C) Above all,
D) Initially,

12
A) NO CHANGE
B) effected the behavior of imminent
C) affected the behavior of eminent
D) affected the behavior of imminent

13
A) NO CHANGE
B) a big deal
C) huge factors
D) befitting

14
A) NO CHANGE
B) revised
C) began anew
D) changed over

19 Transitions

To demonstrate what transitions are and how they're used, let's consider the following sentence:

May's cookies are sweet and sugary. Sam eats them all the time.

In this sentence, it's understood that Sam eats May's cookies *because* they are sweet and sugary. Despite the implied cause and effect relationship here, the reader can't be completely sure. It could be that the two sentences represent two totally independent ideas: May's cookies are sweet and sugary, and it just so happens that Sam eats them all the time. To make the cause-and-effect relationship absolutely clear, we could insert a transition:

*May's cookies are sweet and sugary. **Therefore,** Sam eats them all the time.*

This is a bit of an extreme example, but it illustrates an important point—transitions have meaning. They express how two sentences or paragraphs relate to one another, and they make that connection explicit, even if it's a bit unnecessary to do so. In this case, the *therefore* is probably not needed, but suppose we wanted to imply that sweet and sugary were bad qualities:

*May's cookies are sweet and sugary. **Nevertheless,** Sam eats them all the time.*

With one word, we're able to shift the meaning entirely. Now, sweet and sugary cookies are unhealthy snacks to be avoided.

How sentences connect to one another comes naturally to most students. The hard part is staying aware of the full context. In this one made-up example, we can't be completely sure what the author's intended meaning is, but on the SAT, the author's intention will always be clear. Your job on SAT transition questions is to read the context, figure out the author's meaning, and choose the transition word that conveys that meaning. Always read the sentence before and the sentence after the one in question.

Although you'll typically see transitions at the start of sentences, they can also be inserted into the middle of a sentence:

Every culture holds on to its own myths and superstitions. Many Chinese
people, **for example,** believe the number "4" to be unlucky.

And while there are many transitions out there, as long as you are familiar with the ones in the table below, you shouldn't need to memorize anything. In fact, this table includes almost all the transitions that have shown up on released past exams.

Common Transition Words		
Example	**Transition...**	**Similar Transitions**
I love eating vanilla ice cream. **However**, too much of it makes me sick.	presents an opposing point or balances a previous statement	fortunately, on the other hand, conversely, whereas, while, in contrast, on the contrary, yet
Math trains you to approach problems more analytically. **Furthermore**, it helps you calculate the minimum tip when you eat out.	adds new and supporting information	in addition, also, moreover, and, too, as well, additionally, not to mention
Pandas are rapidly becoming extinct. **In fact**, some experts predict that pandas will die out in 50 years.	gives emphasis to a point by adding a specific detail/case	as a matter of fact, indeed, to illustrate, for instance, for example
The state is facing a flu epidemic. **Consequently**, all hospital rooms are filled at the moment.	shows cause & effect	as a result, because, hence, therefore, thus, accordingly, so, for this reason
Granted, the SAT is a long and tedious exam, but it's necessary for college admissions.	concedes a point to make way for your own point	nevertheless, although, regardless, despite, even if, nonetheless, still, even so
Place the bread on an ungreased baking sheet. **Finally**, bake in a preheated oven for 10 minutes.	shows order or sequence	subsequently, previously, afterwards, next, then, eventually, before
Social security numbers uniquely identify citizens. **In the same way**, IP addresses identify computers.	shows similarity	similarly, likewise, by the same token
In conclusion, the world would be a happier place without nuclear weapons.	gives a summary or restatement	in summary, to sum up, in short, in other words

Some other transitions that didn't quite fit in the table are *meanwhile, instead,* and *otherwise*.

Once you understand all these transition words and how they're used, you'll be well-equipped to handle any SAT question that tests you on them. Just make sure to use process of elimination: plug each answer choice back into the passage and eliminate the ones that don't express the right relationship between the sentences. As always, the best way to get better is to practice and review, practice and review.

Tip

The most commonly tested transition is *however* and it's not even close. It also turns out to be the correct answer most of the time. Know this transition well.

Exercise 1: Choose the best transition. Answers for this chapter start on page 233.

1. Although women in cities from New York to Boston demanded equality in academic opportunities, most East Coast universities did not yield to such demands. <u>In fact,</u> coeducational balance did not become a prominent issue for East Coast admissions officers until the 1960s.

   A) NO CHANGE
   B) In addition,
   C) For example,
   D) Be that as it may,

2. As it turned out, Senator Aldrich did not plan his Jekyll Island trip for relaxation purposes. <u>Therefore,</u> he confidentially planned the weeklong affair to confer with Wall Street executives for a specific purpose—to draft a banking reform bill that would create a centralized American banking system.

   A) NO CHANGE
   B) Nevertheless,
   C) Instead,
   D) Afterwards,

3. Some conservatives claim that America was founded as a Christian nation by devout men who sought to establish a system of law and governance based on the Bible. More secular voices, <u>in summary,</u> have argued that the "Christian nation" concept is a misnomer.

   A) NO CHANGE
   B) likewise,
   C) for instance,
   D) on the other hand,

4. The general knew that the price of victory was enormous. <u>Moreover,</u> there would be over a hundred battles and thousands of deaths by the time the war was over.

   A) NO CHANGE
   B) Yet,
   C) Eventually,
   D) Indeed,

5. Emily Dickinson is known for her reclusiveness, her isolation from the world outside her home. <u>Thus,</u> she did have numerous family members to interact with and keep her company when she needed it.

   A) NO CHANGE
   B) Meanwhile,
   C) Fortunately,
   D) As a result,

6. <u>Even as</u> Emily Dickinson was never recognized as the poet she was during her own lifetime, she is now known as one of the greatest poets ever.

   A) NO CHANGE
   B) Before
   C) Unless
   D) Although

7. Dogs use their excellent sense of smell to detect friends and foe around them. <u>Nevertheless,</u> bats rely on their incredible ears to navigate the world using echolocation.

    A) NO CHANGE
    B) In the same way,
    C) On the one hand,
    D) Otherwise,

8. Jonas became fascinated by the variety of seafood in Japan. <u>Nonetheless, the people</u> there ate everything from raw fish over rice, known as sushi, to dried squid and octopus.

    A) NO CHANGE
    B) Conversely, the people
    C) Additionally, the people
    D) The people

9. The cooks first beat the mixture until the batter comes together in the pan. The pan is then put into the oven and the cake is baked for 30 minutes. <u>Meanwhile,</u> the cake is taken out and put into a decorative box as it cools.

    A) NO CHANGE
    B) Secondly,
    C) Finally,
    D) In conclusion,

10. My cousin in Vietnam told me in advance that a gift would be arriving at my doorstep. <u>Nevertheless,</u> it surprised me to see a package from such a faraway place reach a small suburban town in Minnesota.

    A) NO CHANGE
    B) In fact,
    C) Furthermore,
    D) Therefore,

11. Many students at the university copy their homework assignments, store test answers in their calculators, and collude in groups. <u>Additionally,</u> professors now use multiple versions of their tests, along with questions that are open response and cannot be copied.

    A) NO CHANGE
    B) To illustrate,
    C) As a result,
    D) Just in case,

12. If nothing is done, many sea creatures will soon die off in the face of illegal hunting and the destruction of their natural habitats. <u>Similarly,</u> the leatherback turtle is predicted to be extinct within 20 years.

    A) NO CHANGE
    B) In other words,
    C) In contrast,
    D) In particular,

13. When I visited New York City for the first time, seeing all those densely packed streets didn't intimidate me. Regardless, they just reminded me of my childhood in Hong Kong, where I would walk from shop to shop selling newspapers.

    A) NO CHANGE
    B) They
    C) Similarly, they
    D) Finally, they

14. Even though they all serve sushi, there are many types of sushi restaurants in Japan. Accordingly, kaiten sushi restaurants use a conveyor belt from which customers can pick out what they want to eat.

    A) NO CHANGE
    B) Thus,
    C) Otherwise,
    D) For example,

15. The United States upholds free speech and the right to bear arms. In addition, the Singapore government bans the chewing of gum and fines its citizens if they forget to flush a public toilet.

    A) NO CHANGE
    B) In contrast,
    C) Otherwise,
    D) Similarly,

Exercise 2: Answers for this chapter start on page 233.

1. As most people associate fortune cookies with Chinese cuisine, they were developed entirely in America and are not at all a Chinese invention.

    A) NO CHANGE
    B) Because
    C) So that
    D) Even though

2. Global warming has lead to the melting of the polar ice caps, harming ecosystems and disrupting natural habitats that have existed for centuries. Even so, there has been a scramble to reduce carbon dioxide emissions and slow the rate of environmental change.

    A) NO CHANGE
    B) For this reason,
    C) Meanwhile,
    D) Be that as it may,

3. A vital part of any school curriculum, physical education gives students a much needed break in the middle of the day. Consequently, the classes promote healthy eating and exercise, something most Americans don't get enough of.

    A) NO CHANGE
    B) However,
    C) Likewise,
    D) Moreover,

4. One of the most densely populated areas in the world, Hong Kong is a city bustling with tourists and foreign businessmen, <u>not to mention</u> the 7 million people who live there.

   A) NO CHANGE
   B) furthermore
   C) don't forget about
   D) also plus

5. The President must maintain his position on this issue <u>provided that</u> the public does not think he is indecisive and easily swayed.

   A) NO CHANGE
   B) so that
   C) in spite of the fact that
   D) because

6. <u>Where</u> the government breaks up the monopoly of the cable companies to allow for more competition, service outages and high monthly charges will continue to be the norm.

   A) NO CHANGE
   B) If
   C) Unless
   D) As soon as

7. Sam likes to keep his finances in check with spreadsheets that track where he spends his money, <u>alternatively,</u> Juno impulsively spends money on things she doesn't need.

   A) NO CHANGE
   B) rather than
   C) so
   D) whereas

8. The Mongols are better equipped, have more men, and know exactly how to dismantle our defenses. <u>Anyway,</u> fighting them is a hopeless endeavor.

   A) NO CHANGE
   B) In short,
   C) Nevertheless,
   D) Specifically,

9. Guavas originated from Mexico or Central America and were distributed throughout tropical America and the Caribbean region. <u>They</u> are now cultivated in many different places around the world, including Africa and the Mediterranean coast.

   A) NO CHANGE
   B) Later, they
   C) For instance, they
   D) In summary, they

10. All over the world remain fantastic objects, vestiges of people or forces which the theories of archaeology, history, and religion cannot explain. <u>They</u> have found electric batteries many thousands of years old and strange entities in space-suits with platinum fasteners.

    A) NO CHANGE
    B) In addition, researchers
    C) In particular, they
    D) For instance, researchers

11. The idea that life can flourish only under terrestrial conditions has been made obsolete by space research. <u>Despite the findings,</u> there are forms of life at the bottom of oceans that don't need oxygen.

    A) NO CHANGE
    B) As a specific example,
    C) Even on Earth,
    D) As a result of the research,

12. Both rock and pop can be considered movements in society; the motivations behind these movements, <u>in fact,</u> were not the same.

    A) NO CHANGE
    B) therefore,
    C) however,
    D) furthermore,

13. Four guys were brought together by a few corporate bigwigs to create an American version of The Beetles—The Monkeys. Little did the public know they were not even singing their own songs; they were lip-syncing the whole time. <u>Subsequently,</u> The Monkeys managed to top the charts and make young girls faint.

    A) NO CHANGE
    B) All in all,
    C) Nevertheless,
    D) As a matter of fact,

14. Developed biomedical methods such as cloning are very controversial. <u>Due to this,</u> 93% of all Americans oppose cloning.

    A) NO CHANGE
    B) In fact,
    C) As you can see,
    D) In conclusion,

15. In any organ donation, blood types and other characteristics must match before organs can be transferred. <u>According to some people,</u> unexpected incompatibilities may exist, resulting in further medical problems.

    A) NO CHANGE
    B) In summary,
    C) Similarly,
    D) Even then,

20
Topic, Conclusion, & Transition Sentences

In the previous chapter, we reviewed transition words such as *furthermore* and *however* and how they're used to explicitly connect ideas. Transitions, however, can be more than just one or two words—they can be entire sentences that guide the reader from one thought to another. The more complex ideas get and the more subtle the relationships between them become, the longer the transitions will tend to be. Take a look at the following paragraphs:

> By the time *Heart of Darkness* was published in 1902, a movement was already underway to expose the large-scale theft and murder occurring in the Congo. Dozens of missionaries had begun sending reports, including photographs, to bear witness to the violence. William Sheppard, an African-American Presbyterian, was one of these missionaries. He sent out shocking testimony of lands seized by force, of people living under a reign of terror, and of soldiers cutting off the hands of women and children.

> **An Englishman named E.D. Morel gathered the many reports and photographs and published them.** He gathered crowds to listen to eyewitness accounts of colonial atrocities. He lobbied the British Parliament to denounce the Belgian king's horrifying practices. This became the first modern humanitarian movement, and it successfully exposed the horrendous violence in the Congo. Historians estimate, however, that, by that time, between 10 million and 20 million Congolese people had lost their lives.

Take note of the bolded sentence. This sentence serves as a transition between the two paragraphs, but how do we know? **A good transition sentence references key terms or ideas preceding it and key terms or ideas following it.** It brings together what comes before with what comes after. In this case, the transition brings up not only *E.D. Morel*, who is the primary focus of the second paragraph but also the *many reports and photographs* that were the focus of the first paragraph.

When you're asked to choose the best transition between two paragraphs or even between two sentences within the same paragraph, **always read above and below where the transition will be**. The best transition will be the one that brings together the main elements on either side, leading from the previous topic to the next.

A few more examples:

1.

> Lambert confirmed that we as humans have a finite amount of mental energy and attention. Tough decision making, such as that used when following a diet, saps us of our ability to exercise the same discipline later on. **Based on this research, Lambert designed a diet that minimizes the need for discipline and protects against regression.** Her program has been used by everyone from celebrities to world-class athletes who vouch for its effectiveness.

The bolded sentence is an amazing transition between two topics in the same paragraph. The opening phrase *Based on this research* refers back to the statements on mental energy. In particular, the word *this* makes that reference explicit. The *diet* that Lambert designed leads into the focus of the next sentence: the *program*. In short, this transition guides us from the research she did to the diet program she developed.

2.

> A professor at Harvard and an advocate of human rights, Dr. Joseph remains skeptical of charities that donate haphazardly to impoverished African communities, and **his position has gained traction among other scholars**. Many economists believe that these donations disrupt the local economy and potentially jeopardize businesses that would have to compete against the items being donated.

The bolded phrase is a transition that guides us from Dr. Joseph to other economists, explicitly laying out what the relationship is between them.

Now here's an important concept: **topic and conclusion sentences are just specific types of transition sentences.** The job of a topic sentence is to introduce a paragraph, guiding you from the previous one if necessary. The job of a conclusion sentence is to wrap up a paragraph, guiding you to the next one if necessary. These are transition sentences! The example on the first page of this chapter was a topic sentence.

There is, however, a slight nuance. Though they are just transition sentences, **topic and conclusion sentences are typically more general and less specific than sentences in the middle of a paragraph.** That's because a topic sentence usually tries to capture the entire scope of the paragraph it leads into, and a conclusion sentence encompasses the paragraph that led to it. Note the topic sentence of the paragraph you're reading right now. It's pretty general and even a bit mysterious, isn't it? That's what a topic sentence does. It doesn't tell you everything—it just leads into it.

The following two examples will show topic and conclusion sentences in action:

3.

> Zero population growth was an idea espoused by Dr. Ehrlich at Stanford in the 60's. His argument was that the Earth's resources would soon be exhausted and that everyone would suffer unless measures were taken to slow the rate of population growth. By the 70's, the idea had become mainstream. Everyone knew what zero population growth meant and its implications. People even took to the streets to raise awareness of the impending doom. **Despite the movement's popularity, the predicted apocalypse never happened.**
>
> The world today manages to support over 7 billion people and counting. Through ingenuity and innovation, the human race has developed such improved agricultural practices that increasingly more can be maintained with increasingly less. Technological developments such as the internet have allowed humans to be more efficient in both production and distribution.

The first paragraph talks about the rise of the zero population growth idea whereas the second paragraph talks about the world today. Notice how the bolded sentence serves not only as a conclusion sentence that resolves the first paragraph but also as a transition between the two paragraphs, bridging them together. If you took this sentence out, the shift in topic between the paragraphs would be jarring and confusing for the reader, who would wonder why the writer is suddenly talking about the world supporting 7 billion people right after talking about protests in the streets.

4.

> Computer science is more than just working with computers. It involves computational thinking and algorithms, step-by-step solutions to complex problems. For example, calculating the shortest way from one location to another like a GPS would requires an algorithm. The subject requires patience and extreme attention to detail, especially when it comes to tracking down bugs and cleaning up code.
>
> **From an early age, I knew I wanted to study computer science and so all of my college planning revolved around it.** I asked my math and science teachers to write me recommendations for all the top universities that offered this major. My college essays focused on the applications that I had built and the fun I had on the robotics team. I talked extensively about my passion for problem solving in my interviews. Now I just have to wait for decisions to roll in.

The bolded sentence serves as a transition between what computer science is and the author's personal experience with college planning. Note that this sentence is also a great topic sentence. It's broad and leads directly into the more specific details in the rest of the second paragraph. Hopefully by now, you're really seeing how these transitions work. Bad transitions will either miss the connection altogether or fail to relate both sides in a logical way.

Tip

When you're asked to insert the best transition between two sentences, look for words such as *this*, *that*, and *these*. These reference words must point to other nouns that exist in the surrouding context, which means the transition sentence itself may need to include them. In the last example, the second sentence of the second paragraph contains the words *this major*. But what is *this major*? Notice that the bolded transition defines what *this major* is—computer science. Because it supplies that definition, this is the transition you would pick as the answer if this were a question on the SAT.

Now on the SAT, you'll know you're being tested on transition sentences when you see questions like this:

- The writer wants to link the first paragraph with the ideas that follow. Which choice best accomplishes this goal?

- Which choice best connects the sentence with the previous paragraph?

- Which choice provides the most appropriate introduction to the passage?

- Which choice provides the most logical introduction to the sentence?

- Which choice most effectively sets up the information that follows?

- Which choice most effectively concludes the sentence and paragraph?

- Which choice most smoothly and effectively introduces the writer's discussion of... in this paragraph?

- Which choice most effectively sets up the paragraph?

Your job boils down to choosing the best transition sentence. In answering these questions, there are a few additional things to watch out for. We'll point them out with this last example.

5.

Research has found that expressions of intense enjoyment are most likely the result of finding the solution to a difficult problem. The Greek mathematician and scientist Archimedes is said to have jumped from his bath and run through the streets naked shouting "Eureka!" after his insight into how to measure the volume of objects by submerging them in water. Understanding insight is important because it has led to some of humanity's most important scientific advances. While the modern scientific study of insight has existed since the 1950s, only in the last decade have the powerful tools of cognitive neuroscience been applied to the problem. Tools such as the electroencephalogram (EEG) and functional magnetic resonance imaging (fMRI) are being used to unravel the neural mechanisms that underlie creative insights.

Which choice provides the best introduction to the paragraph?

A) NO CHANGE
B) Many of the scientific insights made by the Greeks were later expanded upon by the Romans.
C) Cognitive neuroscience is the field of study concerned with the brain's mental processes and how they help humans solve problems.
D) Insight is that "a-ha!" moment when we get a joke, recognize a hidden pattern, or solve a problem.

Let's go through the answer choices one by one. Answer A might seem correct because the Archimedes story supports the research, but if we read the whole paragraph, we'll find that the main idea is *the study of insight*, NOT the enjoyment we get from solving difficult problems. Since Answer A steers the paragraph down the wrong path, it makes for a poor introduction. Even though Answer B mentions *insights*, this answer can be discarded because the paragraph has nothing to do with the *Romans* (an irrelevant keyword that allows for easy elimination). Answer C might look correct since it introduces *cognitive neuroscience*, a keyword mentioned later in the paragraph, but it's actually wrong because *cognitive neuroscience* is not the focus of the paragraph. Furthermore, Answer C doesn't lead smoothly into the next sentence about Archimedes. The correct answer is Answer D, which defines what *insight* is. The sentence about Archimedes then serves as an illustration of this definition.

Let's summarize the takeaways:

- For questions that require you to understand/capture the main idea of a paragraph, read the entire paragraph, not just the next sentence.

- Discard answer choices with irrelevant keywords.

- Don't base your answer on keywords mentioned elsewhere in the paragraph if they aren't the focus.

- Always make sure that your answer meshes well with the next/previous sentence.

Exercise 1: Choose the best transition. Answers for this chapter start on page 234.

1. It's well known that cell phone usage correlates with a higher chance of vehicle accidents. <u>No matter how safely people drive, there will always be accidents.</u> Teenagers have the highest level of risk because they're the newest to driving. They're also the ones who tend to text the most. Older drivers, however, are generally more responsible and have the patience to wait.

   A) NO CHANGE
   B) Not all age groups, however, have the same level of risk.
   C) For that reason, many states require seat belt use by law.
   D) Road signs that encourage drivers to put their phones away are marginally effective at best.

2. Since I was a child, I've wanted to see the treasures that were supposedly hidden behind the stone wall. <u>My friends would always say that they'd one day start the journey over the wall, but they never found the courage.</u> Despite these failed attempts, I was determined to find a way in.

   A) NO CHANGE
   B) It's rumored that dragons lay in wait, guarding all the riches beyond imagination.
   C) Local tribesmen gossiped daily of the different ways they would try to get through.
   D) Many men had lost their lives trying to scale it and a half-finished underground tunnel had been given up on years ago.

3. Jacobsen LLC. is a cupcake company that does about a million dollars every year, but <u>the bulk of the revenue doesn't come from the cupcakes that are sold in the stores.</u> Much of the money actually comes from corporate accounts that make sizeable orders for their premier events.

   A) NO CHANGE
   B) customers aren't aware of its finances.
   C) management intends to triple that number in the coming few years.
   D) most orders aren't for the signature cupcake that it promotes.

4. Of all the Indian tribes, the Wampagees designed the most elaborate masks, but their purpose is still unknown. <u>Perhaps the Wampagees created the masks for their ritual dances, which were performed every month for good luck.</u> As one of the smaller tribes, they had to repeatedly stave off invaders that wanted to claim their land. In order to survive, the Wampagees must have sought ways to deal with enemies other than direct combat.

   A) NO CHANGE
   B) Members of the tribe were extremely superstitious.
   C) Some speculate that the masks were worn in times of war to intimidate competing tribes.
   D) They could've been used solely as decorative items, a form of art to line the walls of their huts.

5. The busiest season for our travel agency is spring, cherry blossom season in Japan. During this time, visitors line up outside our doors for the discounts that we offer. Some are headed solely for the temples while others are interested in the local sushi joints and the fascinating shopping malls.

    A) NO CHANGE
    B) the trees in the public parks are in full bloom.
    C) many of the hotels are fully booked.
    D) we arrange plans for hundreds of tourists eager to explore the sites.

6. There were some days when I loved taking public transportation, and other days when I didn't. On a good day, I would sit back and enjoy the coffee sold at the corner store. Today being a good day, I watched an old Vietnamese woman with a cluster of plastic shopping bags gripped tightly in her hand like a cloud of tiny white bubbles. Next to her was the lonely businessman staring longingly across the aisle at the beautiful Mexican girl in the tight jeans standing with her back to him.

    A) NO CHANGE
    B) study the other passengers.
    C) listen to the music stored on my phone.
    D) read the paper for most of the commute.

7. The decline in Pennetta's form, however, is not without its causes. Two years ago, the Italian was involved in a bike accident that left her arm with a severe injury. Doctors said that a full recovery was possible. During the long break, the tennis star kept up a light practice routine and proclaimed that she would come back to the sport stronger than ever.

    A) NO CHANGE
    B) She didn't play any tournaments for the rest of the year.
    C) She used the most advanced treatments of physiotherapy to nurse it back to health.
    D) It crossed her mind a few times after the injury that she may never play professionally again.

8. Serena Williams has come a long way since her childhood days in California. Tournament after tournament, year after year, she continues to prove her dominance over the sport of tennis. Although she cannot equal Maria Sharapova's endorsements, she maintains a crushing 17-2 head-to-head record over the number two Russian. In fact, no other female athlete in any other sport can rival Serena's winnings.

    A) NO CHANGE
    B) she finds the time for projects outside of tennis, such as designing fashionable athletic clothing.
    C) her career prize money exceeds 56 million dollars, almost double that of Sharapova.
    D) her matches command the highest TV ratings, her popularity among American tennis fans being at an all time high.

9. Many students pursuing their doctorate degrees are disheartened by the amount of research professors have to do to maintain their positions, but research is much more than poring over books and writing articles. As a biology professor, I conduct interviews with experts, collect samples from the ocean, and perform experiments in the lab.

    A) NO CHANGE
    B) the compensation and career stability make it worthwhile.
    C) the universities are unwilling to change their requirements.
    D) it shouldn't be thought of as a burden.

10. My doctor has told me that I need to go on a strict diet, no unnecessary snacks and definitely no junk food. I know that controlling calorie intake is important when trying to lose weight. Just last night, even after I had finished my dinner, I drove to the grocery store and wolfed down an entire cheesecake in the parking lot.

    A) NO CHANGE
    B) I also exercise daily to improve my health.
    C) I forced myself to throw away all the chips and candy from the kitchen cabinet.
    D) I try to heed his advice, but it's difficult.

11.   Boston has become the central hub for food, tourism, and entertainment in New England. New businesses and restaurants are popping up all over the place and its sports teams pack the stadiums every week.
        The reasons for Boston's growth can be traced back to excellent state policy decisions a decade ago. Old brownstones, once affordable to even those on government welfare, are being listed for thousands of dollars. Many people who prefer single studios now have no choice but to find roommates to soften the cost of living.

    A) NO CHANGE
    B) Despite the city's modern appeal, Boston's cultural and historical significance cannot be ignored.
    C) Rents for apartments have been on the rise due to the booming economy.
    D) Boston also has a large variety of housing options.

12. A major component of a pilot's flight training is preparing for emergency situations. However, it is not practical to rehearse all the scenarios that might occur. Often, a candidate demonstrates excellent flying skills, but loses composure when under pressure.

    A) NO CHANGE
    B) It is vital that all cabin crew know basic first aid in the event that a passenger becomes ill.
    C) All important flight instruments, such as the course deviation indicator, must be regularly monitored by the co-pilot.
    D) Therefore, assessors will look for candidates who can adjust calmly to unexpected events.

13. The Great Pyramid of Giza is best enjoyed by taking the desert approach on camelback or on foot. Not only does it offer a better view of the monuments, but it also costs much less. On busy days, there are so many visitors that it's impossible to reach the main entrance by the city route.

    A) NO CHANGE
    B) avoids most of the tourist traffic.
    C) provides a local experience.
    D) passes by the Giza plateau, which is home to many fascinating desert animals.

14. The last few years have seen an abundance of new microbial species being discovered. While many discoveries occur in the comfortable surroundings of university research laboratories, still many more are made out in the field. Scientists have developed special vessels to withstand the extreme pressures found at these depths.

    A) NO CHANGE
    B) in jungles and lakes.
    C) on the planet's surface.
    D) on the deep ocean floor.

15. Sherlock Holmes would sometimes use a loose network of casual spies called the "Baker Street Irregulars." These were young boys who provided intelligence to Holmes on an ad hoc basis. After all, even a detective as great as Sherlock Holmes needs help sometimes. But in the event that the amateur sleuths provided a clue of some special importance, they might just find themselves in receipt of a full dollar!

A) NO CHANGE
B) His assistant Watson, however, was the primary companion on most of his cases.
C) Their reward for such services was 25 cents a day.
D) It wouldn't be until the final novel that they would play a crucial role in the mystery.

Exercise 2: Answers for this chapter start on page 234.

1. The body has many defenses. Without the conscious brain knowing, several internal mechanisms come into play: T cells raise the alarm, B cells produce antibodies to stop the virus from replicating, and other white blood cells destroy contaminated cells directly.

Which choice most effectively sets up the examples given at the end of the sentence?

A) NO CHANGE
B) When human beings become unhealthy,
C) A part of the immune system,
D) At the start of an infection,

2. Though it depends on the school, most students do not buy all the textbooks they need. However, it is not always necessary to purchase a book at full price. Used books are often available online at a fraction of their original cost. Similarly, renting textbooks, which allows for semester-long access to relevant information, is becoming much more common. Another option is textbook buyback, in which the university buys the textbook back from the student at the end of the semester. There simply isn't an excuse for students to fall behind in class because they can't get their hands on the required textbooks.

Which choice provides the most appropriate introduction to the paragraph?

A) NO CHANGE
B) Because they can't afford it,
C) Despite some professors' requirements,
D) Regardless of their major,

3. Philosophy is not the same all over the world. Many regard it as the study of knowledge, reality, and existence. In the East, philosophy tends to be more based in the self-realization of spirituality, whereas in the West, philosophy uses a more scientific and logical approach to continually rediscover and rededicate oneself to a higher purpose. Buddhists, for example, focus on meditation and attaining a state of enlightenment. Greek philosophers Socrates and Aristotle, on the other hand, studied logic, debate, ethics, and rationality.

Which choice most effectively sets up the information that follows?

A) NO CHANGE
B) They all eventually converge to a shared vision, though.
C) Eastern philosophy and Western philosophy are particularly distinct.
D) It is not a hard science and, therefore, is not a valuable system of thought.

4. The history of Zydeco music begins with the arrival of the French settlers in Louisiana in the late 1600s. <u>Several instruments make up its characteristic sound,</u> but there is one instrument that is unique to the genre: the vest frottoir, a percussion instrument modeled off of a laundry washboard and worn over the shoulders, extending down the chest. It is usually made of stainless steel and is typically played by stroking spoons down its accordion-style ridges.

Which choice provides the most logical introduction to the sentence?

A) NO CHANGE
B) Many local musicians drew inspiration from its fast tempo,
C) Due to its popularity, it quickly spread to other regions in the South,
D) They reserved it for house dances and social gatherings,

5. Studio Fitness is a small local gym owned by Carolina Teoh. <u>Even when they've switched to other gyms,</u> many clients still seek out Carolina for her fitness and nutrition services, which are time-consuming for her to carry out. By referring new members to her employees, she hopes that by the fifth year, she can move away from customer-facing activities and focus on growing the business. She plans to expand the existing gym and open up new ones in neighboring towns.

Which choice provides the most logical introduction to the sentence and the rest of the paragraph?

A) NO CHANGE
B) Because her competition isn't as knowledgeable as she is,
C) Although she now has her training staff running most of the sessions,
D) Despite the many workout options available,

6. Mrs. Benaroch's amnesia has lead to an almost complete inability to recall the past. It first set in when she was 60 years old and gradually erased her memories to the point where she hardly knew her own self. Since then, over 20 years have gone by and she is still surprised every morning by the face staring back at her in the mirror. <u>She has a few wrinkles but has aged well.</u>

Which choice most effectively concludes the paragraph?

A) NO CHANGE
B) It's like bumping into the same stranger a thousand times.
C) In most cases, amnesia is temporary but Mrs. Benaroch's was particularly acute.
D) She would then brush her teeth and wash her hair.

7. Online piracy is a serious problem. Statistics show that it leads to an estimated loss of $12.5 billion in music industry sales and 71,000 lost jobs per year in the U.S. <u>Despite more important problems in society,</u> various organizations have staged protests warning citizens of the harm done by allowing intellectual property to be downloaded for free. They have also distributed flyers explaining the injustices of depriving many artists of their ability to earn a living.

Which choice provides the most logical introduction to the sentence?

A) NO CHANGE
B) To recoup their losses,
C) To conduct further research,
D) To raise awareness of the issue,

8. It's a misconception that joining the raw food movement would impose dietary limitations that are impossible to meet. There are several reasons a raw food diet is more flexible than most people think. Some eat only raw vegan; others eat only raw meat. Then there are raw vegetarians who eat dairy products, but they require that no cheese or milk be pasteurized. There are also those who will not eat any meat, but will eat sashimi. Everyday, there seems to be a new raw diet being discussed on Internet food forums.

Which choice most effectively sets up the examples that follow?

A) NO CHANGE
B) Though it avoids the pain of cooking, eating raw food is riskier.
C) There are two major raw food websites that provide recipes and guidelines.
D) There is so much variety among raw food diets that it's hard to keep track.

9. Television used to provide endless hours of wholesome distraction for our kids. Well, a lot has changed since the days when the most aggression one would see on TV was Fred and Ethel Mertz squabbling on *I Love Lucy*. The popularity of serial killer thrillers and reality TV dramas exemplifies the brutality and senselessness that have become ubiquitous. Nowadays, there are few shows parents can feel comfortable letting their children watch. It seems that even after-school cartoons include distracting graphics and unrealistic storylines.

Which choice most effectively concludes the sentence and paragraph?

A) NO CHANGE
B) excessive violence and inappropriate humor.
C) complicated plot twists and confusing dialogue.
D) frightening settings and disturbing characters.

10. Though hypnosis is often dismissed as a playful trick used by magicians, it can actually increase a patient's focus and alleviate a wide range of mental issues when used in a serious manner. For example, many people have successfully cured their phobias through hypnosis, whether it be a fear of flying or a fear of water. Others have used it to recover suppressed memories or alter destructive habits such as overeating and smoking. It can instill motivation in athletes and put insomniacs to sleep. While the science behind it remains dubious, there is no question that some people have had dramatic results. Hypnosis, if performed by a competent practitioner, has the potential to reshape the mind to create new responses, feelings, behaviors, and thoughts.

The writer wants a concluding sentence that restates the main argument of the paragraph. Which choice best accomplishes that goal?

A) NO CHANGE
B) The degree to which anyone can be hypnotized depends on many factors.
C) Despite what many think, those who have been hypnotized do not lose control over their behavior.
D) Some doctors now recommend hypnosis as an alternative to expensive drugs and medication.

11. Sumo wrestling started in Japan during the 1600s as a form of entertainment. Many years of highly regimented training are endured for the chance to gain fame and fortune at six Grand Sumo tournaments held each year. Winners can expect adulation and praise, not to mention the right to wear elaborate topknots and silk robes in recognition of their higher ranking. Japanese spectators flock to the arenas whenever these high-profile wrestlers are scheduled for a match.

Which choice most smoothly and effectively introduces the writer's discussion of sumo wrestlers in this paragraph?

A) NO CHANGE
B) To become a master sumo wrestler is to be admired in Japanese society.
C) Because of its popularity, very few fans will acknowledge the dangers of sumo wrestling.
D) Sumo matches consist of just one round and typically last only a few seconds.

12. Many students today are in financial trouble. More and more law school graduates are finding it difficult to land the high-paying positions they had envisioned when submitting their applications. Many have turned to mid-level paralegal positions at smaller firms or have left law altogether for other fields such as information technology, finance, and management. Those fortunate to find employment still have to contend with the crushing burden of student loans. "I thought I'd be driving a Lexus by now," one attorney said. "Instead I'm borrowing my friend's Camry."

Which choice most effectively sets up the paragraph?

   A) NO CHANGE
   B) Despite declining enrollment, law schools continue to raise their tuition.
   C) Law schools are revising their courses to better prepare students for the workforce.
   D) The promise of a law degree has eroded in recent years.

13. Student loan debts—the total having reached an outstanding $1.2 trillion in 2015—are on the rise in the U.S. Trying to take out a mortgage for home repairs or to get a new auto loan is proving harder with hefty student loan debt overshadowing the credit of parents who have co-signed for their child's education. There are options, however, to relieve parents of this burden. For example, the child could eventually take advantage of a co-signer release program to remove the parent from the obligation.

Which choice provides the most appropriate introduction to the paragraph?

   A) NO CHANGE
   B) are having a negative effect on the home improvement and auto industries.
   C) are taking a heavy toll on parents.
   D) are making it impossible for the new generation to live debt-free.

14. The H'mong people are an ethnic group in the mountainous region of Southeast Asia. After China, north Vietnam has the next highest population, with over one million people in the Black H'mong and Flower H'mong tribes, who have adopted decorative jewelry distinct to their respective tribes. The Black H'mong use the indigo they grow to dye their clothes a deep-blue, almost black, while the Flower H'mong's are much more colorful.

Which choice most effectively sets up the information that follows?

   A) NO CHANGE
   B) the most obvious distinction between the two being their traditional wardrobes.
   C) who reside in completely different geographical locations.
   D) who both subsist largely on their crop harvests.

15. The past two decades have seen the birth of an amazing professional phenomenon called the virtual assistant, which is revolutionizing the way that business can be conducted for both the assistant and the client. Highly educated, self-motivated people of diverse talents have been looking for ways to work from the comfort of their own homes for ages, and now it is finally a possibility. In fact, documents can be written, graphics can be designed, and prototypes can be built without ever having to meet in person. In addition, there are agencies that put prospective workers through a thorough recruitment process so that quality and efficiency can be assured. Nothing, however, can replace the speed and productivity of in-person meetings.

Which choice most clearly ends the passage with a restatement of the writer's primary claim?

   A) NO CHANGE
   B) The digital workplace is quickly becoming a trustworthy and viable option that is beneficial to everyone.
   C) Many businesses hire virtual assistants in third world countries, where wages are lower.
   D) Confidentiality and security are ongoing issues in this age of online business.

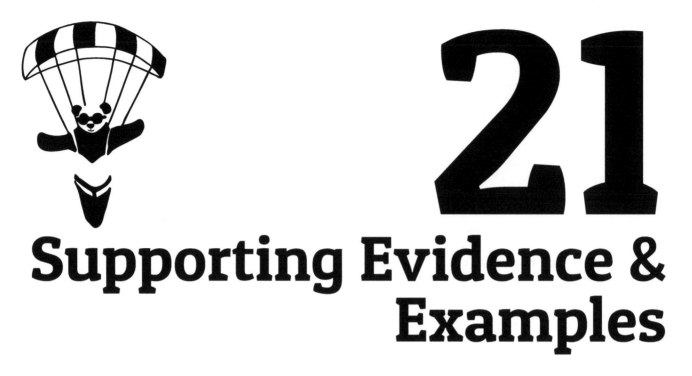

Supporting Evidence & Examples

If topic, conclusion, and transition sentences are the glue, then statements and their supporting evidence, examples, and details are the meat. Last chapter, we talked about choosing the right transitions that lead smoothly to and from certain statements and details. In this chapter, we'll talk about the statements and details themselves and how to choose the right ones.

Whereas previously, we dealt with questions like

> *Which choice most effectively sets up the information that follows?*

Now we're dealing questions like

> *Which choice provides information that best supports the claim made by this sentence?*

It's like we're going in reverse. Instead of setting up the claim, this chapter deals with supporting it. Other questions of this type will look like the following:

- Which choice gives a second supporting example that is most similar to the example already in the sentence?
- Which choice best supports the statement made in the previous sentence?
- Which choice most logically follows the previous sentence?
- At this point, the writer wants to further reinforce the paragraph's claim about.... Which choice most effectively accomplishes this goal?
- Which choice results in a sentence that best supports the point developed in this paragraph?
- Which choice provides the most specific information on...?
- Which choice gives an additional supporting example that emphasizes...?

So how do we handle these types of supporting evidence questions? Let's illustrate the steps with an example:

> A liberal arts education is no longer viewed as a practical one. More and more students are choosing majors that lead directly to employment: engineering, computer science, and business. What was once touted as a well-rounded curriculum to develop culturally literate members of society is now denounced as inapplicable to the workplace. Companies have found that graduates from liberal arts schools—especially those with philosophy, history, and language arts degrees—<u>require more training in order to be effective once they're hired.</u> In light of these findings and trends, many liberal arts programs are expanding their offerings to include more professional development courses, positioning themselves to be more relevant to whatever career paths their students choose to follow.

Which choice results in a sentence that best supports the point developed in this paragraph?

A) NO CHANGE
B) tend to eat lunch and go to outings as a group.
C) express their opinions more openly and eloquently during meetings.
D) possess a wide array of technical skills they've developed outside of school.

1. Underline or work out in your head the claim that you're trying to support

Whatever you're trying to support, whether it be a claim, statement, or point (they're all the same thing), you have to figure out what it is. Sometimes it's as simple as reading the previous sentence, which spells it out for you. Sometimes, it's spelled out in the question! In these cases, don't be lazy—underline it. Other times, you'll have to jump back to the topic sentence or infer the main point from the entire paragraph, in which case you should formulate the main point in your own words.

A main point, however, is NOT a one word answer like "napping" or "pandas." A main point is a sentence or phrase that expresses an argument or opinion. For example,

"Napping during work is good for the productivity of the employees."

"Pandas are rare creatures that we need to save from extinction."

Keep this in mind when you're figuring out the main point yourself. Make it a complete sentence.

Lastly, do this before you look at the answers. Especially on the tougher questions, you don't want the answers to sway your idea of what the paragraph's main point is. If you come up with it independently, you can be that much more confident in choosing an answer that supports what you have in your head.

In our main example, the main point is well expressed by the topic sentence, "A liberal arts education is no longer viewed as a practical one." An even better version might be one you come up with yourself:

> *A liberal arts education is not seen as useful for jobs today.*

2. Eliminate answers that are off-topic

If the question asks for a reinforcement of a claim about the safety of nonorganic food, don't choose answers dealing with organic food. And don't choose answers dealing with all crops in the United States. Choose an answer specific to nonorganic food.

In our example, answer B is off-topic. Eating lunch and company outings aren't really related to the discussion of job performance and liberal arts degrees.

Answer D is also off-topic because it shifts the focus away from the usefulness of what students learn in a liberal arts school to what they learn "outside of school."

3. Eliminate answers that are on-topic but don't support the point

On these questions, remember that you're not trying to add tangential facts or another claim. You're supporting a point. So just because a passage deals with napping doesn't mean any answer related to napping will be the right one. For example, if the main point is that napping during work boosts productivity, an answer that mentions what time most employees nap at is on-topic but not on-point. Instead, the right answer might state, "Employees who take naps meet their deadlines more often." This is on-topic and on-point.

In our example, answer C is on-topic but doesn't support the point we came up with in step 1. In fact, it counters the point. Remember that the main point is that a liberal arts education is not helpful for today's jobs. Answer C implies that it is, in fact, helpful, at least in meetings.

The correct answer is A, which clearly relates to the topic of job performance and supports the point that a liberal arts education is not as useful as others are for today's jobs.

Exercise 1: Answers for this chapter start on page 236.

1. Normally, we think of plants as static beings that do not move and feed only from soil nutrients. However, thanks to evolution, many types of plants have developed animal-like traits that separate them from their conventional image. There are over 600 species of carnivorous plants documented all over the world. Among these, <u>cape sundews are some of the most fascinating because of their sticky tentacles that wrap up prey.</u>

   Which choice best gives a supporting example of the statement made in the previous sentence?

   A) NO CHANGE
   B) tropical pitcher plants, also known as monkey's cup, are a vital source of water for the monkeys that drink from them.
   C) the Portuguese dewy pine requires a certain soil composition to reach the jungle canopy.
   D) cobra plants have balloon-like chambers and long tubes hanging from them.

2. A widespread legend states that food that has fallen to the ground may still be eaten, provided that it is picked up within a few seconds. The underlying reason is that bacteria does not have enough time to cling on to food in such a short amount of time. However, scientific evidence now shows that these claims may just be wishful thinking rather than valid assertions. <u>Instead of taking the risk, we should just eat food from our plates.</u>

   Which choice best supports the statement made in the previous sentence?

   A) NO CHANGE
   B) Experiments have shown that carpets are the least conducive to bacteria on dropped food.
   C) A peer-reviewed study showed that food that had been on the floor had more bacteria, regardless of the contact time.
   D) Food poisoning can cause severe illness in people with compromised immune systems.

3. There are scientific ways to get the most out of studying according to recent studies. There is evidence that study sessions work better when they are done in small short chunks, rather than in one marathon ten-hour session. Too many students are afraid to split up their schedules because they're afraid of forgetting what they've read, but what they don't realize is that study sessions in place of sleep can result in a 20% drop in attention levels.

   Which choice results in a sentence that best supports the point developed in this paragraph?

   A) NO CHANGE
   B) the brain needs time to process information before it can retain it.
   C) routine is the best way to establish a habit in the mind.
   D) rote memorization is not as effective as doing practice tests.

4. Technological advances in robotics have made it inevitable that robots will increasingly be a part of our household life, beyond the dish washers that clean our silverware and the cash registers that calculate our change. But even our jobs are at risk. Research by the BBC shows that 35% of our current occupations could be done completely by machines within the next 20 years. We may soon see drones delivering packages in our neighborhoods and administering shots at the doctor's office.

   Which choice gives a second supporting example that is most similar to the example already in the sentence?

   A) NO CHANGE
   B) the video games that run on our computers.
   C) the solid foundations on which our houses are built.
   D) the air conditioners that regulate the temperature.

5. Traveling in Mongolia can be expensive if activities are booked ahead of time, but it can be quite cheap on site. Inexpensive trips are possible because Mongolia's economy–stimulated by a booming mining sector–is so weak in comparison to those of the majority of western countries. Therefore, prices for tours scheduled remotely are shrewdly designed by travel agencies to reflect the prices in the traveler's home country: a tour that might cost $1000 when booked online might only cost $100 when negotiated with a local business.

   Which choice provides information that best supports the claim made by this sentence?

   A) NO CHANGE
   B) traditionally based on herding and agriculture
   C) considering over 20% of the population lives on less than $1.25 per day
   D) having one of the most promising growth prospects in the near future

6. Dutch Post-Impressionist painter Vincent Van Gogh may be the most celebrated artist of all-time, but he was not one of the happiest. He suffered from severe anxiety and depression throughout much of his life, which is apparent in several of his works.

   Which choice, when inserted afterwards, best gives a supporting example to the underlined portion?

   A) When he moved to the south of France, however, he was greatly enthused by the abundance of light there and began painting orchards in blossom and workers gathering the harvest.
   B) His best works were done in the last two years of his life leading up to his tragic suicide.
   C) Had his fame come during his life, and not posthumously, perhaps he would have been able to better manage his mental illness.
   D) It has been suggested that one of his last paintings, "Wheat Field with Crows," is representative of his suicidal thoughts.

7. People often confuse dark energy with dark matter: to the non-scientist they are often regarded as one in the same, but, in fact, they couldn't be more different. <u>One similarity they share is that they're difficult to detect, hence the nomenclature "dark."</u>

   Which choice best supports the statement made in the previous sentence?

   A) NO CHANGE
   B) One of the most striking differences is that dark energy repels matter while dark matter attracts it, just as normal matter does through gravity.
   C) Everything we see in the universe accounts for approximately 4% of its contents, the rest being made up of about 74% dark energy and 21% dark matter.
   D) Dark energy is what accounts for the expansion of the universe.

8. About half the jobs in the small resort town of Zermatt, Switzerland are within the hotel and restaurant industry. Tourism is the main driver of its economy, with people coming from all over the world to partake in the various activities, most of which involve the mountain made world-famous by the symbol of the Swiss chocolate Toblerone—the Matterhorn.

   After the last sentence, the writer wants to further establish Zermatt as a popular tourist destination. Which choice most effectively accomplishes this goal?

   A) The local fondue is great for relaxing after a day of skiing on the frosty slopes.
   B) Zermatt is also one of the most prestigious ski hubs in the world and the starting point for the Haute Route, a mountain hike passing over the Matterhorn to the Mont Blanc.
   C) The Matterhorn's summit is 4,478 meters high, making it one of the highest mountain peaks in the Alps.
   D) The first expedition that ever reached the top ended dramatically, with only 3 of the 7 climbers surviving the descent.

9. In a recent study using functional magnetic resonance imaging to peer into the effect of specific smells on dogs' brains, scientists found evidence to support the idea that dogs really do love their fellow humans and even consider them family. Of all the smells they took in, dogs actually prioritized the scent of humans over the scent of other animals, both familiar and unknown.

   After the last sentence, the writer wants to further reinforce the paragraph's claim that research done on smell has substantiated dogs' affection for people. Which choice best accomplishes this?

   A) By giving treats to dogs after they perform tricks, humans can strengthen this bond.
   B) These findings are supported by adjacent studies done on dogs' responses to certain human sounds.
   C) Even the distant aroma of a dog's owner can spark activity in the caudate nucleus, also known as the "reward center" of the dog's brain.
   D) Before this study, little was known about canine brain activity in the presence of humans.

10. Project MK-Ultra was an illegal CIA program that started in the early 1950s and lasted for approximately twenty years. The program consisted of experiments on human subjects, intended to explore and determine methods to force confessions through mind control. These experiments called for the development of procedures to be used in interrogations and torture. <u>Years after the termination of the project, many subjects filed lawsuits against the federal government for conducting experiments without consent.</u>

Which choice best supports the previous statement with specific examples?

A) NO CHANGE
B) The program consisted of at least 149 sub-projects which were contracted out to at least 80 institutions and 185 private researchers at various universities and research foundations.
C) The project has become so well-known that it has appeared multiple times in popular culture.
D) The procedures studied included, but were not limited to, hypnosis, sleep deprivation, and isolation.

11. Number one on the 2015 Fortune 500 list, which ranks 500 of the largest U.S. corporations by gross revenue annually, is Wal-Mart, which outperformed petroleum refining mega-corporations Exxon Mobil and Chevron, as well as computer giant Apple. This might be surprising news for some, given that Wal-Mart is a chain of discount department and warehouse stores, but its revenue is based on high volume, not high prices. <u>Each week, more than 260 million customers visit more than 11,500 retail stores and e-commerce websites in 28 countries.</u>

Which choice best supports the statement made in the previous sentence?

A) NO CHANGE
B) Just last year, Walmart increased net sales by 1.9%.
C) The first Walmart opened in Rogers, Arkansas in 1962 and was founded by Sam Walton.
D) Wal-Mart was listed on the New York Stock Exchange in 1972.

12. Widely used in developing countries as a tool for poverty relief, microloans help enterprising individuals <u>who don't have fresh water</u> launch and grow small businesses. The idea is to give just enough so that they can get the business off the ground. The first institution to give funding through microcredit was Grameen Bank of Bangladesh, which won the Nobel Peace Prize in 2006. As of 2009, approximately 74 million individuals held microloans totaling 38 billion dollars.

Which choice results in a sentence that best supports the point developed in this paragraph?

A) NO CHANGE
B) who have a family to take care of
C) who may be in lower castes and tribes
D) who might otherwise not be eligible for a line of credit

Exercise 2: Answers for this chapter start on page 236.

1. The philosophy behind organic architecture, that structures should be designed to be in harmony with humanity and its environment, is attributed to American architect Frank Lloyd Wright. His style had matured to its fullest by the 1920s, and some of his most influential designs were created over the next two decades. His work includes several different structural types, including offices, churches, schools, skyscrapers, hotels, and museums.

   Which choice best gives a supporting example that showcases the expression of Wright's organic architecture?

   A) NO CHANGE
   B) One of these structures, Graycliff, located just south of Buffalo, New York, is a summer estate designed for Wright's long-time patrons, Isabelle and Darwin D. Martin.
   C) One of these structures, a private residence called Fallingwater, was designed to keep occupants close to the home's natural surroundings, with a stream and waterfall running under a portion of the building.
   D) The Taliesin West, Wright's winter home and laboratory, is now the site of the Frank Lloyd Wright School of Architecture.

2. Initiations are present in many different forms across all cultures of the world. From college graduation ceremonies to the coming of age celebrations for 20-year-olds in Japan called *Seijin Shiki*, which are held at local offices and followed by after-parties among family and friends, initiations play an important role in all societies.

   Which choice gives additional examples that support the point that various forms of initiation happen everywhere?

   A) NO CHANGE
   B) from the inductions into the higher ranks of secret societies such as the Freemasons to the tribal rituals of the shamans of the South American jungle,
   C) all of which signify a formal admission to adulthood within a community,
   D) whether they be rites of passage for entering a secret society or a mystical vocation,

3. The coca leaf, notorious for its role in global drug wars, actually has a much different significance for Andean societies native to South America. Unfortunately, this "sacred leaf" has been primarily harvested for the production of cocaine since the beginning of the 20th century. It is also the essential ingredient in chewing coca, which is made by simply mixing the leaf, sodium bicarbonate, and saliva between the cheek and jaw, forming a mass that consists of alkaloids and various nutrients.

   Which choice best supports the paragraph's claim that the coca leaf is significant to Andean societies?

   A) NO CHANGE
   B) The oldest coca leaf, which was found in Peru, dates at least as far back as 2500 BC.
   C) They used it as an anesthetic for wounds and as an offering to the gods under the belief they would be protected from bad luck.
   D) Many members were sent to toil in the fields to harvest this crop.

4. Certain ballets are considered classical because they all have similarities in composition, costuming, and style. Determining factors include whether the music is classical and whether the female dancers dance *en pointe*. Another characteristic of classical ballet is a costume style called *ballet-blanc*, in which the dancers are clothed completely in white. The second act of "Giselle," for example, showcases a group of supernatural women who dance the Waltz of the Wilis all in white, summoning Giselle from her grave. The first act of "Swan Lake" sets up a love story between a prince and a princess who is held captive as a swan.

Which choice gives a second supporting example that is most similar to the example in the previous sentence?

A) NO CHANGE
B) The ballet is one of the most popular of all time and widely considered to be the prototype of *ballet-blanc*.
C) The ballet is centered around a peasant girl named Giselle who dies of a broken heart after finding out that her lover is promised to another.
D) The second act of "La Sylphide", one of the earliest romantic ballets, features a wedding procession in which the cast is dressed in white.

5. Why isn't there a standard voltage around the world? Europe and most other countries in the world use twice the voltage of Japan and the majority of the Americas. To the unsuspecting traveler, this can be disconcerting and even dangerous. Every year, hundreds of people are injured from overheating blow dryers.

Which choice best gives a supporting example to the statement made in the previous sentence?

A) NO CHANGE
B) A burnt transistor can ruin even the most expensive electronic appliance.
C) Fortunately, most modern airports have shops that carry adapters.
D) International travel is already problematic enough without the different standards.

6. Honeybees are dying out at an alarming rate, and experts are not sure why. Because they have such a great impact on the sustainability of the world's ecosystem, their decline is raising great concern over the future of the agriculture industry. The bees are responsible for pollinating about one-sixth of the flowering plant species worldwide and approximately 400 different types of vegetation. As a matter of fact, bats, moths, butterflies, hummingbirds, ants, and beetles contributed to only an estimated $10 billion worth of agricultural revenue in 2010.

At this point, the writer wants to further reinforce the importance of honeybees to the agricultural industry. Which choice most effectively accomplishes this goal?

A) NO CHANGE
B) our world would be much different if bees didn't exist.
C) honeybees helped produce approximately $19 billion worth of crops in the U.S. alone in 2010, which represents about one-third of everything eaten that year.
D) bees contribute more than any other animal to the aesthetic quality of Earth's landscape.

7. The world's governments are often the focus of conspiracy theories that imply that they do not necessarily have the best interest of civilians in mind. Most theories are complete fabrications produced by overactive imaginations, but some seem quite valid. Consider, for example, the case of Aralsk-7 on Vozrozhdeniya Island, a top secret mission to develop biological weapons and test them on innocent people. It was on this island in the Aral Sea of Kazakhstan and Uzbekistan that anthrax spores and bubonic plague bacilli were made into weapons and stored. <u>Scientists also experimented with a variety of other agents, including smallpox, plague, brucellosis, and tularemia.</u>

Which choice best completes the example developed in this paragraph?

A) NO CHANGE
B) Over the last decade, many of the containers have developed leaks.
C) In a scheduled field test, a release of weaponized smallpox infected ten civilians, of whom three died.
D) Eventually, word of the island's danger was spread by Soviet defectors, including the former head of the Soviet Union's bio-weapons program, Ken Alibek.

8. Snow leopards are one of the five species that make up the Panthera genus, commonly referred to as the "Big Cats." They are slightly smaller than the other members, though their tails are relatively long, and their eyes are pale green or gray in color, which is unusual among cats. <u>The defining characteristic of the genus is the dorsal profile of the skull being flattish or evenly convex.</u>

Which choice gives an additional supporting example that illustrates how snow leopards are distinct?

A) NO CHANGE
B) They inhabit alpine and sub-alpine zones at altitudes of 3,000 to 4,500 meters.
C) New studies suggest that they are a sister species of the tiger.
D) Snow leopards also do not have the anatomical structure that allows them to roar like the other cats in the genus.

9. One of the central teachings of Buddhism is the impermanence of everything, illustrated through the active meditation of sand-painting. Over several days or even weeks, elaborate designs called mandalas are created <u>using crushed colored stones or sand.</u>

Which choice provides information that best supports the claim made by the previous sentence?

A) NO CHANGE
B) only to be ritualistically destroyed afterwards.
C) to portray hundreds of deities.
D) as a symbolic offering of the whole universe.

10. Ever since the Soviet-built unmanned Mars-2 rover became the first man-made object to reach the surface of Mars on May 19, 1971, the question has been looming in the minds of citizens across the globe, "when are we going to succeed in putting a man on Mars?" Though NASA claims to be developing the capabilities needed to send humans to an asteroid by 2025 and to Mars by 2040, there are several obstacles that must be overcome. The primary ones include the immense amount of fuel necessary for a round-trip, as well as <u>a habitat that may be home to bacteria life forms.</u>

Which choice offers the most relevant example, in addition to the one already in the sentence?

A) NO CHANGE
B) signs of water on Mars.
C) the thin and shallow Martian atmosphere, which will create extreme heat upon entry.
D) the need for Americans to forget their resentment of the Soviets for landing the first man-made vessel on Mars.

11. There may be no permanent human inhabitants in Antarctica, but there most definitely is an abundance of life that makes its home on Earth's southernmost continent. Exposed rock on land supports vegetation, microbial life, and some hardy insects. Although not a single land vertebrate can survive the winter, <u>a great variety of birds and invertebrates live in the high Arctic year round.</u>

Which choice provides the most specific information on the types of species that thrive in the Antarctic?

A) NO CHANGE

B) Antarctic waters are home to a whole ecosystem of seabirds, seals, penguins, whales, and their prey, which include fish, squid, and krill.

C) special adaptations have developed the ability to survive there in the spring and summer.

D) the Antarctic sea is much more populated by life than the land is.

12. The modern portrayal of Santa Claus is derived from non-Christian origins. For instance, <u>the god Odin– the likely inspiration for Santa Claus–sits on an iron throne with a spear in hand.</u>

Which choice best supports the statement made in the previous sentence?

A) NO CHANGE

B) Santa Claus rides the rooftops on his sled in the same way Odin, a major god among the Germanic people, rides his horses across the sky.

C) the god Odin, considered to be the original Santa Claus, was known in Old English as Wóden in Germanic mythology and paganism.

D) many Christians changed the date for giving gifts from December 6th to the 25th during the Reformation of 16th and 17th-century Europe.

22

Relevance & Purpose

Relevance

While the past few chapters dealt with questions that test you on relevance implicitly—after all, topic sentences, transitions, and supporting details all have to be relevant to the passage in context—you'll encounter quite a few questions that test you on relevance explicitly, as well as questions that test you on both relevance and purpose, in other words, *how* something is relevant. Not only will you have to figure out which answer fits the best, you'll also have to know *why* it fits.

On the SAT, these questions look like the following:

- Which choice provides the most relevant detail?

- The writer is considering deleting the underlined sentence. Should the writer do this?

- The writer is considering deleting the underlined sentence. Should the sentence be kept or deleted?

- At this point, the writer is considering adding the following sentence. ...Should the writer make this addition here?

- The writer is considering revising the underlined portion of the sentence to read.... Should the writer add this information here?

A full example might look like this:

At this point, the writer is considering adding the following sentence:

> Joe then confronted Jane about the money she owed him.

Should the writer make this addition?

A. Yes, because the information clarifies Joe's reasoning for his actions.
B. Yes, because the information helps explain how Joe and Jane originally met.
C. No, because the additional information distracts from the main point of the passage.
D. No, because it's unclear whether Joe wanted to argue with Jane.

When tackling these types of questions, always answer the yes or no part first. Is it relevant? Should it be added or deleted? Yes or no? Don't even read the rest of the words in the answer choices. In your mind, just answer yes or no. That way, you've halved the number of choices under consideration. Usually it's pretty obvious whether a sentence is relevant.

Only after you have answered yes or no should you think about the why (why or why shouldn't the sentence be added?). The reason for doing this is to prevent the answer choices from influencing your reasoning, because once you answer yes or no, you instinctively develop your own reason which you can then compare with the two remaining answer choices. Letting the reason you thought up yourself guide you to the correct answer choice is extremely effective—your instincts are often right. Reading the full answer choices before you've had time to think for yourself has a way of playing with your mind.

If your reason doesn't line up with the reasons in the two remaining answer choices, it's a sign you need to reconsider the yes or no part.

Most irrelevant sentences come in the form of random facts that come out of nowhere. Here are some examples (irrelevant parts are italicized):

- Last Monday, I went to my high school reunion. I was excited about meeting old acquaintances and friends. *Afterwards, I went back home with my wife.* I had lost touch with them after so many years.

- My dad runs a bakery in Boston's Chinatown, *but there's also a Chinatown in Toronto.* He sells freshly baked pork buns, egg tarts, and cakes to the locals everyday.

- Because *All the King's Men* was released as a movie before I could read the book, *which is often available in used book stores*, I decided to watch the movie first. I wish I hadn't though because the book turned out to be far more entertaining.

- Since its inception, Cathay Pacific airlines has served millions of customers worldwide. *Obviously, flying is faster than driving.* The company continues to offer world class service, comfortable seating, and delicious meals on all flights.

The best way to spot irrelevance is to evaluate the key words in the sentence in question. If those key words aren't referred to in some way in the previous sentence or the following sentence, chances are that it's irrelevant. Notice in the respective examples above that:

- There is no reference to *home* or *wife* in the surrounding sentences.

- There is no reference to *Toronto* in the surrounding sentences.

- There is no reference to *used book stores* in the surrounding sentences.

- There is no reference to *driving* in the surrounding sentences.

Also notice how the italicized portions interrupt the flow of the passage; they are abrupt shifts in topic. Relevant content will stay on topic; irrelevant content will not.

Another sign that something is irrelevant is a sudden shift in scope—how general or specific something is. The last example above starts out by talking about one specific airline, Cathay Pacific, but all of a sudden, it jumps into something extremely general, that flying is faster than driving. Be wary of these sudden shifts in scope.

At the end of the day, there is no magic formula for determining whether something is relevant. After lots of practice, your intuition will be your best guide.

Purpose

Ok, so now you've determined whether something is relevant or not. More often than not, you'll have to know why.

Here are some typical reasons for adding/not deleting something:

- because it provides specific examples of...
- because it defines a term that is important to the passage
- because it provides a detail that supports the main topic of the paragraph
- because it helps explain why...
- because it provides context for...
- because it provides support for the claim made in the previous sentence
- because it establishes the relationship between...
- because it elaborates on...
- because it provides a logical introduction to the paragraph
- because it serves as a transitional point in the paragraph
- because it adds a relevant research finding
- because it introduces a new idea that will become important later in the passage
- because it acknowledges a common counterargument to the passage's central claim
- because it sets up the main topic of the paragraph that follows

Here are some typical reasons for not adding/deleting something:

- because it blurs the paragraph's main focus with a loosely related detail
- because it blurs the paragraph's main focus by introducing a new idea that goes unexplained
- because it interrupts the flow of the sentence by supplying irrelevant information
- because it provides background information that is irrelevant to the paragraph
- because it interrupts the paragraph's description of...
- because it interrupts the discussion of...
- because it fails to support the main argument of the passage
- because it repeats information that has been previously provided
- because it introduces a term that has not been defined in the passage
- because it would be better placed elsewhere in the passage
- because it makes a claim about... that is not supported by the passage
- because it does not provide a transition from the previous paragraph
- because it does not logically follow from the previous paragraph
- because it contradicts the claim made in the previous paragraph
- because it contradicts the passage's claim about...

You don't need to memorize any of these. Just familiarize yourself with them.

Tip

The most common reason by far for not adding/deleting something is irrelevance. If the question asks whether to add a given sentence and your answer is no, the reason will likely be that it blurs the paragraph's main focus or supplies irrelevant information, so gravitate towards that answer choice first.

The three most common reasons for adding something are defining a term, offering specific examples, and adding supporting detail to a claim. As you go through practice questions, familiarize yourself with what these questions and answers actually look like so that you develop an intuition for how they're tested.

When you encounter purpose questions, always read the surrounding sentences and determine what function the given sentence plays. If possible, try to make this determination before you actually read the answer choices. The purpose of a given sentence or phrase will usually fall under one of the following categories:

- an explanation of a certain term or phenomenon
- further description
- introduction of a topic
- emphasis of a previous point
- effective transition
- specific evidence or supporting detail
- conclusion of a paragraph or passage

Again, there is no magic formula for consistently determining what the purpose of a sentence is. A lot of it comes down to logic and judgment, which is best improved through practice.

Exercise 1: Answers for this chapter start on page 237.

Fishing on Grandmother's River

My favorite place to visit during my childhood was my grandparents' house, [1] which overlooked a coastal river in North Carolina. I spent many summers there fishing from the dock in the peaceful mornings and evenings when the river had calmed to a still surface broken only by the jumping mullets. [2]

Flowing over a mucky, silty bed, the river usually appeared a dark bluish-brown. We couldn't see the bottom, so we fished with bobbers floating above the wormed hook. Who can express the excitement of a small child when he sees the bobber jerk down suddenly, its whiteness turning golden in the brown murk? [3] I experienced this excitement more times than I can recall, though I eventually learned to temper my joy when I more often than not pulled up an empty hook, [4] which became rustier with every use.

1

The writer is considering deleting the underlined portion (ending the sentence with a period). Should the writer make this deletion?

A) Yes, because the underlined portion interrupts the narrative.

B) Yes, because the information fails to explain the initial statement in the sentence.

C) No, because the underlined portion offers important descriptive details.

D) No, because the underlined portion provides an explanation of a key term.

2

At this point, the writer is considering adding the following sentence.

A mullet is a chiefly marine fish that is widely caught for food.

Should the writer make this addition?

A) Yes, because it describes what was fished for.

B) Yes, because it explains a term that is important to the passage.

C) No, because it interrupts the description of the river with a loosely related detail.

D) No, because there is no indication that the mullets were caught for food.

3

At this point, the writer is considering adding the following sentence.

Not many can.

Should the writer make this addition?

A) Yes, because it answers an important question.

B) Yes, because it gives a sense of how many people can express a certain level of excitement.

C) No, because it is unnecessary to address a rhetorical question that is used to convey an experience.

D) No, because it repeats information elsewhere in the passage.

4

Given that all of the choices are true, which one provides the most relevant detail?

A) NO CHANGE

B) one of the many I had bought at the store.

C) which I had planned on replacing.

D) a clear sign that the fish had escaped with the bait.

Sometimes, my sisters and I would sit together and wait **5** for hours on end. With every fresh catch, we ran over to each other to celebrate, happy that our patience had paid off. **6** Our hooks would bring in bream, bass, and even flounders that had washed in with the brackish water of high tide. We let the smaller ones go but collected the bigger ones **7** . My parents enjoyed crabbing from the dock, using old chicken bones with scraps left on them as the bait. If we ever got drowsy waiting for the next bite, they would sneak up behind us with a crab in hand and scare us awake. **8**

5

At this point, the writer wants to show the extent of his patience while he caught fish. Given that all of the choices are true, which one best accomplishes that goal?

A) NO CHANGE

B) while we chatted about books we had read.

C) until one of us felt a tug.

D) for a while.

6

The writer is considering deleting the underlined sentence. Should the writer make this deletion?

A) Yes, because it does not warn of the dangers of fishing during high tide.

B) Yes, because it introduces information that is irrelevant at this point in the passage.

C) No, because it provides information regarding what types of fish were caught.

D) No, because it serves as a transition to the later discussion of eels.

7

At this point, the writer is considering adding the following information.

for what would become a delicious meal back at the house

Should the writer make this addition?

A) Yes, because it expresses how hungry the narrator was after a long day of fishing.

B) Yes, because it explains why the bigger fish were kept instead of let go.

C) No, because it contradicts the earlier point that fish should be kept as pets rather than eaten.

D) No, because it goes beyond the scope of the passage, which focuses on fishing and not eating.

8

At this point, the writer is considering adding the following sentence.

They also did a lot of other things for their own amusement.

Should the writer make this addition?

A) Yes, because it reinforces the parents' personalities as they are portrayed.

B) Yes, because it reveals just how boring crabbing and fishing can be.

C) No, because it distracts from the focus of the paragraph by introducing a loosely related detail.

D) No, because it suggests that the narrator didn't have any fun, which is not true.

One afternoon, I felt a great tug on the line and excitedly began reeling it in. I thought for sure I had caught a good-sized fish, but instead it was a [9] long, muscular, snake-like creature that flailed and twisted, flapping its tail of a body against the wood. [10] An oily substance covered every place it touched, leaving a powdery, slate-blue residue upon drying. Too disgusted to touch it, I trapped the eel under my foot. [11] Meanwhile, my sister was reeling in a large catch of her own. Once it looked dead, we brought it to my grandmother, who had us leave it in a bucket for her gardener, [12] who liked receiving food as gifts.

9

The writer is considering deleting the underlined portion. Should the writer make this deletion?

A) Yes, because it provides description information that could be inaccurate from another point of view.

B) Yes, because it interrupts the flow of the sentence by supplying irrelevant information.

C) No, because it reinforces the contrast between what the narrator expected and his actual catch.

D) No, because it indicates the type of fish the narrator typically caught.

10

The writer is considering deleting the underlined sentence. Should the writer make this deletion?

A) Yes, because it blurs the paragraph's main focus with loosely related details.

B) Yes, because it's unclear whether the narrator is describing a fish or an eel.

C) No, because it provides additional description that helps explain the narrator's reaction in the next sentence.

D) No, because it provides details that support the idea that fishing is not always enjoyable.

11

The writer is considering deleting the underlined sentence. Should the sentence be kept or deleted?

A) Kept, because it sets up the main topic of the paragraph that follows.

B) Kept, because it provides relevant background information.

C) Deleted, because it should be placed earlier in the passage.

D) Deleted, because it detracts from the paragraph's focus on the eel.

12

Given that all of the choices are true, which one provides the most relevant information with regard to the gardener?

A) NO CHANGE

B) who was referred to us by a friend.

C) who often bought clams at the seafood market.

D) who thought of eels as a delicacy.

That evening, when we came up to the house for dinner, the gardener called us over. "I thought you said you killed that eel," he said. "We did," I answered. He pointed to the bucket: the eel was thrashing like it was possessed. Apparently, eels are hard to kill **13** . We all had a good laugh about it. Then he sliced it in half and threw a piece onto the frying pan.

13

At this point, the writer is considering adding the following information (adding a comma after *kill*).

a fact I could've looked up in a book

Should the writer make this addition here?

A) Yes, because it provides a reference for more information about eels.

B) Yes, because it reinforces how accessible certain information is.

C) No, because it fails to specify which book.

D) No, because it weakens the focus of the passage with a loosely related detail.

Exercise 2: Answers for this chapter start on page 237.

The Economics of the Black Death

Life for an English peasant during the feudal era was brief and taxing. Treated as slaves, peasants performed many tasks for their rich lords **1** . In return, peasants had places to live, a little bit of land to scrape a living from, and the lord's protection. There was very little chance that peasants would rise above their social class— **2** imagine how they must have felt. **3** With social structures seemingly set in stone, no one could have predicted the violent changes that soon came.

1

At this point, the writer is considering adding the following information (adding a comma after *lords*).

providing them with food, clothing, weaponry, and any other materials the nobles wanted

Should the writer make this addition?

A) Yes, because it offers specific details that clarify a broad statement.

B) Yes, because it helps clarify the basic needs of the feudal lords.

C) No, because it blurs the focus of the passage with irrelevant details.

D) No, because it gives examples that are a minor portion of the peasants' work.

2

Given that all of the choices are true, which one provides the most relevant detail?

A) NO CHANGE

B) they played games together to pass the time.

C) bread and porridge was the typical meal.

D) a middle class was nearly non-existent.

3

The writer is considering deleting the underlined sentence. Should the sentence be kept or deleted?

A) Kept, because it reinforces the paragraph's claim about the unpredictability of peasant life.

B) Kept, because it sets up the main topic of the paragraph that follows.

C) Deleted, because it weakens the focus of the passage by introducing a subject other than peasant life.

D) Deleted, because it does not logically follow from the previous sentence.

From 1346 to 1353, the Black Death, carried by rats and fleas, decimated Europe, killing as many as one-third of its inhabitants. **4** It likely originated in the dry plains of Central Asia. But this disease, a massive pandemic of bubonic plague, also reshaped the social landscape and brought new opportunities to impoverished workers. **5** Could death be a solution to most problems? It was a matter of simple economics.

4

At this point, the writer wants to further emphasize the catastrophic impact of the Black Death. Which choice best accomplishes this goal?

A) NO CHANGE

B) Symptoms included acute fever and the vomiting of blood, with death approaching two to seven days later.

C) Everyone lived in fear as family members lost their loved ones and even whole villages were wiped out.

D) Because doctors at the time could not explain the cause, people turned to religion and fanaticism.

5

At this point, the writer wants to add a question that reflects the likely skepticism the previous sentence may have been met with. Which choice best accomplishes this goal?

A) NO CHANGE

B) So how exactly did such a terrible disaster end up helping the very group of people it killed?

C) How did peasants react to these sudden changes in society?

D) How come the feudal lords, with all their power, weren't able to prevent the rise of the peasants?

The feudal lords relied on their peasants to supply all their wants and needs.   [6]   As the plague raged on, they had fewer and fewer people to work their lands and manufacture the goods their lifestyle required. Though the plague struck both rich and poor, the disparity in their population sizes meant that the plague had disproportionate effects on the demand for labor and on the supply of labor. There were fewer nobles to begin with, and they were better equipped to shield themselves from the masses of dying people, so [7] they were insulated from the sadness and chaos around them. The much larger population of peasants, on the other hand, decreased severely, [8] which in turn reduced the labor supply.

[6]

At this point, the writer is considering adding the following sentence.

They were addicted to snacking on caviar and wearing fancy robes.

Should the writer make this addition?

A) Yes, because it further illustrates the extravagance of the feudal lords.

B) Yes, because it offers examples of a typical feudal lord's daily activities.

C) No, because it is inconsistent with the tone and focus of the paragraph.

D) No, because the basic needs of the feudal lords were more important than the luxuries they enjoyed.

[7]

Given that all of the following statements are true, which one provides the most relevant detail?

A) NO CHANGE

B) the peasants had even more reason to harbor resentment towards them.

C) their daily routines were, for the most part, uninterrupted.

D) their collective demand for labor did not change radically.

[8]

The writer is considering deleting the underlined portion. Should the writer make this deletion?

A) Yes, because blurs the focus of the paragraph with a loosely related detail.

B) Yes, because it unnecessarily repeats information from earlier in the passage.

C) No, because it provides an important consequence that supports the main point of the paragraph.

D) No, because it illustrates an important economic principle.

As a result, the peasants now had the ability to leave the lords they worked for [9] . There were many other lords eager to find new workers to replace the dead ones. While life remained rather grim for them, peasants had suddenly gained mobility and the ability, however small, to seek better employment and better lands. [10] For those who survived, it's as happy an ending as anyone could have hoped for.

9

At this point, the writer is considering adding the following information.

without putting their livelihoods at risk

Should the writer make this addition?

A) Yes, because it offers an example of the daily struggles faced by peasants.
B) Yes, because it makes explicit why peasants were previously tied to their lords.
C) No, because it shifts the focus of the paragraph from the lords to the peasants.
D) No, because it contradicts a point made in a previous paragraph.

10

Which choice most clearly ends the passage with a restatement of the writer's primary claim?

A) NO CHANGE
B) It's too bad they had to contend with the trauma left by the plague.
C) This change in the social landscape laid the ground work for the middle class and the fall of the feudal system.
D) Many were able to start their own businesses as independent blacksmiths, merchants, and cooks.

Exercise 3: Answers for this chapter start on page 237.

Harvesting Asparagus

Asparagus is not like other vegetables. [1] Because it's more difficult to grow asparagus from seeds, farmers typically buy crowns, [2] dormant roots ready to be planted. They place them in deep trenches, wait several years for them to mature, and then finally cut the plants in the spring, [3] when artichokes are also in season. I learned about the entire process one year when I applied for a job on a busy asparagus farm during harvest time. [4] There was asparagus on this farm that was ready to be harvested.

1

At this point, the writer is considering adding the following sentence.

It isn't planted in the spring to be harvested in the fall.

Should the writer make this addition?

A) Yes, because it emphasizes the importance of the seasons in growing vegetables.

B) Yes, because it provides a specific justification for the previous statement.

C) No, because it does not specify which vegetables follow the usual harvest schedule.

D) No, because it does not clarify when asparagus is planted and harvested.

2

The writer is considering deleting the underlined portion (ending the sentence with a period). Should the writer make this deletion?

A) Yes, because it distracts from the focus of the paragraph by introducing irrelevant material.

B) Yes, because it implies that growing asparagus is easy.

C) No, because the underlined portion defines a term that is important to the paragraph.

D) No, because it serves as a transition to the next sentence.

3

Given that all of the following statements are true, which one provides the most relevant detail?

A) NO CHANGE

B) my favorite season of the year.

C) when they've grown strong enough to be harvested.

D) just in time for the opening of the farmer's market in many cities.

4

The writer is considering deleting the underlined sentence. Should the writer make this deletion?

A) Yes, because it offers information that is repetitive and obvious.

B) Yes, because it is inconsistent with the style and tone of the passage.

C) No, because it reinforces the difference between asparagus and other vegetables.

D) No, because it helps establish the setting of the passage.

[5] The pay wasn't much but I saw the job as an opportunity to learn about farming and agriculture. The manager explained to me that the crowns had been planted five years ago. During the first year, asparagus can look like a field of weeds. Those weeds have to be cut down so that they don't sap the nutrients from any developing asparagus roots. The next spring, small sprouts, also known as spears, start appearing but none of them should be picked as the plants are still establishing themselves in the soil. They grow a little bit each year but are cut down because they still aren't tall enough for harvest. During this phase, [6] it's difficult to predict how many plants will survive long enough to fully mature.

5

At this point, the writer wants to convey the fact that he was fortunate to get the job. Given that all of the choices are true, which one best accomplishes this goal?

A) NO CHANGE

B) Before I got hired, I introduced myself to all the crew members, who all thought I'd work well with them in a team.

C) On my first day of work, I felt intimidated by the long stretches of farmland that we needed to clear.

D) Despite my inexperience, I landed the job because there was a larger yield than the farm anticipated.

6

At this point, the writer wants to reinforce the idea that growing asparagus is a delicate process that requires a lot of attention. Which of the following most effectively accomplishes this goal?

A) NO CHANGE

B) fertilizer can be especially helpful in stimulating their growth.

C) farmers must check everything from the moisture in the soil to the diameter of the spears to ensure they are growing properly.

D) a lack of sunlight can lead to a variety known as white asparagus.

In the next phase, **7** when the spears are a few inches apart, the asparagus is ready to be harvested. As with all vegetables, some of the plants are ready to be cut before others. This is why one harvest can last up to six weeks. Farmers get up by five in the morning everyday **8** to avoid the midday heat. Spears are cut or snapped just above soil level, leaving benign stubs. The spears are then collected in crates for cleaning and packaging. **9** Five years to wait for one crop to mature seems like a very long time, but once it is established, it can keep on reproducing for up to twenty years. Working on this farm was a great learning experience, but I haven't been able to eat asparagus since.

7

The writer is considering deleting the underlined portion. Should the writer make this deletion?

A) Yes, because it unnecessarily repeats information from earlier in the passage.

B) Yes, because it does not describe any other aspects of the asparagus.

C) No, because it specifies an important condition that is relevant to the sentence.

D) No, because it establishes that spears are the outgrowth of an asparagus plant.

8

Given that all of the choices are true, which one most clearly provides a reason for the prior statement in this sentence?

A) NO CHANGE

B) to brush their teeth.

C) to the sound of rooster's crow.

D) to find breakfast waiting for them.

9

At this point, the writer is considering adding the following sentence.

Asparagus grows the best when the nights are cool and the days are hot.

Should the writer make this addition?

A) Yes, because it elaborates on the conditions needed for the successful growing of asparagus.

B) Yes, because it explains why asparagus is grown only in certain regions of the world.

C) No, because it diverts the focus from the harvesting process back to the growing process.

D) No, because it contradicts the previous point that asparagus requires stable conditions to grow in.

23
Placement

Every sentence has its place. Sure, sometimes the order in which you present your thoughts doesn't matter, but more often than not, it impacts the meaning and clarity of what you have to say.

Here is how sentence placement questions on the SAT are phrased:

- *To make this paragraph most logical, sentence 4 should be placed...*
- *Where is the most logical place in this paragraph to add the following sentence?*
- *The writer wants to add the following sentence to the paragraph. ...The best placement for the sentence is...*

And then the answer choices will consist of the number labels of the sentences in the passage.

The most important thing is to read the sentences before and after the insertion point. So if you're considering inserting the given sentence after sentence 5, make sure to read sentences 5 and 6. Those sentences will often be the deciding factor. If they support the given sentence or clearly transition to or from it, you know you've arrived at the answer.

Handling these types of questions is a lot like selecting the best transition, except you're now working backwards. Instead of choosing which sentence to insert, you're figuring out the best place to insert a given sentence. All the same thinking you exercised back in those transition chapters carries over to these questions.

In particular, look for these cues:

1. *this, that, these, those*

Example 1

[1] During a visit to my son's school, I was able to eat lunch in the cafeteria. [2] When I went there at noon, students were lined up single file to pick out their meals. [3] There were four counters, each serving something different. [4] I picked up a side of salad at the first, some rice at the second, and a chicken sandwich at the third. [5] At that point, I was eager to find a seat and enjoy my meal. [6] What made me upset, however, was the fourth counter, which was serving cake, ice cream, and cookies. [7] I called up the school office to file a complaint, but nobody would listen to me. [8] The fourth counter was the most popular one in the cafeteria.

Where is the most logical place in this paragraph to add the following sentence?

> Desserts like these are bound to make students unhealthy.

A) After sentence 2
B) After sentence 3
C) After sentence 4
D) After sentence 6

When you read the sentence in question, your first thought should be *Desserts like what? What are these?* The sentence only makes sense if it's placed next to another sentence that defines what *these* are. The only sentence that does so logically is sentence 6 (*cake, ice cream, and cookies*), answer **D**.

Example 2

[1] After a year of living on futons and eating ramen, the founders at Hourglass decided that antique watches weren't profitable enough to sustain a business. [2] Instead, they decided to invest in modern designs, create new watches, and market them at a discount online. [3] Hourglass soon skyrocketed to success. [4] Within a year, it broke ten million dollars in revenue and announced its intent to expand overseas. [5] A lot of existing watch companies are now looking to buy out this company that was once on the verge of bankruptcy. [6] With those plans in place, the company began to attract the young and fashionable crowd, as well as celebrities looking for the next trend.

To make this paragraph most logical, sentence 6 should be placed

A) where it is now.
B) after sentence 1.
C) after sentence 2.
D) after sentence 4.

Note that sentence 6 refers to *those plans*, so your natural thought should be *What plans?* Sentence 6 only makes sense if it's placed next to another sentence that defines what *those plans* are. The only sentence that does so logically is sentence 2 (*invest in modern designs, create new watches, and market them at a discount online*), answer **C**.

2. Nouns or pronouns in need of clarification

Example 1

[1] The Large Hadron Collider, the most powerful particle collider in the world, was built to test theories of particle physics. [2] In particular, it was used to prove the existence of the Higgs Boson, a new type of particle that helps explain why things have mass. [3] The Collider is based at the CERN Laboratory and contains four types of detectors. [4] Having more than one detector carry out the same tests gives scientists the ability to cross-check results and identify any anomalies in the data they generate.

Where is the most logical place in this paragraph to add the following sentence?

> Two of them, the ATLAS and CMS detectors, are very similar and can run the same class of experiments.

A) After sentence 1
B) After sentence 2
C) After sentence 3
D) After sentence 4

The key word is *them*—what's *them*? Detectors, obviously. So we must put this sentence after one that brings up detectors, sentence 3. The answer is **C**. The important take-away here is that *them* was a pronoun in need of a clarifying reference.

The first cue in this chapter—*this, that, these, those*—is just a more specific version of this second cue. After all, *this, that, these,* and *those* are all pronouns that are in need of a reference that clarifies them.

Example 2

[1] Hong Kong has long been criticized for its citizens' taste for rare ocean delicacies, especially shark fin soup. [2] People pay hundreds of dollars to enjoy one bowl of the soup, which symbolizes wealth and power. [3] But overfishing and a love for seafood have disrupted many underwater habitats in Asia, endangering much of the marine life, including local sharks. [4] Last October, the Hong Kong government decided to prohibit all imports of shark fin. [5] Biologists are closely monitoring the shark population to see if it recovers.

Where is the most logical place in this paragraph to add the following sentence?

> Environmental activists praised the ban as a crucial step towards protecting the underwater ecosystem in Asia, but more should be done.

A) After sentence 2
B) After sentence 3
C) After sentence 4
D) After sentence 5

The noun that needs clarification here is *the ban*. Reading the sentence by itself, we're not sure what *the ban* refers to. That's why we need to place this sentence next to one that provides that clarification, sentence 4, which specifies that it's a shark fin ban. The answer is **C**.

3. Chronological order

Example 1

[1] The Mongols tried to conquer Vietnam at various points in the second millennium. [2] The first time, they were repelled by the unknown landscape and intemperate climate. [3] When they came back better prepared, the Vietnamese scared them off by setting fires to their encampments. [4] The Mongols finally succeeded twice in the late 13th century, but mysteriously left each time. [5] It wasn't until the 19th century that the Vietnamese were fully conquered—by the French. [6] On their third return, they were routed by the genius of the Vietnamese generals at the battle of Bach Dang.

To make this paragraph most logical, sentence 6 should be placed

A) where it is now.
B) after sentence 1.
C) after sentence 2.
D) after sentence 3.

This is an example of putting things in chronological order, from first to last. Sentence 6 begins with *On their third return*, which means that it should be placed after the narrator has talked about the first and second times. The second time the Mongols tried to conquer Vietnam is discussed in sentence 3, so the answer is **D**.

Example 2

[1] John dusted himself off and returned to the tractor for a flashlight and a length of rope. [2] We tied the end of the rope to the rear of the tractor. [3] I lead the line for John while he went down for a look around. [4] He had discovered one of the largest cave systems in all of New York State. [5] It would take years to map and would be an adventure even more profitable than the original goal that had lead us to discover it.

Where is the most logical place in this paragraph to add the following sentence?

When John returned to the surface, he was grinning ear to ear.

A) After sentence 1
B) After sentence 2
C) After sentence 3
D) After sentence 4

Consider the logical sequence of events. The sentence in question states that "John returned to the surface," which means he had to have gone below the surface sometime before that point. Sentence 3 is the only place where that event is stated. The answer is **C**. Why not place it later, after sentence 4, for example? Because placing the sentence after sentence 3 then allows sentence 4 to explain why John was "grinning ear to ear." Also note that the first half of the paragraph is action, whereas the latter half is more reflection. The given sentence belongs in the "action" half.

4. Lead/Topic sentences

Example 1

[1] Clinical studies have shown that squatting is better than any other lower-body movement for muscle hypertrophy. [2] In fact, the rate of muscle growth can be up to three times as fast if squats are done correctly as part of a regular workout routine. [3] The back-squat is considered the king of all bodybuilding movements. [4] Most injuries in the gym, however, stem from accidents caused by poor form. [5] As a result, runners will rarely use squats as part of their training.

To make this paragraph most logical, sentence 3 should be placed

A) where it is now.
B) before sentence 1.
C) after sentence 4.
D) after sentence 5.

Sentence 3 is a good example of a lead sentence—a more general sentence that leads into more specific details or supporting evidence, sort of like a topic sentence. It sets the stage for the more specific reasoning in sentences 1 and 2. The answer is **B**.

The only reason I like to call it a lead sentence rather than a topic sentence is that most students think a topic sentence must start a paragraph. Lead sentences, however, can be in the middle of the paragraph. Take a look at the following example:

Example 2

[1] My freshman year of college was quite intimidating. [2] Not only did I have to adjust to a new setting, but I also had to make sure I did well in my classes. [3] Professor Kwok always had a weird experiment to illustrate the concept of the day. [4] To teach us about speed and rates of change, he swung a bowling ball from the ceiling until it collided with the door. [5] Another time, he made explosives out of liquid nitrogen so that we could apply the Gurney equations to them. [6] He was fired after that.

Where is the most logical place in this paragraph to add the following sentence?

> I had many teachers, but my favorite was my math professor.

A) After sentence 1
B) After sentence 2
C) After sentence 4
D) After sentence 6

The sentence in question is a lead sentence—it introduces what the author will talk about next, his math professor. Because everything after sentence 2 talks about Professor Kwok, after sentence 2 is exactly where the sentence should be inserted. The answer is **B**. This lead sentence is essentially a transition sentence.

5. Supporting sentences

A supporting sentence is the opposite of a lead sentence. It offers additional details and specific facts or examples in support of a more general statement that comes before it. Let's take a previous example and change the question:

Example

[1] My freshman year of college was quite intimidating. [2] Not only did I have to adjust to a new setting, but I also had to make sure I did well in my classes. [3] I had many teachers, but my favorite was my math professor. [4] Professor Kwok always had a weird experiment to illustrate the concept of the day. [5] One time, he made explosives out of liquid nitrogen so that we could apply the Gurney equations to them. [6] He was fired after that.

Where is the most logical place in this paragraph to add the following sentence?

> To teach us about speed and rates of change, he swung a bowling ball from the ceiling until it collided with the door.

A) After sentence 1
B) After sentence 3
C) After sentence 4
D) After sentence 5

The sentence in question is a supporting sentence—it provides an example that backs up some point made before it. Because it's an example of one of Professor Kwok's "weird experiments," it belongs after sentence 4. The answer is **C**. Note that sentence 4 serves as a lead sentence. Writing can be funny that way. Sentence 4 is a supporting sentence to sentence 3, but it's a lead sentence to the one we're inserting.

6. Transition words

Example

[1] Barbary falcons are a particular kind of hunting bird used in the desert kingdom of Saudi Arabia. [2] Their nimble flight mechanics make them the perfect predators for hunting smaller birds. [3] Although they live in dry open hills and deserts, they make their nests on cliffs and breed throughout the year. [4] The Barbary falcon is often mistaken for the peregrine falcon, even though the former has a smaller wingspan.

Where is the most logical place in this paragraph to add the following sentence?

> However, they are less valuable for catching land based mammals like foxes or mice, as their larger size often warns potential prey of their approach.

A) After sentence 1
B) After sentence 2
C) After sentence 3
D) After sentence 4

Note the word *However*. This indicates that wherever the sentence is placed, it must serve to offset or counter the sentence before it. The best insertion point is after sentence 2, answer **B**. While barbary falcons are the "perfect predators for hunting smaller birds," they are "less valuable for catching land based mammals." Side by side, the two sentences offer a strength and then a weakness, which makes the *However* fit quite logically.

Exercise 1: Answers for this chapter start on page 238.

1.   [1] Machines that play chess have been around for a long time, but never have they been as powerful as they are today. [2] Given that level of computing power, they usually win. [3] But a new type has been designed that is intended to lose. [4] The idea is aimed at novice players, who would benefit from a boost in confidence by beating a computer. [5] Grandmaster Garry Kasparov thinks the new machine is a great invention and intends to use it with his beginner students in the near future. [6] They are now able to perform millions of calculations within seconds in order to determine what moves to play.

To make this paragraph most logical, sentence 6 should be placed

A) where it is now.
B) after sentence 1.
C) after sentence 2.
D) after sentence 4.

2.   [1] Chloe smiled, but didn't reply to his joke. [2] Erik searched her face for a clue as to what she was thinking. [3] Silently, they strolled on, Erik walking a little behind her in the dying light of the day. [4] Chloe turned to ask him something, but he was gone. [5] She called his name, but no response. [6] She knew then that she'd lost him forever.

To make this paragraph most logical, sentence 6 should be placed

A) where it is now.
B) after sentence 1.
C) after sentence 2.
D) after sentence 4.

3.   [1] Four workmen stand on a road in front of a small steel-mill. [2] They have a tricky problem. [3] How do they lift a weighty piece of machinery onto the second floor of the factory without the aid of a mechanical vehicle? [4] Even if it could be held up, it would be impossible to carry it up the steep, narrow stairs to where it needs to be fitted. [5] It is extremely heavy, too heavy to lift.

To make this paragraph most logical, sentence 5 should be placed

A) where it is now.
B) after sentence 1.
C) after sentence 2.
D) after sentence 3.

4.   [1] The Prince built a barracks adjacent to the castle and stationed a garrison of men there to carry on the assault in his absence. [2] After he left north to negotiate with Edwin of Lancaster, the soldiers surprised the opposing province in a daring, early morning ambush. [3] According to the rules of medieval chivalry, he could not be pursued by the Prince's soldiers once he was there. [4] But the soldiers ignored these conventions, stormed the monastery, and captured him. [5] The duke escaped and fled to a nearby monastery.

To make this paragraph most logical, sentence 5 should be placed

A) where it is now.
B) after sentence 1.
C) after sentence 2.
D) after sentence 3.

5.   [1] The drier conditions of the Ice Age suited one of the larger mammal species that made it to the Central American archipelago—the tree sloth. [2] However, there were a number of evolutionary relatives of this creature that didn't survive. [3] Was it the animal's unusual metabolism that gave the tree sloth a competitive advantage? [4] We can't know for sure. [5] What we do know from fossil findings is that the morphological characteristics of this kind of sloth are the same today as they were fifteen thousand years ago.

To make this paragraph most logical, sentence 5 should be placed

   A) where it is now.
   B) after sentence 1.
   C) after sentence 2.
   D) after sentence 3.

6.   [1] The city was established in 1781, when a group of Spanish colonialists came up from Mexico and built a small town of mud houses with red tile roofs. [2] Would you recognize the name El Pueblo de Nuestra Senora La Reina de Los Angeles de Porciuncula? [3] You've probably heard of it before. [4] In fact, it's the Spanish name for what is now known as the city of Los Angeles. [5] It wasn't until 1847, after the Mexican-American War, that the city came under U.S. control, with the signing of the Treaty of Cahuenga finally confirming American ownership and the name change to Los Angeles.

To make this paragraph most logical, sentence 1 should be placed

   A) where it is now.
   B) after sentence 2.
   C) after sentence 4.
   D) after sentence 5.

7.   [1] Plantation owners typically divided their fields between coffee beans and the native rubber crop. [2] In the 1800s, however, a coffee crop disease which spread throughout the region wiped out much of the farmland devoted to it. [3] The renewed taste for coffee elsewhere meant that it didn't take long for Sri Lanka's farms to recover with a complete shift to coffee production. [4] New, blight-resistant strains were re-planted where old ones had been decimated. [5] During that time, coffee was becoming more and more popular overseas, with the middle-class in America selecting it as its drink of choice. [6] Those who remembered the earlier blight thought this reliance on one export was foolish, but their warnings would go unheeded.

To make this paragraph most logical, sentence 5 should be placed

   A) where it is now.
   B) after sentence 2.
   C) after sentence 3.
   D) after sentence 6.

8.   [1] In Spanish soccer teams, to score without the right aesthetic and technique is almost frowned upon. [2] Juande Ramos, the Real Madrid coach who previously led Seville to the UEFA Cup final in 2006, disagrees. [3] His utilitarian approach to management—to win at all costs, even if it isn't pretty—has predictably lost him favor with the fans. [4] But silverware and trophies are what count in the long-run, and many journalists, and even some spectators, are beginning to warm to him. [5] The Spanish believe that a victory in soccer must be achieved in style, that winning with flair is the only way to win.

To make this paragraph most logical, sentence 5 should be placed

   A) where it is now.
   B) after sentence 1.
   C) after sentence 2.
   D) after sentence 3.

9.   [1] The Earth's poles may appear permanent, but they have reversed many times in the planet's history. [2] The North becomes the South, and the South becomes the North. [3] It is not known why this happens, just that it does. [4] Without this vital physical clue, it would've been impossible to tell whether this phenomenon had really occurred. [5] Magnetized rock on the ocean floor serves as a record for the changing orientation of the Earth's magnetic field.

To make this paragraph most logical, sentence 5 should be placed

   A) where it is now.
   B) after sentence 1.
   C) after sentence 2.
   D) after sentence 3.

10.   [1] Many people mistakenly believe a wave is just a mass of water careening across the surface of the sea. [2] There's a much deeper science behind it. [3] If one observes a bird bobbing on the waves, it appears as if it's going to be carried away to another place. [4] If one keeps on looking, however, it looks like it's actually staying in the same place, not heading towards shore or anywhere else. [5] If they could just find a way to replicate the motions of an ocean wave in laboratory conditions, they could begin to investigate this peculiar phenomenon in more detail.

Where is the most logical place in this paragraph to add the following sentence?

   It was this lack of movement that first gave scientists an insight into how waves behave.

   A) After sentence 1
   B) After sentence 2
   C) After sentence 3
   D) After sentence 4

11.   [1] The ships developed out of a maritime "arms-race" of sorts, in what was a unique set of economic circumstances at the time. [2] Tea drinking was quickly replacing beer as the national drink of England, and the tea came mostly from China. [3] Buyers were desperate to be the first to try a new variety of tea arriving in port, and so the ships that could deliver their cargo the fastest could charge the highest prices. [4] One such merchant was the flamboyant Irving Ironhammer, who had made his name in the cotton trade and now sought his riches from tea plantations in remote areas of China, far up the Yangtze River.

Where is the most logical place in this paragraph to add the following sentence?

   Merchants were willing to invest in building the sleekest ships to compete with one another.

   A) After sentence 1
   B) After sentence 2
   C) After sentence 3
   D) After sentence 4

12.   [1] Oil is utilized in many industrial processes. [2] It provides fuel for heavy machinery used in the agriculture and farming sectors. [3] Much of the oil we extract from nature provides energy for the nation's power stations, which in turn provide heat and light for our homes and places of work. [4] It might surprise some people to discover that crude oil is also a crucial part of the plastic manufacturing process. [5] Hydrocarbons found in oil are the raw ingredients used to synthesize common household necessities, such as kitchenware and furniture. [6] They are also increasingly being used to create sophisticated biomedical devices, such as pacemakers and artificial limbs.

To make this paragraph most logical, sentence 5 should be placed

A) where it is now.
B) after sentence 2.
C) after sentence 3.
D) after sentence 6.

13.   [1] The active ingredient in this medicine is Chlorphenamine Maleate. [2] Symptoms of an allergic reaction include itching, streaming eyes, and a blocked nose. If you suffer from hayfever, allergies, or insect bites, this drug may be of help. [3] Remember, do not give this medicine to anyone else whom it has not been prescribed to by a health professional. [4] Do not take this medication if you are taking any other treatment that your pharmacist or doctor has not been informed of.

Where is the most logical place in this paragraph to add the following sentence?

> An antihistamine, the drug blocks the effects of a compound that can cause allergic reactions in some people.

A) After sentence 1
B) After sentence 2
C) After sentence 3
D) After sentence 4

14.   [1] They reached the door of the hunting lodge. [2] Daisy dropped her bucket and looked around. [3] No one had been here for a long time. [4] She really couldn't remember. [5] The door was still unlocked, just as it had been when they were there last year. [6] She peered through the dusty window. [7] The bed had been made. [8] Had she left it like that?

To make this paragraph most logical, sentence 4 should be placed

A) where it is now.
B) after sentence 2.
C) after sentence 5.
D) after sentence 8.

15.   [1] Because of his reputation as a great artist, Michelangelo was eventually pardoned and resumed work for the Medicis again. [2] During this period, he spent time crafting the tomb of Lorenzo de Medici. [3] His sculpture of Lorenzo seeks to capture the inner personality of the dark, pensive, and brooding man. [4] Indeed, Lorenzo's nickname, "The Thoughtful One," wasn't given to him for no reason.

Where is the most logical place in this paragraph to add the following sentence?

> He would never finish the project during his lifetime, but scholars still acknowledge it as one of his finest pieces ever.

A) After sentence 1
B) After sentence 2
C) After sentence 3
D) After sentence 4

Exercise 2: Answers for this chapter start on page 238.

1. [1] India is a land of riches. [2] Precious metals and priceless stones have been mined from the earth there for as long as anyone can remember. [3] Yet the natural bounty that gave rise to its wealth has also brought with it a dark side. [4] However, the people have not surrendered so easily; even Alexander the Great was driven out, never to return. [5] Invaders have sought to conquer her lands to possess the riches underground.

To make this paragraph most logical, sentence 5 should be placed

 A) where it is now.
 B) after sentence 1.
 C) after sentence 2.
 D) after sentence 3.

2. [1] It is impossible to differentiate between cane sugar and beet sugar. [2] Cane molasses are what we know as the treacle in our puddings and desserts. [3] Beet molasses are not typically consumed by humans but go towards producing cattle food when mixed with beet pulp. [4] Both cane and beet molasses can be used to produce alcohol as well. [5] However, the molasses obtained from each are somewhat different.

To make this paragraph most logical, sentence 5 should be placed

 A) where it is now.
 B) after sentence 1.
 C) after sentence 2.
 D) after sentence 3.

3. [1] One of the saddest stories in Greek mythology is that of Echo the nymph. [2] Echo liked to have the last word in every conversation, but upon upsetting the goddess Hera, her punishment was to never speak again, except to repeat the last words spoken by other people. [3] But Narcissus cared only for himself and sat admiring his reflection on the surface of a pond until he died. [4] Echo was heartbroken and died not long after, the only remaining trace of her being the anguished cry heard between the mountains of her home. [5] One day, she encountered the handsome Narcissus and was smitten with his youth and beauty.

To make this paragraph most logical, sentence 5 should be placed

 A) where it is now.
 B) after sentence 1.
 C) after sentence 2.
 D) after sentence 3.

4.   [1] Along the beaches of the Pribilof Islands is a sea creature prized for its luxuriant fur. [2] The bulls, or males, arrive first. [3] Snorting and threatening other males, they battle for prime territory. [4] Then, packs of females return to the islands, completing their winter migration from the north. [5] The bulls pack them into harems and spend the rest of their time defending their territory and mating with the females.

Where is the most logical place in this paragraph to add the following sentence?

> Northern fur seals, as they are known, gather here every year to play out their violent breeding ritual.

A) After sentence 1
B) After sentence 2
C) After sentence 3
D) After sentence 4

5.   [1] Many of Charles Dicken's characters are as famous today as they were when he wrote them into his books over a century ago. [2] Despite the great fortunes he made from his writings, Dickens always felt a special concern for the plight of the poor. [3] Characters like Tiny Tim and Oliver Twist portray the harsh lives that children suffered in Victorian times. [4] Dickens himself had a childhood not unlike those depicted in *A Christmas Carol* or *The Old Curiosity Shop*. [5] He never forgot those times and used the experiences as a resource for his works of fiction.

Where is the most logical place in this paragraph to add the following sentence?

> After his father went to debtors' prison, young Charles had to work long hours in dismal conditions to pay back what the family owed.

A) After sentence 1
B) After sentence 2
C) After sentence 4
D) After sentence 5

6.   [1] In 1849, the British government repealed the British Navigation Acts and opened up previously inaccessible tracts of the global marketplace to foreign traders. [2] Suddenly, merchants in the United States and all over Europe were free to compete with British businessmen on level terms, and they wasted no time in building even faster ships to capitalize on the situation. [3] They were still admired, but their aura of invincibility had gone. [4] The golden age of the British vessel was over; the new age of the steam ship was just around the corner.

Where is the most logical place in this paragraph to add the following sentence?

> Soon, the ships of Great Britain were no longer the envy of the world.

A) After sentence 1
B) After sentence 2
C) After sentence 3
D) After sentence 4

7.   [1] You do not want to be overly relaxed when executing a maneuver. [2] But nor do you want to be too tense. [3] You should be able to "relax into tension," to enable proper breathing while exerting sufficient muscle strength. [4] The concept seems like an oxymoron, but once you begin kettlebell training, you will start to understand. [5] In kettlebell training, you must keep a special balance between tension and relaxation.

To make this paragraph most logical, sentence 5 should be placed

A) at the beginning of the paragraph.
B) after sentence 1.
C) after sentence 2.
D) after sentence 3.

8.   [1] The Brazilian portion of the Amazon is enormous, but it contains only about 7 percent of the country's population. [2] Much of that 7 percent is concentrated around the town of Belen. [3] Belen is known mostly for its tree farming industry. [4] Somehow, the seeds of its magnificent trees were stolen and later taken abroad where they were grown in special tree-nurseries, ending the monopoly Belen had enjoyed. [5] The timbers from that region of the Americas were once the finest in the world.

To make this paragraph most logical, sentence 5 should be placed

A) where it is now.
B) after sentence 1.
C) after sentence 2.
D) after sentence 3.

9.   [1] The cat is often portrayed as a creature of leisure, stretching itself before a cozy fire, or curled up beside its owner. [2] Yet this animal, though it appears tame, is still a semi-wild pet, not reliant on its "master" as much as we'd like to think. [3] The cat has hardly changed in 4000 years of domestication. [4] Many farm cats, for instance, are fed sporadically so that they keep on catching mice and other countryside rodents.

Where is the most logical place in this paragraph to add the following sentence?

  Its hunting instinct is still strong.

A) After sentence 1
B) After sentence 2
C) After sentence 3
D) After sentence 4

10.   [1] It was once believed that fermentation was caused by little creatures living within substances in which gases or acids are formed. [2] Louis Pasteur discovered that it was actually due to tiny organisms floating in the air. [3] He tested his hypothesis by heating a liquid, like wine or milk, very rapidly. [4] He found that the microorganisms that soured the liquid were killed and that further contamination depended on whether the bottle was open to the air. [5] This process of treating foods with heat, pasteurization, still bears his name to this day.

To make this paragraph most logical, sentence 5 should be placed

A) where it is now.
B) after sentence 1.
C) after sentence 2.
D) after sentence 3.

11.   [1] Tanks have been used as fighting vehicles in every modern war. [2] Compared to the latest designs, which incorporate electric range-finding devices and laser gun-control technology, those older models may seem like relics of the past. [3] Nevertheless, human beings are still required to drive the machines, no matter how technologically advanced they currently are. [4] But with automation science and remote-controlled drone-like piloting now being developed, tanks may become independent weapons of destruction sooner than we think.

Where is the most logical place in this paragraph to add the following sentence?

> Early versions were pedal-powered and demanded a great deal of physical effort to propel them.

A) After sentence 1
B) After sentence 2
C) After sentence 3
D) After sentence 4

12.   [1] The tabor is a small, drum-like instrument. [2] It can be held aloft with one hand, or rested in the crook of an arm. [3] Should the musician play both instruments at the same time, he or she would use crooked drumsticks to make it easier to blow the pipe. [4] Evidence from manuscript records shows that the tabar was used nearly 1000 years ago. [5] It is even mentioned in some of Shakespeare's plays!

Where is the most logical place in this paragraph to add the following sentence?

> Beaten with either a drumstick or the palm of an opposing hand, the tabor would sometimes be accompanied by a flute or three-holed pipe, often played by the same musician.

A) After sentence 1
B) After sentence 2
C) After sentence 4
D) After sentence 5

13.   [1] Soil provides a medium in which plants and other living things can grow. [2] The basis of all soil is rock. [3] These particles, over time, mix with other rocks, plants, bacteria, and a variety of organic materials. [4] The resulting soil rarely comprises more than a layer 10 inches thick, but it is a complete, functioning, living environment in and of itself. [5] When water and wind break rock down, finer and finer pieces are formed.

To make this paragraph most logical, sentence 5 should be placed

A) where it is now.
B) after sentence 1.
C) after sentence 2.
D) after sentence 3.

14.   [1] Numerology is the belief that numbers have an inherent mystical dimension over and above their significance to mainstream mathematics. [2] There was a strong belief around that time that the universe could be understood through numbers, though this stemmed from a religious concept of the divine, in which man could be united with God through numerical relationships. [3] The idea was that the human understanding of numbers was a God-given attribute, put there to better appreciate the world that God created. [4] Yet it would be the early Church councils of the 4th century AD that eventually condemned this notion as superstitious nonsense, a move that many people today might find hard to believe. [5] Despite its unscientific character, numerology has a history going back to the Pythagorean school of philosophers of the 6th century BC.

To make this paragraph most logical, sentence 5 should be placed

A) where it is now.
B) after sentence 1.
C) after sentence 2.
D) after sentence 3.

15.   [1] There is still no definitive cause of aging. [2] One theory is that cells have a pre-determined lifetime. [3] Some cells, like those that make up skin and blood, can be replaced, while others, such as nerve cells, cannot. [4] If a cell is damaged, and it cannot be replaced, it is lost forever. [5] This division process allows subsequent generations of cells to carry errors caused during replication. [6] These errors may degrade the quality of the duplicated cells, leading to what we know of as aging.

Where is the most logical place in this paragraph to add the following sentence?

      But cells that can be replaced do so by splitting in two.

A) After sentence 2
B) After sentence 4
C) After sentence 5
D) After sentence 6

24
Singular Plural Noun Inconsistency

Example 1

Wrong:	The three boys want to become a superhero.
Correct:	The three boys want to become **superheroes**.

It doesn't make much sense to say that three boys want to become one *single* superhero (unless they happen to be the pandas in this comic strip). Each boy wants to become his or her own superhero, so the plural *boys* should be followed by the plural *superheroes*.

Example 2

Wrong:	The teacher gave the students who aced the test a high-five.
Correct:	The teacher gave the students who aced the test **high-fives**.

Example 3

Wrong:	Witness testimony, documents, and a consumer guarantee have been a key piece of evidence in many major landmark trials involving corporations and their customers.
Correct:	Witness testimony, documents, and a consumer guarantee have been **key pieces** of evidence in many major landmark trials involving corporations and their customers.

Exercise: Correct the noun inconsistency errors in the following sentences. There may be more than one error in each sentence. Answers for this chapter start on page 240.

1. The football players put on their helmet and grabbed their water bottle.

2. The two students put their mind to the test by participating in the state chess competition.

3. Revered as talented magicians who can do much more than card tricks, David Blaine surprises audiences with superhuman feats of endurance.

4. The caterpillars that emerged from their cocoon will soon turn into a butterfly.

5. Environmental scientists are currently promoting ethanol, natural gas, and chemically stored electricity as an alternative to fossil fuels.

6. Mary and Ann dreamed of blossoming into a princess and being rescued by a prince.

7. We competed in many exciting baseball games this year, but our win against last year's champions is by far the most memorable victories.

8. Curiosity, diligence, and the willingness to think on one's feet are a strong prerequisite for a successful career in any industry.

9. An expert in the federal tax code, the bank's financial advisors can tell you where to put your investments to maximize your deductions.

10. You will not be able to pass the preliminary background check unless the document you provide is a driver's license, passport, or other valid forms of identification.

11. The two teams from Pittsburgh won the first and second place prize in the international robotics competition.

12. Two out of every fifteen college students who major in computer science will go on to become a small business owner at some point in their lives.

25
Who vs. Whom

Now's a good time to introduce an error you'll probably encounter just once on the SAT, but probably hundreds of times in your life: *who* vs. *whom*.

Rule

Use *whom* after a preposition (*to, for, of,...*). Use *who* for all other cases. Note that this rule is not always correct, but it's easier to memorize and it will get you through all SAT questions related to this error.

Example 1

Wrong:	Jane is the girl for **who** I brought these gifts.
Correct:	Jane is the girl for **whom** I brought these gifts.
Correct:	Jane is the girl **whom** I brought these gifts for.

Note the exception to the rule in the second correct version. Sometimes, the preposition (*for*, in this case) is moved to someplace later in the sentence, so just watch out. Here's another example of this:

Example 2

Wrong:	The chaperones **who** the students were assigned to made sure they walked in a single file.
Correct:	The chaperones **whom** the students were assigned to made sure they walked in a single file.
Correct:	The chaperones **to whom** the students were assigned made sure they walked in a single file.

In the example above, the preposition to look out for is *to*. Notice that the preposition can be moved back in front of the *whom*.

Example 3

Wrong:	The boys **whom** robbed the store should be thrown in jail.
Correct:	The boys **who** robbed the store should be thrown in jail.

Example 4

Wrong:	To **who** should I send these flowers?
Correct:	To **whom** should I send these flowers?

Example 5

Wrong:	The librarian yelled at the boy **whom** never returned his books.
Correct:	The librarian yelled at the boy **who** never returned his books.

Example 6

Wrong:	He is the man **who** I love.
Correct:	He is the man **whom** I love.

This is an example of an exception to the rule. Because *the man* is the object of your love, we have to use *whom*. These cases pretty much never come up on the SAT, so just trust in the rule above. However, knowing this exception will give you added confidence on the small chance it actually comes up.

Exercise: Answers for this chapter start on page 240.

1. The agency recruited overseas teachers (*who/whom*) would be able to demonstrate a native fluency in English.

2. At Kim's birthday party were millionaires and celebrities, some of (*who/whom*) had flown in from New York to attend.

3. Julie's math teacher was a graduate student (*who/whom*), after completing his finance degree, decided to get into teaching instead.

4. The police officers, (*who/whom*) were eating donuts at the time, didn't hear the cries for help.

5. The girl (*who/whom*) Dave was matched with was unimpressed by his sense of humor.

6. Anyone (*who/whom*) has read the book will say that it's much better than the movie.

7. Reflecting on all her past accomplishments, the winner thanked everyone with (*who/whom*) she had been associated.

8. Can you tell the boys (*who/whom*) are at the door to go away?

9. The girls with (*who/whom*) I'm going shopping need to borrow money.

10. I want to hire those chefs (*who/whom*) cooked the perfect pasta at the restaurant we ate at last week.

26 Combining Sentences

You'll typically get two questions that ask you to choose the best way of combining two sentences. Below are examples of the most common ways of doing so. Of course, the best strategy will depend on the sentences you're working with. You've seen a lot of these before in previous chapters.

1. Use a trailing phrase

This method is by far the most commonly tested.

Example 1

Before:	To get the gun-control law passed, the President pointed out the numerous shootings that happen every year. He illustrated the dangers of having few restrictions.
After:	To get the gun-control law passed, the President pointed out the numerous shootings that happen every year, **illustrating the dangers of having few restrictions**.

Example 2

Before:	Students often see the complex theorems of physics as useless and tiresome. They don't know that every piece of modern technology is founded on the discoveries of quantum physics.
After:	Students often see the complex theorems of physics as useless and tiresome, **not knowing that every piece of modern technology is founded on the discoveries of quantum physics**.

Example 3

Before:	The monkey was tied down because other animals were distracted by its eating habits. It was not because of its tendency to escape.
After:	The monkey was tied down because other animals were distracted by its eating habits, **not because of its tendency to escape**.

Example 4

Before:	Inside the dusty cabinet was a map of the Underground Railroad. It was a network of underground tunnels slaves once used to escape from the South.
After:	Inside the dusty cabinet was a map of the Underground Railroad, **a network of underground tunnels slaves once used to escape from the South**.

2. Use a preposition

Example 5

Before:	Joseph finished his homework. His teacher helped him.
After:	Joseph finished his homework **with the help of his teacher**.

Example 6

Before:	He is one of the fastest runners in the world. His accomplishments are demonstrated by his numerous world records.
After:	He is one of the fastest runners in the world **as demonstrated by his numerous world records**.

3. Turn one of them into a dependent clause or modifier

Example 7

Before:	Jacob has decided to avoid snacks and soda. The reason for the diet is that he wants to lose weight.
After:	**Because he wants to lose weight,** Jacob has decided to avoid snacks and soda.

Example 8

Before:	The giant panda is the rarest bear in the world today. It has large, distinctive, black patches around its eyes, strong jaw muscles, and a long tail.
After:	**The rarest bear in the world today,** the giant panda has large, distinctive, black patches around its eyes, strong jaw muscles, and a long tail.

4. Use a conjunction

Example 9

Before:	On the surface, Seinfeld is most famous for its light-hearted dialogue. Included among the many episodes is an assortment of comments on racism, homosexuality, and death.
After:	On the surface, Seinfeld is most famous for its light-hearted dialogue, **but** included among the many episodes is an assortment of comments on racism, homosexuality, and death.

5. Link two verbs with *and*

Example 10

Before:	The people sitting in front of me on the train were talking throughout the ride. They would not turn their cell phones off even after being told to do so.
After:	The people sitting in front of me on the train were talking throughout the ride **and** would not turn their cell phones off even after being told to do so.

6. Use a relative clause

Example 11

Before:	John Durgin worked as an accountant for ten years and then became a math teacher. He first learned to calculate in his head by reciting multiplication tables at home.
After:	John Durgin, **who worked as an accountant for ten years and then became a math teacher**, first learned to calculate in his head by reciting multiplication tables at home.

Example 12

Before:	Every car is powered by an engine. The engine converts fuel and heat into mechanical motion.
After:	Every car is powered by an engine, **which converts fuel and heat into mechanical motion**.

7. Use an infinitive to express purpose

Example 13

Before:	The little boy happily ran home. He would tell his mom he had found the last golden ticket.
After:	The little boy happily ran home **to tell** his mom he had found the last golden ticket.

8. Use an appropriate punctuation mark (dash, colon, or semicolon)

Example 14

Before:	The fighter defended his title by taking his opponent to the ground. This is the same strategy he used in his last championship match.
After:	The fighter defended his title by taking his opponent to the **ground—the same strategy** he used in his last championship match.

Here are some tips and guidelines:

1. The fewer pronouns, the better (especially *this, these, they, it*)

Note the pronoun *it* in the following example.

Example 14

The arctic owl's coat of snow-white feathers acts as camouflage. It keeps the owl hidden by blending the animal in with its surroundings.

A) NO CHANGE
B) camouflage, and it keeps
C) camouflage; it keeps
D) camouflage, keeping

Answer D is the best because it avoids using the unnecessary pronoun *it*.

Nearly all the examples in the strategy section above involve unnecessary pronouns.

2. Keep the intended meaning

Don't combine sentences in such a way that the intended meaning is altered.

Example 15

Chinese families get ready for Mid-Autumn Festival by doing several things. They light lanterns, prepare mooncakes, and arrange flowers.

A) NO CHANGE
B) Chinese families get ready for Mid-Autumn Festival to light lanterns, prepare mooncakes, and arrange flowers.
C) Chinese families get ready for Mid-Autumn Festival by lighting lanterns, preparing mooncakes, and arranging flowers.
D) Chinese families get ready for Mid-Autumn Festival for lighting lanterns, preparing mooncakes, and arranging flowers.

Notice how answers B and D change the intended meaning. Chinese families don't get ready for the Festival **in order to** light lanterns, prepare mooncakes, and arrange flowers. That would be backwards. They get ready for the Festival **by** lighting lanterns, preparing mooncakes, and arranging flowers. Those activities are HOW they get ready, not WHY they get ready. The answer is C.

3. Avoid repeated words

Alarm bells should go off anytime you see repeated words.

Example 16

The restaurant was highly recommended by the food critics. These critics stayed there for four hours to savor every dish.

A) NO CHANGE
B) critics, who
C) critics, and these critics
D) critics after the critics

The answer is B because it doesn't repeat *critics*.

4. The fewer words, the better

This is a general rule of thumb. More words imply complexity and when you're combining sentences, you're trying to make things less complicated, not more.

Example 17

The new hardware runs at a faster rate when compared to the old one. This increased speed reduces costs in our technology department, where we have the most overhead.

A) NO CHANGE
B) When compared to the old one, the new hardware runs at a faster rate, which reduces costs in our technology department, where we have the most overhead.
C) The new hardware runs at a faster rate when compared to the old one, and this increased speed reduces costs in our technology department, where we have the most overhead.
D) The new hardware runs at a faster rate when compared to the old one; by increasing the speed, we reduce costs in our technology department, where we have the most overhead.

Answers A, C, and D are all wordy compared to answer B. The words *increased speed* are unnecessary and should be cut out.

In general, the answer will usually involve the fewest number of words and the least amount of effort, which means you should be eliminating words, not adding them. This is the over-arching guideline that all the above guidelines fall under—take it to heart.

Exercise 1: Which choice most effectively combines the two sentences at the underlined portion? Answers for this chapter start on page 241.

1. Water filters are designed to handle any tap water that flows <u>through. They eliminate</u> the chlorine and bacteria growth that can affect the taste of drinking water and cause infections in humans.

    A) through; they can eliminate
    B) through, which is eliminating
    C) through, eliminating
    D) through, so they eliminate

2. Many of the courses in law schools today are purely theoretical <u>exercises. These exercises</u> have little to do with their initial purpose.

    A) exercises that
    B) exercises, so they
    C) exercises; they
    D) exercises, being so these

3. In addition to farming crops, slaves in Egypt during the rise of Mesopotamia had the mundane tasks of cleaning the <u>house. They also cooked the food.</u>

    A) house, but also cooked the food.
    B) house and cooking the food.
    C) house, and the food was cooked by them.
    D) house and food being cooked.

4. Jane had originally intended to completely wash her large aquarium by <u>hand. She</u> decided against doing so because it would have taken too much effort.

    A) hand: she
    B) hand while she
    C) hand, but she
    D) hand unless she

5. Since Joan took office as governor, some public issues have been solved in very clever <u>ways. Others</u> have been completely ignored.

    A) ways, whereas others
    B) ways, since others
    C) ways, provided that others
    D) ways, considering that others

6. Jojoba oil is made from the seeds of jojoba <u>plants. These plants</u> are sometimes mistaken for boxwood shrubs.

    A) plants; these
    B) plants, for they
    C) plants, which
    D) plants as they

7. Located near the abundant coasts of Maine, the town of Portland is a famous fishing <u>port. That is where</u> lobstermen set their traps in the early morning.

    A) port, which is where
    B) port, the location where
    C) port, a place at which
    D) port where

8. The online retailer Amazon completely has changed how many consumers purchase <u>goods. They managed to make</u> the whole online buying and selling experience trustworthy and easy.

    A) goods; they made
    B) goods by making
    C) goods to make
    D) goods, and this made

9. Debbie has a habit of giving long speeches during her <u>performances. They are so long</u> in fact that her regular clients have stopped inviting her to perform at their dinner parties.

    A) performances, and these are so long
    B) performances, which are so long
    C) performances, so long
    D) performances as so long

10. The planet of Venus, which routinely revolves around the Sun in an ellipse, has many active <u>volcanos. One of them</u> is taller than Mount Everest.

    A) volcanos, one of which
    B) volcanos; there is one that
    C) volcanos, and one
    D) volcanos, such that one

11. Language is the door to other <u>cultures. It is</u> a means of understanding other perspectives and traditions.

    A) cultures,

    B) cultures, and it is

    C) cultures, being

    D) cultures while serving as

12. After a month of deliberation, the prime minister unveiled his prescription for revitalizing the <u>economy. His economic plan entails</u> lower interest rates, higher tax cuts, and less government spending.

    A) economy such as

    B) economy:

    C) economy—entailing

    D) economy; it entails

Exercise 2: Which choice most effectively combines the underlined sentences? Answers for this chapter start on page 241.

1. <u>There were more than 80 applications for the elite summer English program. Megan's essay was proclaimed most eloquent by the committee of admissions officers.</u>

    A) Of the more than 80 applications for the elite summer English program, Megan's essay was proclaimed most eloquent by the committee of admissions officers.

    B) Megan's essay was proclaimed most eloquent by the committee of admissions officers, which there were more than 80 applications for the elite summer English program.

    C) The committee of admissions officers, who are at the elite summer English program, which had more than 80 applications, proclaimed Megan's essay most eloquent.

    D) The committee of admissions officers proclaimed it to be most eloquent; Megan's essay was one of 80 applications for the elite summer English program.

2. <u>My financial advisor has a suggestion. Before selling an old house, have it carefully evaluated by a real estate expert.</u>

    A) My financial advisor has an old house carefully evaluated by a real estate expert before selling it.

    B) To have a real estate expert carefully evaluate an old house before selling it is a suggestion from my financial advisor.

    C) My financial advisor suggests that before selling an old house, have it carefully evaluated by a real estate expert.

    D) My financial advisor's suggestion is to sell an old house before it is carefully evaluated by a real estate expert.

3. <u>Influenza is a well-known, contagious virus that is transmitted through the air. It can infect large groups of pigs, birds, and even horses.</u>

    A) Infecting large groups of pigs, birds, and even horses is a well-known, contagious virus, which is transmitted through the air and called influenza.

    B) It is a well-known, contagious virus that is transmitted through the air; influenza can infect large groups of pigs, birds, and even horses.

    C) Influenza is a well-known, contagious virus that is transmitted through the air by infecting large groups of pigs, birds, and even horses.

    D) A well-known, contagious virus that is transmitted through the air, influenza can infect large groups of pigs, birds, and even horses.

4. New evidence confirms that blood was not found on the defendant's clothes. The prosecutor's earlier claim that the defendant physically wounded the victim is now contradicted.

   A) New evidence, which is contradicting the prosecutor's earlier claim that the defendant physically wounded the victim, confirms that blood was not found on the defendant's clothes.

   B) In a contradiction to the prosecutor's earlier claim that the defendant physically wounded the victim, new evidence confirms that blood was not found on the defendant's clothes.

   C) What's contradicted by the new evidence confirming that blood was not found on the defendant's clothes is the prosecutor's earlier claim that the defendant physically wounded the victim.

   D) New evidence confirms that blood was not found on the defendant's clothes, contradicting the prosecutor's earlier claim that the defendant physically wounded the victim.

5. Often advertised as the most luxurious hotel in the world, the Four Seasons is completely averse to serving anything in moderation. That is unlike most other hotel chains.

   A) Unlike most other hotel chains, often advertised as the most luxurious hotel in the world, the Four Seasons is completely averse to serving anything in moderation.

   B) Often advertised as the most luxurious hotel in the world, the Four Seasons is, unlike most other hotel chains, completely averse to serving anything in moderation.

   C) Often advertised as the most luxurious hotel in the world, most other hotel chains are unlike the Four Seasons, which is completely averse to serving anything in moderation.

   D) Most other hotel chains are unlike the Four Seasons in that the Four Seasons is advertised as the most luxurious hotel in the world and completely averse to serving anything in moderation.

6. The author of the study guide knows that there are students who must take the test on short notice. For that reason, the author has included an index of the most common grammar rules.

   A) The author of the study guide has included an index of the most common grammar rules for the students who must take the test on short notice.

   B) The reason the author has included an index of the most common grammar rules is because he knows that there are students who must take the test on short notice.

   C) The author has included an index of the most common grammar rules, the reason being that he knows that there are students who must take the test on short notice.

   D) The author of the study guide knows that there are students who must take the test on short notice because he has included an index of the most common grammar rules.

7. A survey of human buying behavior that raises interesting questions about the mental processes was done. These processes govern the spontaneous and quick judgments we make when we see a product.

   A) A survey of human buying behavior that raises interesting questions about the mental processes was done, and these are what govern the spontaneous and quick judgments we make when we see a product.

   B) A survey of human buying behavior raises interesting questions about the mental processes we make when we see a product and have spontaneous and quick judgments.

   C) A survey of human buying behavior raises interesting questions about the mental processes governing the spontaneous and quick judgments we make when we see a product.

   D) A survey of human buying behavior—about the mental processes—raises questions that govern the spontaneous and quick judgments we make when we see a product.

8. Rosa Park's refusal to obey led to a fight for racial equality that forever changed the cultural and political landscape of America. It was the start of the Civil Rights movement.

   A) Rosa Park's refusal to obey led to a fight, the start of the Civil Rights movement, for racial equality that forever changed the cultural and political landscape of America.

   B) The fight for racial equality that forever changed the cultural and political landscape of America was the Civil Rights movement that Rosa Park's refusal to obey started.

   C) Rosa Park's refusal to obey led to the start of the Civil Rights movement, a fight for racial equality that forever changed the cultural and political landscape of America.

   D) Rosa Parks refused to obey and it led to a fight for racial equality that forever changed the cultural and political landscape of America; it was the start of the Civil Rights movement.

9. Many immigrants work long hours at menial jobs despite the low wages. They hope to provide a better life for their kids.

   A) Hoping to provide a better life for their kids are many immigrants, despite the low wages, who work long hours at menial jobs.

   B) Despite the low wages, many immigrants work long hours at menial jobs in the hopes of providing a better life for their kids.

   C) Hoping to provide a better life for their kids, long hours are worked, despite the low wages, at menial jobs by many immigrants.

   D) Many immigrants working long hours at menial jobs and having low wages hope to provide a better life for their kids.

10. Today's restaurants' ordering systems maximize efficiency both in the kitchen and behind the counter. Many of which have expanded their seating spaces to accommodate the increasing number of customers.

   A) Today's restaurants' ordering systems maximize efficiency both in the kitchen and behind the counter; seating spaces have been expanded by them to accommodate the increasing number of customers.

   B) Ordering systems maximize efficiency both in the kitchen and behind the counter; many restaurants have expanded their seating spaces in the accommodation of the increasing number of customers.

   C) Ordering systems maximizing efficiency both in the kitchen and behind the counter are why many restaurants have expanded their seating spaces, accommodating the increasing number of customers.

   D) Today's restaurants, whose ordering systems maximize efficiency both in the kitchen and behind the counter, have expanded their seating spaces to accommodate the increasing number of customers.

Data Interpretation

Data interpretation questions will ask you to analyze tables, charts, and graphs in the context of the passage.

The correct answer to this type of question will satisfy the first or both of the following criteria:

1. It reflects the data accurately.
2. It supports the point being made in context.

For the easier data interpretation questions, all you will have to do is choose the answer that makes an accurate statement about the data. For the harder questions, you might get several choices that make an accurate statement, but only one will support the point being made in context.

To illustrate, we'll use the following chart for Examples 1 and 2.

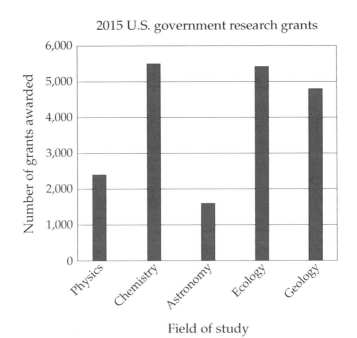

2015 U.S. government research grants

Example 1

In 2015, the U.S. government awarded <u>1,600 grants for geology research, half as many as</u> the number awarded for astronomy research.

A) NO CHANGE
B) 1,600 grants for geology research, about 3,000 fewer than
C) 4,800 grants for geology research, about 3,000 more than
D) 4,800 grants for geology research, twice as many as

This question is just asking you to make an accurate interpretation of the data. Looking at the chart, we can see that about 4,800 grants were awarded for geology research and about 1,600 were awarded for astronomy research, which means geology research grants outnumbered astronomy research grants by $4,800 - 1,600 = 3,200 \approx 3,000$. Therefore, the answer is C. The answer is not D because 4,800 is much more than twice 1,600.

Example 2

Because of how profitable new advances in the pharmaceutical industry can be, companies and institutions typically pursue grants for chemistry research. But given the growing public concern for the environment over the past few years, researchers' interests have started to shift. In 2015, <u>the U.S. government awarded 5,500 grants for chemistry research.</u>

A) NO CHANGE
B) chemistry research grants awarded by the government outnumbered physics research grants by more than 3,000.
C) more government grants were awarded for ecology research than for geology research.
D) there was hardly a gap between the number of government grants awarded for chemistry research and the number awarded for ecology research.

In this question, all the answer choices happen to be accurate statements about the data, so we need to choose the one that best supports the surrounding context. The second sentence (... *researchers' interests have started to shift.*) indicates that there is a trend away from chemistry research and towards environmental research. Since ecology is the field of study most concerned with the environment (at least among the ones in the chart), we're looking for an answer choice that discusses both chemistry research and ecology research in terms of that trend. The only answer that does so is D. The other answer choices bring up at least one field of study that isn't relevant.

Exercise 1: Which choice offers the most accurate interpretation of the data in the chart? Answers for this chapter start on page 243.

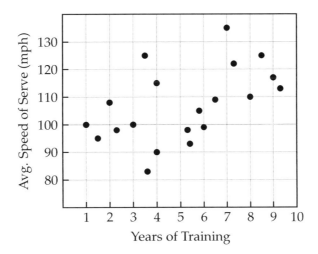

1. The average speed of serve was measured for each player in a sample of professional tennis athletes and the results were graphed with his or her number of years of training. The data indicate that <u>the player with the least number of years of training had the slowest serve.</u>

    A) NO CHANGE
    B) the player with the highest number of years of training had the fastest serve.
    C) players with the same years of training can have average serve speeds that are different.
    D) all the professionals surveyed average a serve above 100 miles per hour.

Percentage of Adults who report consuming fruits and vegetables less than one time daily			Percentage of Adolescents who report consuming fruits and vegetables less than one time daily		
State	Fruits	Vegetables	State	Fruits	Vegetables
Alabama	43.8	28.3	Alabama	44.4	45.7
Maryland	36.4	22.8	Maryland	38.7	38.9
Hawaii	39.5	22.6	Hawaii	45.1	48.8
Ohio	40.5	26.0	Ohio	42.4	40.2
Texas	34.3	21.8	Texas	42.1	47.5
Georgia	41.9	23.2	Georgia	42.9	43.1

2. A recent study indicated that across all six states, <u>adults are more likely to consume fruits than vegetables at least once per day.</u>

    A) NO CHANGE
    B) adults are more likely to consume vegetables than fruits at least once per day.
    C) adolescents are more likely to consume fruits than vegetables at least once per day.
    D) adolescents are more likely to consume vegetables than fruits at least once per day.

3. Doctor Andrews has argued that as people grow up, they tend to make healthier choices, citing evidence that among six states surveyed, the percentage of adults who ate vegetables less than once per day was smaller than the percentage of adolescents.

    A) NO CHANGE
    B) adolescents avoided vegetables and fruits almost equally.
    C) adults ate fruits at least once per day more frequently than vegetables.
    D) the percentage of adults who ate fruits less than once per day was greater than the percentage of adolescents.

4. If a population's eating habits were judged by the percentage of adults who eat fruits and the percentage of adults who eat vegetables at least once per day, the state with the best eating habits among those surveyed would be Hawaii.

    A) NO CHANGE
    B) Alabama.
    C) Texas.
    D) Maryland.

5. Researchers can likely conclude that as adolescents transition to adulthood, they tend to eat roughly the same amount of fruits as vegetables.

    A) NO CHANGE
    B) more and more fruits relative to vegetables.
    C) more and more vegetables relative to fruits.
    D) less fruits but more vegetables.

Percentage of High School Students Who Drank a Specific Beverage in the Past Week						
	Water	Milk	Fruit Juice	Soda	Sports Drink	Coffee
Female	71.8	49.1	26.5	20.3	11.1	15.7
Male	72.9	58.9	33.9	28.4	21.1	12.1
Total	72.4	54.2	30.2	24.3	16.1	13.8

6. The study suggests that the least frequently consumed beverages are unhealthy drinks like fruit juice, soda, and sports drinks.

    A) NO CHANGE
    B) high school boys are more accustomed to having
    C) high school girls are more accustomed to having
    D) high school boys and girls are equally likely to have

7. Among the two genders, the common denominator was water, which, compared to other drinks, was consumed by nearly equal percentages of male and female students in the past week.

    A) NO CHANGE
    B) milk,
    C) fruit juice,
    D) coffee,

8. In general, a higher percentage of males than females consumed each drink that was listed. In fact, the only drink more common among females than males was <u>water.</u>

    A) NO CHANGE
    B) soda.
    C) sports drink.
    D) coffee.

9. In the 1990s, the famous "Got Milk?" campaign was a massive success among high school students. In a study done after the campaign, <u>milk was the most common drink.</u>

    A) NO CHANGE
    B) milk was consumed by three times as many students as soda.
    C) milk was as commonly chosen as water when it came to beverages.
    D) more than half of those surveyed had consumed milk within the past week.

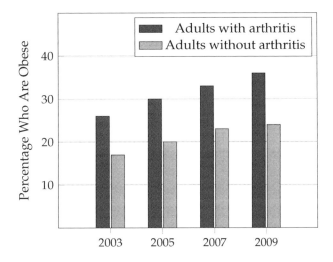

10. Hospitals have long studied the relationship between obesity and other ailments like arthritis. For example, doctors have gathered enough data to conclude that <u>those who are obese are about 10 percent more likely to have arthritis.</u>

    A) NO CHANGE
    B) obesity rates among those who have arthritis are about 10 percent higher than for those who don't.
    C) those who have arthritis are roughly 10 percent less likely to be obese than those who don't.
    D) the percentage who are obese among people who suffer from arthritis is double than that among people who don't.

11. Throughout the years, obesity has become an increasingly widespread problem, <u>but only among those without arthritis.</u>

    A) NO CHANGE
    B) but only among those with arthritis.
    C) regardless of the presence of arthritis.
    D) more so in 2005 than in any other year.

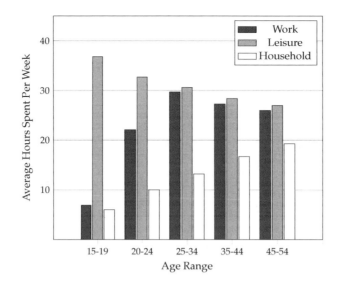

12. Teenagers should be encouraged to take on more responsibility. The average hours that 15-19 year olds spent on <u>work turned out to be more than the average hours they spent on leisure and household activities</u> combined.

   A) NO CHANGE
   B) leisure was more than the leisure time spent by 20-24 year olds and 25-34 year olds
   C) leisure exceeded the average hours they spent on work and household activities
   D) household activities eclipsed the average hours they spent on work and leisure

13. As people get older, they spend <u>more and more time on work and less and less on household activities.</u>

   A) NO CHANGE
   B) more and more time on household activities and less and less on leisure.
   C) more and more time on work and less and less on leisure.
   D) more and more time on household activities and less and less on work.

14. Because of complaints about work-life imbalance among employees, the director believed that his workers weren't getting enough leisure time to relax from a long workday. A study he conducted, however, found that his employees as a whole <u>spent more time on leisure than on household activities,</u> even though average leisure time went down as the age range went up.

Which choice best fits the sentence with accurate information from the graph above?

   A) NO CHANGE
   B) spent more time on leisure than on work,
   C) spent more time on work than on household activities,
   D) spent more time on household activities than on leisure,

15. The company has decided to give special benefits to those who work at least 25 hours a week. On the average, employees above the age of <u>15</u> will be able to receive these benefits.

   A) NO CHANGE
   B) 20
   C) 25
   D) 35

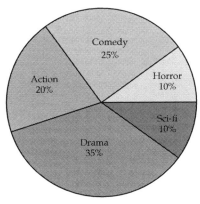

American Movies by Genre

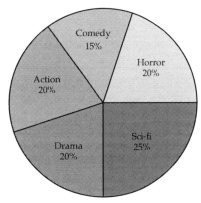

Korean Movies by Genre

16. In following the American movie industry, Korean studios are encouraging directors to make less action and comedy movies.

    A) NO CHANGE
    B) action and drama
    C) horror and sci-fi
    D) drama and horror

17. When critics looked at the distribution of genres in different countries, they found that over a third of the movies in Korea fall under the sci-fi genre.

    A) NO CHANGE
    B) sci-fi is the most common genre in Korea but one of the least common in America.
    C) sci-fi is as popular as comedy among American audiences.
    D) American cinemas are more likely to show sci-fi movies than action movies.

18. In Korea, action and horror make up over half of the movie offerings.

    A) NO CHANGE
    B) sci-fi and drama
    C) drama and action
    D) no two genres

Exercise 2: Which choice offers the most accurate interpretation of the data in the chart? Answers for this chapter start on page 243.

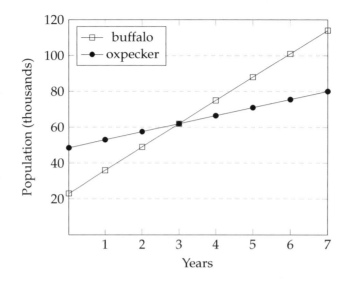

1. Oxpecker birds and buffalo form one of nature's most successful symbiotic relationships. Oxpeckers rid the buffalo of parasites and alarm them when predators are near. In return, the buffalo naturally attract insects and parasites that serve as food for the oxpeckers. Over the years, as the population of oxpeckers declined, so too did the population of buffalo, though at a slower rate.

   A) NO CHANGE
   B) as the population of oxpeckers grew, so too did the population of buffalo,
   C) as the population of buffalo grew, so too did the population of oxpeckers,
   D) as the population of buffaloes declined, so too did the population of oxpeckers,

2. By the seventh year, the oxpeckers outnumbered buffaloes by about thirty-eight thousand.

   A) NO CHANGE
   B) At the start, the buffalo population exceeded the oxpecker population by roughly thirty thousand.
   C) In the fourth year, the oxpecker population surpassed the buffalo population.
   D) By the third year, there were equal numbers of buffaloes and oxpeckers.

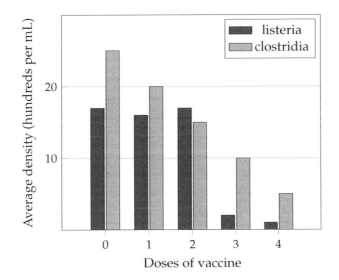

3. A selected group of patients were prescribed different dosages of a new vaccine. To test its effectiveness, doctors measured the presence of harmful bacteria listeria and clostridia in a milliliter of blood drawn from each patient. They found that <u>at least two doses of the vaccine are necessary to significantly reduce the number of listeria bacteria.</u>

A) NO CHANGE
B) the vaccine is effective in reducing listeria only after three or more doses.
C) the vaccine is capable of completely eliminating listeria bacteria with enough doses.
D) the vaccine has no effect on the number of listeria bacteria, regardless of the number of doses.

4. The data also show that <u>the vaccine has no influence on the amount of clostridia bacteria.</u>

A) NO CHANGE
B) the vaccine encourages the growth of more clostridia bacteria.
C) clostridia density decreases proportionally as the doses of vaccine increase.
D) after three doses, the number of clostridia bacteria decreases substantially.

5. The doctors decided to recommend the vaccine for mass production once the study showed that <u>five doses will completely rid a patient of clostridia.</u>

A) NO CHANGE
B) one dose is just as effective in combating clostridia as it is clearing listeria.
C) four doses are enough to completely eradicate both types of bacteria.
D) it is capable of reducing both listeria and clostridia.

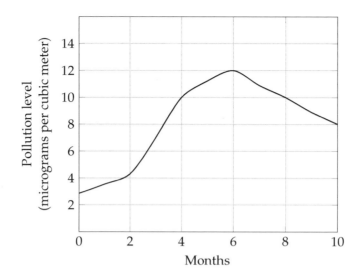

6. Environmentalists measured the air pollution in Beijing over 10 months. Pollution levels above 10 micrograms per cubic meter of air are considered to be dangerous. The data show Beijing was exposed to dangerous levels for <u>two months.</u>

    A) NO CHANGE
    B) four months.
    C) six months.
    D) eight months.

7. Pollutions levels were at their highest <u>after six months and at their lowest at the start.</u>

    A) NO CHANGE
    B) six months in and at their lowest after 10 months.
    C) at the start and at their lowest after 10 months.
    D) after ten months and at their lowest at the start.

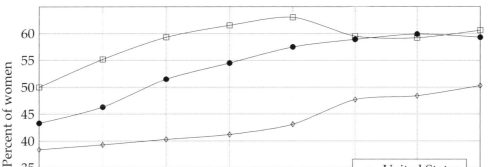

Women's Labor Force Participation Rates

8. Which of the following correctly ranks the countries from lowest to highest with respect to women's average participation rates in the labor force since 1970?

   A) Sweden, United States, Germany
   B) Germany, United States, Sweden
   C) Germany, Sweden, United States
   D) United States, Germany, Sweden

9. After 1995, Germany had more than half of its women in the labor force.

   A) NO CHANGE
   B) Sweden's proportion of women in the labor force dropped to less than 50 percent.
   C) the United States had a smaller proportion of women in the workforce than Germany.
   D) the United States had roughly the same proportion of women in the labor force as Sweden.

10. Historically speaking, never has there been a time in the United States when the majority of women were in the labor force.

   A) NO CHANGE
   B) Germany's proportion of women in the labor force has always been above 40 percent.
   C) women's labor force participation rates have always increased in all three of the countries studied.
   D) women in Germany were always less likely to be in the labor force compared to those in the United States and Sweden.

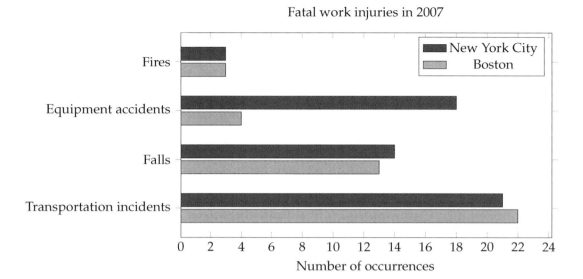

Fatal work injuries in 2007

11. Several New York City companies are making it mandatory that employees wear protective gear when working with machinery after a report indicated that there were more equipment related accidents than transportation incidents in New York City.

   A) NO CHANGE
   B) there were over 20 fatal equipment accidents in New York City.
   C) the number of fatal equipment accidents in New York City were over triple the number in Boston.
   D) a few fires occurred in both Boston and New York City.

12. Residents in both New York City and Boston are pushing city officials to expand the budget for public transit infrastructure, citing evidence that transportation accidents led to as many deaths as fires.

   A) NO CHANGE
   B) over half of all fatal work injuries were transportation related.
   C) transportation incidents were the leading cause of fatal work injuries.
   D) other cities did not have as many fatal transportation incidents.

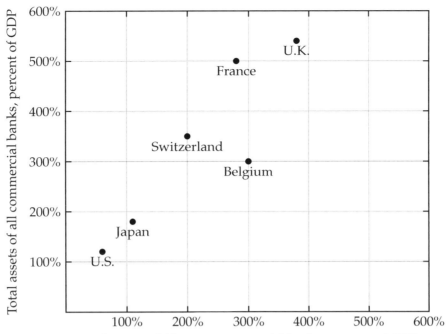

13. As a percentage of GDP (gross domestic product), the banking system of <u>Switzerland</u> is the smallest of all the advanced economies that were studied.

    A) NO CHANGE
    B) Belgium
    C) Japan
    D) the U.S.

14. <u>Belgium has the largest banking system relative to its GDP.</u>

    A) NO CHANGE
    B) The four largest banks in Belgium control all of the commercial banking assets in the country.
    C) Relative to GDP, Japan has a larger banking system than Belgium.
    D) Belgium's banking system is proportionally equal in size to Switzerland's.

15. France has a banking system that is roughly <u>five times</u> its GDP.

    A) NO CHANGE
    B) four times
    C) three times
    D) two times

28

Odds and Ends You Must Know for the Perfect Score

1. Avoid the passive voice

Here's an **active** sentence:

I ate chicken wings.

Here's the **passive** version:

Chicken wings were eaten by me.

Notice how the passive version is a not only wordier but also more awkward. Passive sentences usually contain the word *by*.

On the SAT, you want to **choose active sentences over passive ones**. To make a sentence active, move the "main actor" to the front.

Example 1

Passive:	Eye contact with the raging bull was avoided by me.
Active:	I avoided eye contact with the raging bull.

Example 2

Passive:	There is a wide variety of cuisine cooked by the chef.
Active:	The chef cooked a wide variety of cuisine.

Example 3

Passive:	It was decided by the jury that the defendant was innocent.
Active:	The jury decided that the defendant was innocent.

Example 4

Passive:	We were invited by our coworkers to attend the dinner party.
Active:	Our coworkers invited us to attend the dinner party.

The passive voice, however, is NOT grammatically incorrect. Many students think that a passive sentence is always wrong. That's not the case. It's just that the passive voice is usually not the best way to express your thoughts. If you're given three grammatically incorrect answer choices and one that is passive, choose the passive one. Most of the time though, there will be an answer choice in the active voice.

2. Beware of double main verbs

Example 5

Wrong:	One of our school's students, came from India, was awarded the national scholarship.
Correct:	One of our school's students, **who** came from India, was awarded the national scholarship.

Example 6

Wrong:	The dire warnings serve as reminders of our purpose in life is survival.
Correct:	The dire warnings serve as reminders of our purpose in **life:** survival.

If you're lazy and just read the second half of the sentence, *our purpose in life is survival*, you might think the sentence is fine. Don't fall victim to such trickiness.

Example 7

Wrong:	The central train stations, which service thousands of people each day, need to expand the tracks, are undergoing construction.
Correct:	The central train stations, which service thousands of people each day, need to expand the tracks **and** are undergoing construction.

3. Question Marks

When we report what people say, expressing their questions in *direct speech*—quoting something exactly as it was said—requires a question mark at the end of the question. Expressing their questions in *indirect speech*—describing what they said without quoting them exactly—does not require a question mark.

Basically, if a reported question is an exact quote from someone, use a question mark. If it isn't, don't.

Direct Speech	**Indirect Speech**
"Where do you live?" she asked me.	She asked me where I lived.
The passenger asked, "What time does the train leave?"	The passenger asked what time the train left.
"Did you finish your homework?"	Tony wanted to know if Eric had finished his homework.

Example 8

Wrong:	Many sci-fi authors have wondered what it would be like to live on Uranus?
Correct:	Many sci-fi authors have wondered what it would be like to live on Uranus.

Example 9

Wrong:	Yuzuru asked Tamami whether she enjoyed the party?
Correct:	"Did you enjoy the party?" Yuzuru asked Tamami.
Correct:	Yuzuru asked Tamami whether she enjoyed the party.

The following examples are weird blends of direct speech and indirect speech. Watch out for this type of faulty construction.

Example 10

Wrong:	Tony wanted to know did Eric finish his homework.
Correct:	Tony wanted to know if Eric had finished his homework.

Example 11

Wrong:	Alice was wondering what are you doing today?
Correct:	Alice was wondering what you were doing today.

4. Shift in Point of View

Keep the point of view the same within sentences and within paragraphs.

Example 12

Wrong:	If one does not believe, you will not succeed.
Correct:	If **one** does not believe, **one** will not succeed.
Correct:	If **you** do not believe, **you** will not succeed.

Example 13

Wrong:	If someone wants to play tennis, you should know how to serve.
Correct:	If **someone** wants to play tennis, **he or she** should know how to serve.
Correct:	If **you** want to play tennis, **you** should know how to serve.

5. Prepositions with Multiple Idioms

Example 14

Wrong:	I am interested and familiar with graphic design.
Correct:	I am interested **in** and familiar with graphic design.

Example 15

Wrong:	He always complains yet insists on my presence.
Correct:	He always complains **about** yet insists on my presence.

Example 16

Wrong:	The son of immigrant parents, Jacob felt a need to reconnect and learn from the past.
Correct:	The son of immigrant parents, Jacob felt a need to reconnect **with** and learn from the past.

Example 17

Wrong:	Ironically, the movement was both a revolt and a celebration of our cultural values.
Correct:	Ironically, the movement was both a revolt **against** and a celebration of our cultural values.

The following example is correct because both idioms take on the preposition *of.* In this case, the preposition does not need to be written twice.

He is both a supporter and critic of the new law.

6. Defining Phrases

Example 18

Wrong:	An aspiring filmmaker, Michael purchased a *Cinefex* subscription, a trade magazine that covers news and trends in the film industry.
Correct:	An aspiring filmmaker, Michael purchased a **subscription to** *Cinefex*, a trade magazine that covers news and trends in the film industry.

The defining phrase here is *"a trade magazine that covers ..."* Since it defines *Cinefex* and NOT *a Cinefex subscription*, it must be placed next to *Cinefex*. This concept is very similar to the ones we covered in the modifiers chapter.

Example 19

Wrong:	Giving children intravenous fluids as a ketoacidosis treatment (an emergency complication of untreated diabetes) does not appear to worsen the brain swelling that may accompany the condition.
Correct:	Giving children intravenous fluids **to treat ketoacidosis** (an emergency complication of untreated diabetes) does not appear to worsen the brain swelling that may accompany the condition.

Thd defining phrase "*(an emergency complication of untreated diabetes)*" must be placed next to *ketoacidosis*.

Exercise 1: Answers for this chapter start on page 245.

1. James hopes that <u>what the political activists are doing will be enough to inspire change.</u>

    A) NO CHANGE
    B) will what the political activists are doing be enough to inspire change?
    C) what the political activists are doing will be enough to inspire change?
    D) if what the political activists are doing will be enough to inspire change.

2. The employees at the after-school daycare were required to <u>take in and abide</u> the new safety rules and regulations.

    A) NO CHANGE
    B) take and abide in
    C) take and abide by
    D) take in and abide by

3. In France, a tourist can spend a romantic night overlooking the Eiffel tower and <u>you</u> can also enjoy delicious coffee at all the cafes.

    A) NO CHANGE
    B) one
    C) he or she
    D) we

4. Some doctors claim that eating <u>lutein-containing foods</u> (an antioxidant related to beta-carotene and vitamin A) can improve eyesight and decrease the risk of macular degeneration.

    A) NO CHANGE
    B) foods high in lutein
    C) lutein-rich food
    D) foods that increase lutein intake

5. Delirium, also known as acute confusional state, is an organically caused decline in mental <u>function must</u> be treated aggressively with the effective tools that are available.

    A) NO CHANGE
    B) function and
    C) function, must
    D) function that must

6. The host inquired <u>why we threw blueberry muffins on the living room floor during his dinner party with the managers?</u>

    A) NO CHANGE
    B) why did we throw blueberry muffins on the living room floor during his dinner party with the managers?
    C) why did we throw blueberry muffins on the living room floor during his dinner party with the managers.
    D) why we threw blueberry muffins on the living room floor during his dinner party with the managers.

7. <u>One is</u> more likely to come back to the store when they are treated with respect.

    A) NO CHANGE
    B) We are
    C) He is
    D) Customers are

8. The members of the community service group are great role models because they show <u>concern of their fellow students and respect in</u> their teachers.

   A) NO CHANGE
   B) concern of their fellow students and respect for
   C) concern for their fellow students and respect
   D) concern for their fellow students and respect in

9. The couple asked the salesperson whether an air handler—the NP2900 model in particular—<u>quietly and efficiently could circulate conditioned air throughout an entire building?</u>

   A) NO CHANGE
   B) quietly and efficiently could circulate conditioned air throughout an entire building.
   C) could quietly and efficiently circulate conditioned air throughout an entire building.
   D) could quietly and efficiently circulate conditioned air throughout an entire building?

10. In the face of declining business, the publisher cut costs by as much as 30 <u>percent, laid</u> off more than 20 staff writers in the process.

   A) NO CHANGE
   B) percent, laying
   C) percent to lay
   D) percent: laid

Exercise 2: Answers for this chapter start on page 245.

1. Even when we arrive ahead of time at the doctor's office, the receptionist makes <u>you</u> wait at least 15 minutes.

   A) NO CHANGE
   B) us
   C) me
   D) one

2. Even though we grew up in a country different from theirs, we have chosen to <u>comply rather than deviate from</u> our parents' cultural norms and expectations.

   A) NO CHANGE
   B) comply with rather than deviate from
   C) comply rather than deviate against
   D) comply with rather than deviate against

3. Although Dr. Kiln is aware that the <u>research was published</u> today in the *Annals of Internal Medicine,* shows significant process irregularities in the development of the new treatment, he still believes that it is more effective than the alternatives.

   A) NO CHANGE
   B) research, was published
   C) research, published
   D) research published

4. The optometrists collected data from 80 patients to examine <u>what is the effect of switching from eye-glasses to contact lenses on myopia progression as children reach adolescence.</u>

    A) NO CHANGE

    B) what is the effect of switching from eyeglasses to contact lenses on myopia progression as children reach adolescence?

    C) what effect switching from eyeglasses to contact lenses might have on myopia progression as children reach adolescence.

    D) whether switching from eyeglasses to contact lenses might have an effect on myopia progression as children reach adolescence?

5. The tulip orchid grows at a rate that depends greatly on the amount of sunlight available in <u>their</u> environment.

    A) NO CHANGE

    B) one's

    C) our

    D) its

6. Over the past few years, audio downloads have increased by more than 300%, thereby highlighting <u>pod-casting's popularity,</u> the practice of distributing audio files to users over the Internet, in the United States.

    A) NO CHANGE

    B) popular podcasting,

    C) the popularity of podcasting,

    D) how popular podcasting has become,

7. It's amazing Drew hasn't been punished yet given his blatant <u>disregard and distaste for</u> the rules.

    A) NO CHANGE

    B) disregard and distaste in

    C) disregard in and distaste for

    D) disregard with and distaste for

8. "How were the speeds of light and sound first determined and <u>measured," she wondered?</u>

    A) NO CHANGE

    B) measured," she wondered.

    C) measured?" she wondered?

    D) measured?" she wondered.

9. To truly appreciate computer programming as a craft, software engineers must take the time to study higher-level algorithms and data structures, regardless of whether <u>one finds</u> them useful on the job.

    A) NO CHANGE

    B) he or she finds

    C) they find

    D) you find

10. It wasn't until her groundbreaking <u>phytochemistry research</u>—the study of chemicals derived from plants—was published that Lynette finally received the recognition she deserved.

    A) NO CHANGE

    B) phytochemistry research,

    C) research in phytochemistry,

    D) research in phytochemistry—

Review Cheat Sheet

This chapter consists of a lot of incorrect example sentences from previous chapters. They cover most of the hard-and-fast rules you'll encounter on test day, so it's a great review for the day before the test. See if you can fix these sentences without looking back at the corresponding chapter. Answers are at the end of this chapter.

Idioms

- The Olympic athlete was capable ~~in~~ *of* climbing Mt. Everest.
- The public was opposed ~~against~~ *to* the war.
- The children were prohibited ~~against~~ *from* playing outside at dark.
- Unless you comply ~~to~~ *with* those food safety standards, we will shut you down.

Subject-Verb Agreement

- The diner near the dorms which (*houses*/*house*) the students (*serves*/*serve*) breakfast all day.
- The widely recognized red coloring of stop signs everywhere (*alerts*/*alert*) people who can't even read them to stop.
- Each team made up of one girl and one boy (*has*/*have*) to reenact a scene from Romeo and Juliet.
- Her jewelry, in addition to her pokemon cards, (*was*/*were*) stolen by the robber.
- Beside the bins, where one could smell the stench of rotten eggs, (*was*/*were*) a pack of philosophy majors gathering cans for recycling.

Modifiers

- The magician dazzled and surprised the audience members wearing a cloak and top hat.
- Decorated with colorful ornaments and stars, we took pictures by the Christmas tree.
- After missing an easy goal, the crowd booed the soccer player.

Run-ons

- He was hungry, he bought a Chipotle burrito.
- In New York, the train system is difficult to learn, however the food is fantastic and diverse.
- He believed that a career in nursing would guarantee a stable job, Joseph applied to nursing school.

Fragments

- In the middle of the night, when most people are sleeping while I sneak to the kitchen to eat.
- Although pandas are one of the most likable mammals but are one of the most rare.

Redundancy

- The reason why red pandas have ringed tails is because they are relatives of both the giant panda and the raccoon.

- After hearing the spy's information, the general knew that an attack was imminent in the future.

- In her biography about her life, she writes about overcoming poverty and fear.

- It's only on the night before the test that I wish my notes had been more clearer.

Parallelism I – Lists

- That she looks beautiful and her charm help her get out of speeding tickets.

- In chess, remember these three goals: get your pieces to the center, capture the opposing pieces, and attacking the opposing king.

- The 300 men trained diligently, screamed fiercely into battle, and valiantly fights.

Parallelism II – Pairs

- It's so hard to decide between the cheaper priced meal or the higher quality one.

- The candidate ran for office not only because he was power-hungry and also his belief that he could do a better job.

- Neither the fierce yelling nor the screams that were loud could wake Travis from his midday nap.

Parallelism III – Faulty Comparisons

- Characters in Chekhov's plays have always been crazier than Vogel's plays.

- Like the underwear made by Hanes and Armani, Calvin Klein makes you feel comfortable.

- The competition among recreational chess players is much more intense than recreational bingo players.

Pronoun Reference

- Whenever Jason and Alexander sit down at a buffet, he eats way more food.

- Even if a student gets in early, they still have to maintain good grades during senior year.

- At the police station, they found a pile of cash stashed in her bra.

- Although it is small and furry, koalas are able to protect themselves from predators by quickly climbing trees.

Tenses

- Although the cheetah holds the record for fastest land animal, many other mammals outlasted it.

- Whenever we stopped by the market, my mom always tries to negotiate the prices.

- She bought her dress at Wal-Mart yet it impresses everyone at the party.

Commas, Dashes, and Colons

- The platter was filled with berries, crackers; and cheese.

- Trapped in a mine the victims found it hard to see and breathe.

- Great white sharks the most fearsome creatures of the sea are actually less dangerous than they appear.

- The guy, cleaning the room, is the janitor.

- Runners around the world participate in the Boston Marathon which is 26 miles long.

- Penguins unlike most other birds cannot fly.

- Most bats are blind. Their sense of hearing however is amazing.

- The report indicates, that the pollution above Beijing has reached an all-time high.

- The Thai restaurant serves noodle dishes such as: pad thai, pad see ew, and kua gai.

- Cambridge is home to two of the best universities in the world MIT and Harvard.

- What you should remember from this whole ordeal is: that there can be no progress without sacrifice.

Apostrophes

- Tonys hat is on the floor.
- Louis' scarf is 3 feet long.
- Both players's jerseys were soaked with sweat.
- The book has a cool picture on it's cover.
- He is the actor whose most known for his role in *Batman*.

Word Choice

- The start of the tennis tournament was effected by the rain.
- The apartment in North Quincy has a nicer view then the one in Brighton.

Singular Plural Noun Inconsistency

- The three boys want to become a superhero.
- Witness testimony, documents, and a consumer guarantee have been a key piece of evidence in many major landmark trials involving corporations and their customers.

Who vs. Whom

- The agency recruited overseas teachers (*who/whom*) would be able to demonstrate a native fluency in English.
- Jane is the girl for (*who/whom*) I brought these gifts.
- The chaperones (*who/whom*) the students were assigned to made sure they walked in a single file.

Odds and Ends

- One of our school's students, came from India, was awarded the national scholarship.
- Many sci-fi authors have wondered what it would be like to live on Uranus?
- Tony wanted to know did Eric finish his homework.
- If someone wants to play tennis, you should know how to serve.
- I am interested and familiar with graphic design.
- An aspiring filmmaker, Michael purchased a *Cinefex* subscription, a trade magazine that covers news and trends in the film industry.

Model Answers to the Review Cheat Sheet:

Idioms

- The Olympic athlete was capable **of** climbing Mt. Everest.

- The public was opposed **to** the war.

- The children were prohibited **from** playing outside at dark.

- Unless you comply **with** those food safety standards, we will shut you down.

Subject-Verb Agreement

- The diner near the dorms which **house** the students **serves** breakfast all day.

- The widely recognized red coloring of stop signs everywhere **alerts** people who can't even read them to stop.

- Each team made up of one girl and one boy **has** to reenact a scene from Romeo and Juliet.

- Her jewelry, in addition to her pokemon cards, **was** stolen by the robber.

- Beside the bins, where one could smell the stench of rotten eggs, **was** a pack of philosophy majors gathering cans for recycling.

Modifiers

- **Wearing a cloak and top hat,** the magician dazzled and surprised the audience members.

- We took pictures by the Christmas tree, **which was decorated with colorful ornaments and stars.**

- After **he missed** an easy goal, the crowd booed the soccer player.

Run-ons

- He was hungry, **so** he bought a Chipotle burrito.

- In New York, the train system is difficult to learn**;** however the food is fantastic and diverse.

- **Because** he believed that a career in nursing would guarantee a stable job, Joseph applied to nursing school.

Fragments

- In the middle of the night, when most people are sleeping, ~~while~~ I sneak to the kitchen to eat.

- Although pandas are one of the most likable mammals, **they** are one of the most rare.

Redundancy

- ~~The reason why~~ Red pandas have ringed tails ~~is~~ because they are relatives of both the giant panda and the raccoon.

- After hearing the spy's information, the general knew that an attack was imminent ~~in the future~~.

- In her biography ~~about her life~~, she writes about overcoming poverty and fear.

- It's only on the night before the test that I wish my notes had been ~~more~~ clearer.

Parallelism I – Lists

- **Her beauty** and her charm help her get out of speeding tickets.

- In chess, remember these three goals: get your pieces to the center, capture the opposing pieces, and **attack** the opposing king.

- The 300 men trained diligently, screamed fiercely into battle, and **fought valiantly**.

Parallelism II – Pairs

- It's so hard to decide between the cheaper priced meal **and** the higher quality one.

- The candidate ran for office not only because he was power-hungry **but also because he believed that he could do a better job.**

- Neither the fierce yelling nor **the loud screaming** could wake Travis from his midday nap.

Parallelism III – Faulty Comparisons

- Characters in Chekhov's plays have always been crazier than **characters in Vogel's plays**.

- Like the underwear made by Hanes and Armani, **underwear made by Calvin Klein** makes you feel comfortable.

- The competition among recreational chess players is much more intense than **the competition/that among recreational bingo players**.

Pronoun Reference

- Whenever Jason and Alexander sit down at a buffet, **Jason** eats way more food.

- Even if a student gets in early, **he or she** still **has** to maintain good grades during senior year.

- At the police station, **the officers** found a pile of cash stashed in her bra.

- Although **they are** small and furry, koalas are able to protect themselves from predators by quickly climbing trees.

Tenses

- Although the cheetah holds the record for fastest land animal, many other mammals **outlast** it.

- Whenever we **stop** by the market, my mom always tries to negotiate the prices.

- She bought her dress at Wal-Mart yet it **impressed** everyone at the party.

Commas, Dashes, and Colons

- The platter was filled with berries, crackers, and cheese.

- Trapped in a mine, the victims found it hard to see and breathe.

- Great white sharks, the most fearsome creatures of the sea, are actually less dangerous than they appear.

- The guy cleaning the room is the janitor.

- Runners around the world participate in the Boston Marathon, which is 26 miles long.

- Penguins, unlike most other birds, cannot fly.

- Most bats are blind. Their sense of hearing, however, is amazing.

- The report indicates that the pollution above Beijing has reached an all-time high.

- The Thai restaurant serves noodle dishes **such as** pad thai, pad see ew, and kua gai.

- Cambridge is home to two of the best universities in the world: MIT and Harvard. (A dash also works.)

- What you should remember from this whole ordeal **is that** there can be no progress without sacrifice.

Apostrophes

- **Tony's** hat is on the floor.

- **Louis's** scarf is 3 feet long.

- Both **players'** jerseys were soaked with sweat.

- The book has a cool picture on **its** cover.

- He is the actor **who's** most known for his role in *Batman*.

Word Choice

- The start of the tennis tournament was **affected** by the rain.

- The apartment in North Quincy has a nicer view **than** the one in Brighton.

Singular Plural Noun Inconsistency

- The three boys want to become **superheroes**.

- Witness testimony, documents, and a consumer guarantee have been **key pieces** of evidence in many major landmark trials involving corporations and their customers.

Who vs. Whom

- The agency recruited overseas teachers **who** would be able to demonstrate a native fluency in English.

- Jane is the girl for **whom** I brought these gifts.

- The chaperones **whom** the students were assigned to made sure they walked in a single file.

Odds and Ends

- One of our school's students, **who** came from India, was awarded the national scholarship.

- Many sci-fi authors have wondered what it would be like to live on Uranus.

- Tony wanted to know **if Eric had finished** his homework.

- If someone wants to play tennis, **he or she** should know how to serve.

- I am interested **in** and familiar with graphic design.

- An aspiring filmmaker, Michael purchased a **subscription to** *Cinefex*, a trade magazine that covers news and trends in the film industry.

30

Answers to the Exercises

Chapter 3: Relative Clauses

Exercise:

1. ~~Although it may better mankind~~, some critics of animal testing, ~~which is sometimes harmful to the animals~~, claim it is cruel and inhumane.

2. ~~After running the Boston marathon~~, Jack Kunis drank all the water ~~that was left in his bottle~~ and fell to his knees.

3. The lost ship and its treasure ~~that had fallen to the bottom of the ocean~~ were never found again.

4. Frank, ~~in addition to his cousins~~, suffers from a condition known as hyperthymestic syndrome, ~~which prevents one from ever forgetting anything~~.

5. ~~Starting at the age of 10~~, Mrs. Smith kept a daily diary, ~~which allowed her to recall the happy memories in life~~.

6. For years the chairman remained anonymous, ~~referred to only by initials even within his inner circles~~.

7. Students ~~whose grades are low~~ will have to report to me, ~~the principal of the school~~.

8. Every detail about every day since 1976, ~~ranging from the time she got up to what she ate~~, has forever ingrained itself into her mind.

9. ~~Ever since it allowed internet games, which were previously blocked~~, the library has been the place everybody wants to be nowadays.

10. ~~With such sadness occupying her thoughts~~, Erika, ~~a poor single mother of two~~, struggles to sleep at night, ~~even when the babies themselves are fast asleep~~.

11. Farmers ~~who want a good yield~~ should use fertilizers ~~that enrich the soil with nutrients~~.

12. ~~Having worked so hard with blood, sweat, and tears,~~ I long for the day I can finally say the SATs are over.

13. Culture shock, ~~in some cases,~~ can be severe enough to trigger mental breakdowns.

14. Mastery of martial arts requires a dedication ~~that many do not have.~~

15. Mrs. Daughtry, ~~a 74-year old married housewife recently discharged from a local hospital after her first psychiatric admission,~~ came to our facility for a second opinion, ~~one that she hoped would be different.~~

Chapter 4: Prepositional Phrases

Exercise:

1. Hillary got ~~into the boat for the short trip to Haiti.~~

2. If you do business ~~with me,~~ you'll never get the better end ~~of the deal.~~

3. We'll need to see the receipts ~~for the underwear~~ you bought ~~on Monday.~~

4. I drove ~~by my house~~ to check if the package ~~from Amazon~~ had arrived.

5. The eleven robbers broke ~~into the casino vault with their perfectly executed plan.~~

6. Since the hypothesis ~~of string theory,~~ scientists have been back ~~at the drawing board.~~

7. Everything that man creates carries ~~within it~~ the seeds ~~of its own destruction.~~

8. Kelvin snuck ~~out the door during the school assembly.~~

9. ~~Within seconds of hearing about the trip to Antarctica,~~ Charlotte packed shorts and sunglasses.

10. We found Teddy ~~in a broken elevator at a rundown hotel in Thailand.~~

Chapter 5: Idioms

Exercise 1:

1. I don't care about your opinion **of** me.

2. Your ability **to get** the perfect cards has caught the attention of casino surveillance.

3. The Olympic athlete was capable **of** climbing Mt. Everest.

4. The public was opposed **to** the war.

5. The children were prohibited **from** playing outside at dark.

6. Unless you comply **with** those food safety standards, we will shut you down.

7. Those who don't abide **by** the rules are often the ones who successfully innovate.

8. China is becoming an economic hegemony **over** foreign rivals who dare to compete.

9. By taking good care of pandas, zoos have succeeded **in saving** pandas from extinction.

10. I hope you are aware **of** the raccoons that are mating in your basement.

11. She has lived **on** Broome street for over fifty years.

12. She managed to get a position **as** the director of the engineering department.

13. He was inclined **to accept** the new job offer, but wanted to wait.

14. The young graduate yearned **for** the days when he didn't have to worry about the bills.

15. Because she had many toxic relationships, Jane became accustomed **to** yelling her way through arguments.

Exercise 2:

1. D	9. B
2. A	10. B
3. C	11. C
4. B	12. D
5. C	13. B
6. D	14. C
7. A	15. B
8. C	

Chapter 6: Subject Verb Agreement

Exercise 1:

		To Be	To Go	To Have	To Win	To Kiss
Present Tense	He	is	goes	has	wins	kisses
	They	are	go	have	win	kiss
Past Tense	He	was	went	had	won	kissed
	They	were	went	had	won	kissed

Exercise 2:

1. **Participants** in the charity organization **were** angry when no one donated.

2. The **habit** of hugging your pillow while sleeping **indicates** that you miss someone.

3. Elderly **criminals** in Florida sometimes **lead** the police on chases at speeds of 10 to 15 mph.

4. **Bonnie and her boyfriend Clyde like** to jump into ponds to avoid the cops, often forgetting that they can't swim.

5. **Every** Bentley, Lamborghini, and Porsche **is** owned by Volkswagen.

6. **Propaganda** that's played off as the truth **has** been used throughout history to persuade the masses.

7. **Forcing** yourself to forget the pain someone else has caused you only **hurts** you more.

8. **One** of the skills I would like to learn **is** the ability to talk while inhaling through the nose.

9. **Some** of the superpowers I dream of having **include** summoning jack o' lanterns on people's lawns during Halloween and making people burst into the Gangnam style dance.

10. **Each** iPhone 5 **costs** Apple $168 and **costs** us $699.

11. **Each** of the three little pigs **was** afraid of the big bad wolf.

12. According to the phonebook, **the number** of Americans named Herp Derp **is** four.

13. **A good cook** rinses the dishes and **repeats** the same recipes to perfection.

14. Please let me know if **the group stumbles** upon or **manages** to find the train station.

15. **A number** of people **have** hyperthymesia, **a condition** that **allows** them to remember every detail of their lives. *(A number...have, a condition...allows)*

16. There **was** an awkward **silence** when Mike's date told him she was actually a man.

17. **A flock** of birds **and a bear have** been captured in the field.

18. There **are three types** of people in this world: those who can count and those who can't.

19. There **is** stashed below the frigid depths of the arctic a magnificent **treasure** that no one has ever been able to recover.

20. There **is** in the works of Emerson an underlying **tone** of quiet appreciation.

21. *Snow White and the Seven Dwarves* **was** purportedly based on cocaine; the seven dwarves were each side effects of the drug.

22. **Harry**, along with Ron and Hermione, **attends** Hogwarts School of Wizardry.

23. **Frodo**, as well as Merry and Pippin, **fights** to protect the one ring of power.

24. This picture **book** on the art of nudity in the modern age **is** a thought-provoking read.

25. The **extent** of our universe and those beyond constantly **amazes** me.

26. We found out that **his mother**, as well as his friends, **was** covering for Mike's crime.

27. **Aliens** from another planet **have** come here to kill us all.

28. The **pigs** you will be dissecting in this class **are** available as take-home dinners afterwards.

29. **Human brain cells, the universe, and the internet** all **have** similar structures.

30. **Each team** made up of one girl and one boy **has** to reenact a scene from Romeo and Juliet.

31. **Speaking** more than one language **makes** the brain more flexible and agile.

32. **Getting** to stuff my face silly with delicious food **is** the best part of being an obese food critic.

33. When **were the cowboy and the Indians** last here?

34. The class **bully** laughs at and then **interferes** with those trying to get work done.

35. **Brendan and Brianna** are out of money and **have** used up all possible guesses.

36. **Paris and Nicole** grew up rich and **were** sheltered all throughout life.

37. What **does** that **fact** have to do with anything we just talked about?

38. **He** sets his alarm but, when the morning comes, **fails** to wake up.

39. **Marcie and Michael** exercise everyday and, in doing so, **improve** their stamina.

40. **Alice**, in addition to a scarecrow, a tin man, and a lion, **tries** to find the Wizard of Oz.

41. **A jar** of hearts **is** on the counter.

42. **Several trucks and an oil tanker** near the highway exit **were** flipped on their sides.

43. **Dreams** within **a dream** that **is** spliced and diced up inside another dream **confuse** me. *(Dreams. . . confuse, a dream. . . is)*

44. **A herd** of cows **and** a slow moving **tortoise are** relaxing at the beach.

45. **The lines** for **the elevator** that normally **carries** just five passengers **were** reinstated because **the crowd** of fat commuters **was** too heavy for it. *(The lines. . . were, the elevator. . . carries, the crowd. . . was)*

46. **The diner** near **the dorms** which **house** the students **serves** breakfast all day. *(The diner. . . serves, the dorms. . . house)*

47. The widely recognized red **coloring** of stop signs everywhere **alerts** people who can't even read them to stop.

Exercise 3: The answers go in the format of *subject...verb*.

1. reference books... **are**

2. a stack... **sits**

3. variety... **is**

4. the act... **is**

5. the notion... **misrepresents**

6. research and investigation... **play**

7. perfect grammar and well-crafted sentences... **do**

8. education... **encompasses**

9. education... **fosters**

10. attention... **rivals** (the key here is the singular *that*, which means the clause only applies to *attention* and not *dedication and attention*)

11. this dedication (to the craft) and attention (to detail)... **require**

12. authors... **have equated**

13. writers... **do**

14. answers... **are**

15. the belief... **persists**

Chapter 7: Modifiers

Exercise 1:

1. Hunting for deer, Julian misfired his rifle which then burst into flames.
   While Julian was hunting for deer, his rifle misfired and burst into flames.

2. Having finished the SAT, I found the rest of life to be easy.

3. Having had no water for five days, we squeezed the steak and cheese sandwich for the grease that we could drink.

4. Active in community service and local affairs, Obama had a passion for politics that would eventually lead him to the presidency.

5. By blasting music at home, you will see that the neighbors will start to acquire your musical taste.

6. Because I majored in basket weaving, a lifetime of regret and despair awaits.

7. After catching a cold, I found that my lung surgery was the perfect cure.
   After I caught a cold, my lung surgery was the perfect cure.

8. While the talk show host was on air at the radio station, his microphone exploded.

9. As a young child growing up in Massachusetts, Mitt received airplanes as gifts from his father.

10. Hidden far from sunlight in the caves of Mars, an E.T. colony has been uncovered by scientists.
    Scientists have uncovered an E.T. colony, hidden far from sunlight in the caves of Mars.

11. Looking outside the window, Chris saw the march of marines as crowds cheered on either side.

12. Gordon Ramsay swore at the cook and dumped the fish that was overcooked and over-seasoned into the garbage.

13. Tiffany loved the soft feel of her teddy bear dressed in a cute outfit and filled with cotton.

14. Wearing a cloak and top hat, the magician dazzled and surprised the audience members.

15. We took pictures by the Christmas tree, which was decorated with colorful ornaments and stars.

16. After he missed an easy goal, the crowd booed the soccer player.
    After missing an easy goal, the soccer player was booed by the crowd.

17. Having forgotten about the homework assignment, he made comments on the book in class that were general statements that could apply to any book.
    Because he had forgotten about the homework assignment, his comments on the book in class were general statements that could apply to any book.

18. To get the best view of the movie, we reserved our seats in the front and center.

19. The scientist followed the deer prancing joyously from field to field.

20. Though skinny and awkward from the outset, Conan had a sense of humor that made him a television success.
    Though Conan was skinny and awkward from the outset, his sense of humor made him a television success.

21. The explorers avidly watched the red pandas climbing from tree to tree.

Exercise 2:

1. $\boxed{C}$ *Since the age of 10* is the modifer that must be placed next to *my daughter Cayla*.

2. $\boxed{B}$ Choices A, C, and D make it seem like Serena and Venus were watching something live, whereas it was Cayla who watched them.

3. $\boxed{A}$ Choice A is the only one that makes logical sense.

4. $\boxed{D}$ The modifier *as encouraging parents* needs to placed next to *we*.

5. $\boxed{B}$ The modifier *a simple sport* needs to be placed next to *tennis. The rules* themselves are not a sport.

6. $\boxed{C}$ The modifier *made and shaped from wood* needs to be placed next to *the first racquets*, not *players*. Choice C is much more concise than choice D.

7. $\boxed{D}$ The modifier *by improving the underlying technology* needs to be placed next to a person/people, namely *today's racquet creators*. After all, it's humans who improve the technology, not the racquets themselves.

8. $\boxed{D}$ The modifier *hitting the ball* must be placed next to *a player*.

9. $\boxed{D}$ It's a little confusing to see *squinting at the sky* describe *the tennis ball*. It should be placed at the start to modify a person, *she*. Choice B makes it sound like she deliberately squinted at the sky to miss the ball. Choice C is awkward because the modifier needlessly interrupts the verb and direct object.

10. $\boxed{B}$ The modifier *searching for one that was more patient* should be placed next to *we*.

11. $\boxed{D}$ Choices A and B make it sound like the teacher taught with spin and power. Choice C is an awkward placement because it interrupts the verb and object. The modifier should be placed at the end to describe how Cayla serves the ball.

12. $\boxed{C}$ The modifier *growing in confidence* should be placed next to a person, *she*.

Chapter 8: Run-ons

Exercise 1:

1. A caller from Memorial Park reported a man beating his head against a wall, he was heading to work.
   ⇑

2. A completely naked long-haired brunette in her 20s was pumping gas into a Hummer on the corner of Beachmont, no one got a good look at the vehicle's license plate.
   ⇑

3. In New York, the train system is difficult to learn, however, the food is fantastic and diverse.
   ⇑

4. When a man became so upset with the lack of parking enforcement in his town, he reported his own parking violation, and the police showed up to subdue him with a stun gun, apparently, he became
   ⇑
   combative and screamed at the officers that they weren't doing their job.

5. There's a big chance that if you're 16 or older, you've already met the person you'll marry. *CORRECT*

6. Wanting to be sure that what he had been sold was real weed, Phillip Donahue approached two officers and asked them to test his pipe, as a result, he was arrested and charged with drug possession.
   ⇑

7. Jimmy hid in the dumpster when Mr. Trump, his boss, walked by, unfortunately, Mr. Trump had to
   ⇑
   throw something away and saw him crouching there, forcing Jimmy to confess that he actually lived there.

8. Zoe likes to ace her tests but resents it when her classmates ask her how much she studied, sometimes
   ⇑
   Zoe will just say that she didn't study at all when in fact she had stayed up all night.

9. At the time, discovering quantum physics looked like a waste of time and money, but it is now the foundation of all modern technology**,** thus, when people claim that math and science are of no relevance, it drives Dr. Tyson into a deep rage.
⇑

10. Playing them day and night, Shawn and his video games were inseparable**,** however, once he got a girlfriend, everything changed.
⇑

11. Despite his friends' tearful pleas for forgiveness, Jonathan maintained a deep grudge against everyone who had ever asked for a pencil and never returned it, an act he considered a crime against humanity. *CORRECT*

12. Suddenly realizing the movie was too scary for her, Maya panicked and looked at her watch**,** there was still 20 minutes left, enough time to still make her uneasy about what was to come.
⇑

13. The salesman, aware that he was going to lose a sale if he didn't make something up, claimed that the laptop could not be customizable and that the only options were in the store. *CORRECT*

14. As a young girl, Lindsay was praised as a talented and burgeoning actress**,** as an adult, she fell into the dark world of sex, drugs, and alcohol and would never reclaim her former glory.
⇑

15. Omega-3 fish oil provides essential fatty acids for your nutritional health**,** furthermore, it soothes back pain and muscle aches.
⇑

16. Last Saturday, Peter Parker was bit by a spider**,** after that incident, he would never be the same again.
⇑

Exercise 2:

1. C	7. D	13. B
2. C	8. B	14. A
3. C	9. D	15. B
4. D	10. D	16. B
5. C	11. D	
6. A	12. B	

Exercise 3:

1. B	6. D	11. C
2. A	7. B	12. B
3. D	8. A	13. D
4. C	9. B	
5. C	10. C	

Chapter 9: Fragments

Exercise 1:

1. Tony's toys ~~which~~ were hidden in the cupboard so that nobody could get to them.

2. ~~When~~ I was given the opportunity to speak in front of the graduating class as if I were some celebrity or movie star.
   When I was given the opportunity to speak in front of the graduating class as if I were some celebrity or movie star, **I couldn't have felt more honored.**

3. **She dumped** him on the first date because he smelled so bad even though she knew he had just returned from a wrestling match.

4. It is very convenient that the grocery store I live next to **and** the surrounding malls and restaurants are open late at night.

5. In the middle of the night, ~~when~~ most people are sleeping while I sneak to the kitchen to eat.
   In the middle of the night, when most people are sleeping, ~~while~~ I sneak to the kitchen to eat.

6. Like the moment you realize your cereal is soggy because you left it in the milk too long, **the realization you're old comes quietly but swiftly.**

7. The butler who served the Wright family for several years ~~and~~ later became a successful businessman.

8. The tennis champion **waved** his racquet up towards a roaring crowd with his right hand and **lifted** the trophy with his left.

9. Even though Aaron fully believed that his actions, now the cause of much public controversy, were morally and ethically right, ~~but~~ the prosecutors would hear none of it.

10. The negative thoughts ~~that~~ were constantly on Floyd's mind as he got into the ring.
    The negative thoughts that were constantly on Floyd's mind as he got into the ring **made him even more nervous.**

11. **I was** disgusted by the lack of cleanliness in the men's bathroom yet curious about the sanitation in the ladies' room.

12. I wore the pants you bought me **and** the purple tie that the saleswoman picked out.

13. ~~As~~ They walked down the street, checked out the stores, and talked about life.
    As they walked down the street, checked out the stores, and talked about life, **they remembered how much they loved each other**.

14. ~~Although~~ Pandas are one of the most likable mammals but are one of the most rare.

Exercise 2:

1. C	5. B	9. B	13. B
2. C	6. C	10. D	14. D
3. A	7. B	11. B	15. C
4. D	8. B	12. D	

Chapter 10: Redundancy

Exercise 1:

1. In her biography ~~about her life~~, she writes about overcoming poverty and fear.

2. During high school, I sung in a trio ~~that consisted of three people~~.

3. Scratching the rash made it ~~more~~ worse than before.

4. ~~The reason why~~ Most people give up on New Year's resolutions ~~is~~ because they're too accustomed to old habits.
   The reason ~~why~~ most people give up on New Year's resolutions is **that** they're too accustomed to old habits.

5. The plagiarist ~~who copied the works of others~~ was banned indefinitely from the journalism industry.

6. There's a good chance that an earthquake ~~has the possibility of happening~~ **will happen** within the next week.

7. After her graduation speech, Zoe was thirsty ~~and needed to drink something~~.

8. Because James was an optimist ~~with a positive outlook on life~~, he faced his struggles with a smile on his face.

9. Seafood restaurants are becoming less and less expensive due to the abundance ~~and oversupply~~ of fish.
   Seafood restaurants are becoming less and less expensive due to the ~~abundance and~~ oversupply of fish.

10. ~~Her verbal statements in~~ Her conversation with me led me to believe that she was holding something from me.

11. The sisters reunited at the house where they grew up ~~as siblings~~ upon their father's death.

12. Building his own motorcycle, ~~which would belong to him,~~ Quentin looked forward to the day when he would be old enough to drive it.

13. My aunt ~~is a beginner who~~ just started learning about photography.

14. The president gave a strong message ~~that was quite powerful~~ to the world in his speech yesterday.

15. This year, the volcano came alive as if it were angry and the eruption lasted for days, ~~which numbered quite a few~~.

16. In 1472, Christopher Columbus set sail ~~and thereby rigged a boat~~ and charted a course towards India.

17. Since he quit his job, his savings have suffered~~, decreasing the balance in his bank account quite a bit~~.

18. When she walked into the room, he lost his concentration ~~and couldn't focus~~ on the task at hand.

Exercise 2:

1. The plane that had crash-landed was found **in** New Hampshire.

2. On ~~the occasion of~~ July 4th, the residents of Lynn waited along the beach to see the massive fireworks display.

3. Linzy completed the 100 mile trail by ~~means of~~ bike.

4. Marine biologists estimated that the beached whale weighed ~~in the rough neighborhood of~~ about 200 tons.

5. The director decided to give the aspiring journalist a job **because** he was so persistent.

6. The child continued to ask his mother for chocolate chip cookies in spite of ~~the nature of~~ her initial rejection.

7. When it comes to college applications, all decisions made are **final**.

8. If ~~it can be determined to be~~ feasible, a flexible work arrangement allows employees the freedom to work on a schedule suited to them.

9. As police officers, we ~~express our desire to~~ have a commitment to public safety.

10. If Michelle answers the last question correctly, she stands to win **over** a million dollars.

11. With a booming agricultural sector, China exports rice, wheat, potatoes, tea, and other crops ~~in addition to them~~.

12. Do not lift the pressure valve **until** the astronaut has landed safely.

13. As shown by ~~the one particular case of~~ the Black Plague, one disease can kill millions of people.

14. Weightlifting is more physically demanding and harder on the bones than ~~the people who would rather go~~ swimming.

15. The case was solved when several eyewitnesses decided to **cooperate** with the police.

Exercise 3:

1. [D] *Famous for* means the same thing as what's underlined.

2. [B] *Separation* means the same thing as *division*.

3. [C] *Heir* implies *next in line* or *successive*.

4. [B] *Died* is all that's needed. *Perished* and *fatally* both imply death.

5. [C] *Recently* means the same thing as *a short time ago*.

6. [D] *Father* implies that Henry was his son.

7. [B] *King* implies that he ascended to the throne.

8. [D] *Over the years* is the same thing as *throughout their time together*.

9. [C] *Worried* and *troubled* mean the same thing.

10. [A] *Sole* implies *only*, which is a word in all the answer choices except A.

11. [B] *Declaring, announcement, proclaiming* all imply the same thing.

12. [B] *Unswayed* means the same thing as *unconvinced*.

13. [D] *His own hands* implies *on his own* or *by himself*.

14. [C] *All he needed* means the same thing as *that would be sufficient, enough,* or *adequate*.

15. [C] The exact year adds information here so it should be kept. However, *after that* and *subsequently* mean the same thing as *later*, which is found earlier in the sentence.

16. [D] *Which led the way* offers nothing in the context of this sentence. The cause and effect relationship between Henry's actions and altering the future of his country is already clear.

17. [B] If the number of years is going to be stated, there's no point in also saying that it was a *few* years.

Chapter 11: Parallelism I - Lists

Exercise 1:

1. **Her beauty** and her charm help her get out of speeding tickets.

2. Visitors to my hometown in the middle of nowhere can experience rides on the bus, drinks at the tavern, and **meals** at the McDonald's.

3. Because of their amazing sense of smell, quick agility, and ~~they have~~ **fierceness** when protecting themselves, lions are the kings of the savannah.

4. My tasks today are to file for divorce, burn my house down, and ~~to~~ start all over.
   My tasks today are to file for divorce, **to** burn my house down, and to start all over.

5. By investing in nuclear energy, we can save the environment, jobs, and **money**.

6. In his free time, Wild Bill likes smoking Cuban cigars and **drinking** the finest red wine Martha's Vineyard has to offer.
   In his free time, Wild Bill likes **to smoke** Cuban cigars and to drink the finest red wine Martha's Vineyard has to offer.

7. Quickly and **silently**, Jesse and Walt snuck by the sleeping police officers and made off with a barrel of methylamine.

8. Inspired by the hard work of his immigrant father, Jeremy wanted to pay for college, find a job, and **buy** a new house.

9. According to Apple, Samsung's directors need to admit they violated Apple's patent, pay the fines, and ~~also needed is to~~ recall all their products.

10. Samsung's executives responded by completely rejecting Apple's ultimatum in court and **countersuing** Apple back for patent infringement.

11. The 300 men trained diligently, screamed fiercely into battle, and **fought valiantly**.

12. At the yard sale, Jimmy found dusty writings of Einstein, containers of fossils, and **boxes of Chinese opium**.

13. American immigrants took huge risks to leave their homelands and **search** for a better life elsewhere.

14. Come to the next party prepared to eat a lot, to dance a lot, and **to drink a lot**.

15. As soon as he graduated from high school, he packed all his belongings, rushed to the college campus, and **left** his parents behind.

Exercise 2:

1. B	5. B	9. B	13. A
2. C	6. A	10. D	14. D
3. D	7. C	11. B	15. D
4. A	8. B	12. C	

Chapter 12: Parallelism II - Pairs

Exercise:

1. The college experience is not only an exciting time to meet new people **but also** a stressful one because of the level of independence required.

2. Oleg works out daily not only to improve his physique but also **to improve his cardiovascular strength**.

3. The massive data breach reminded us not only of the need for better digital security but also **of the need for data retention policies**.

4. Critics have to rate both the food at the restaurant itself and **the food at other competing restaurants with the same cuisine**.

5. Though a horror fan, she preferred happy children's books **to Stephen King's books**.

6. She wasn't a fan of either the pizza at Domino's **or the pizza at Reggie's**.

7. I hope you suffer neither the pain of breaking up nor **the regret of lost love**.

8. Winston Churchill is known not only for his eloquence but also **for his charisma**.

9. Fruits aren't actually **as** necessary to one's diet as most doctors would have you believe.

10. Just as most politicians come from a law background, **so most doctors come from a biology background**.

11. Apple products are not so much a statement of technological performance as **a statement of style and status**.

12. Having a GPS system is not only convenient but also **necessary** when driving to new places.

13. There is no comparison between China's economic power and **Japan's (economic power)**.

14. My new book is not only comprehensive but also **concise**.

15. Not only were the books the most widely read, **but they also** influenced much of the philosophical thought during that time.

Chapter 13: Parallelism III - Faulty Comparisons

Exercise:

1. When the tour guide brought up how similar Edison's inventions were to the inventor Nikola **Tesla's**, Jimmy suggested that Edison might have just taken the idea from Tesla.

2. No personality is as weird as **the personality of the** physics teacher at my school, Mr. Greenman.

3. Gina's skill in archery pales in comparison to her **skill in rifle-shooting**.

4. At the festival, Abraham rocked out to Cannibal Corpse's death metal music, which he thought was less stale than the **other groups' music**.

5. Clothes worn by young adults in the 80's were much wilder than **those worn by the teenage crowd now**.

6. For some people, giving gifts is far easier than **receiving** them.

7. With the popularity of iPhones and iPads, Steve Jobs's legacy may surpass Microsoft founder **Bill Gates's**.

8. Efforts made by activists to curb global warming have been less effective than **efforts (those) made by environmentally-conscious consumers**.

9. Geographers have shown that the area of Australia is more than 20 times **the area of Japan**.

10. In France, public supply of water is run more efficiently than **that of electricity and heating**.

11. The gummy bears that Syed ordered off of Amazon turned out to be cheaper and of higher quality than **those ordered off of eBay**.

12. The molecular structure of Carbon is considered superior in terms of reactivity compared to **the molecular structures of most other elements**.

13. The percentage of the U.S. budget devoted to health care far exceeds **the percentage devoted to education**.

14. It's far more entertaining to watch a football game than **to actually play** in one.

Chapter 14: Pronoun Reference

Exercise 1: Correct answers are bolded along with their references, if applicable.

1. When I looked up at **the stars**, I couldn't believe **they were** so many light-years away.

2. Although many people believe **the tiger** is fierce and ferocious, **it is** actually quite peaceful.

3. **Anyone** who misses **his or her** parents can just go home.

4. The toxic level of **water bottles** isn't apparent to most people because they assume **their** plastic content is harmless.

5. After searching the whole day for my brother's **shoes**, I told him I wasn't able to find **them**.

6. **Birds** must migrate south during the winter season because **they manage** to survive only in warmer climates.

7. Until technological advances enable **them** to consume less fuel for thrust and power, the possibility of **space rockets** to Mars will remain remote.

8. By the time **they** can be fixed up, cleaned, and upgraded, old **cell phones** will be completely irrelevant compared to newer ones.

9. The food that **the chefs** serve at the restaurant is absolutely delicious.

10. The secretary unplugged the keyboard from the computer and cleaned **the computer**.

11. Joey was required to go to a meeting but **the announcement** never stated the location.

12. Before **the state university** could open up a new program in astrophysics, **it** needed funding from alumni.

13. **The government** is so arrogant in **its** ability to solve problems that **it has** silenced the voice of the people.

14. The show *American Idol* has as **its** premiere judge a man who can't sing himself.

15. Elle told the teacher that **the teacher** had made a mistake.

16. My iPhone fell onto the glass plate, but thankfully **the phone** didn't break.

17. **Some spiders** can inject **themselves** with poison to enact revenge on their predators.

18. Anthony used to hang out all the time with Albert until **Albert** got the big promotion at work.

19. When **a person** dies, **his or her** sense of hearing is the last to go whereas touch and sight are the first.

20. **The city** of Boston, which weathered the American Revolution, regularly offers tours that honor **its** local heroes.

21. One of the unique features of **the red panda**, an exotic creature that lives in the eastern Himalayas, is **its** ringed tail, which is used as a blanket in the cold.

22. **The health department** should be able to handle the paperwork by **itself**.

23. My mom cooked some traditional Russian **dishes**, but I hate eating **them**.

24. I took my old computer to the store and luckily **the engineers** were able to fix it.

Exercise 2: If applicable, the relevant reference is in parentheses.

1. $\boxed{D}$ *They* needs to be defined.

2. $\boxed{B}$ (*Seattle Police Department*)

3. $\boxed{C}$ *It* needs to be defined.

4. $\boxed{C}$ *That* should be defined. That what?

5. $\boxed{B}$ (*the writing style*)

6. $\boxed{D}$ (*the characters*)

7. $\boxed{A}$ (*a movie*)

8. $\boxed{B}$ (*the script*)

9. $\boxed{C}$ (*actors*)

10. $\boxed{C}$ *Their* has no reference in the passage so we must define it.

11. $\boxed{A}$ (*book signings*)

12. $\boxed{B}$ There is no clear reference for *them*, so we have to define it.

13. $\boxed{A}$ (*any reader*)

Chapter 15: Tenses

Exercise 1:

1. When Columbus and his crew discovered America in 1492, many Indian tribes **welcomed** them graciously.

2. The United States is considered the melting pot because its inhabitants **include** immigrants from all over the world.

3. Although the giant panda's diet consists primarily of bamboo, most other bears **hunt** for their food.

4. The door was decorated with ornate imprints of animals and **had** a stained glass window in the middle.

5. Every Sunday, Jane cleans the house and does the laundry at the same time her dad **mows** the lawn.

6. She bought her dress at Wal-Mart yet it **impressed** everyone at the party.

7. Every year he wishes for an end to world hunger and **prays** for a cure for cancer.

8. Whereas astronomers focus on the stars to advance the frontier of science, astrologists **study** the constellations to predict whether bad things will happen today.

9. To create the bracelet, Jane carefully slipped beads onto the band and then **twisted** it into a circular shape.

10. It's easy to tell when the teacher is being boring because some students start to fidget with their pens while others **yawn**.

11. Admissions officers **look** at several factors when determining whether to admit an applicant.

12. In today's fast-paced world, news sometimes spreads on social media faster than it **travels** through traditional media.

Exercise 2:

1. $\boxed{B}$ Past tense.

2. $\boxed{D}$ Present tense.

3. $\boxed{D}$ The last train leaving happened before Rick reached the train station, so the past perfect should be used.

4. $\boxed{B}$ Present tense.

5. $\boxed{D}$ Past tense.

6. $\boxed{C}$ Because James is continuing to live in the house, the present perfect is needed. The keyword *for* is a good indicator that the present perfect tense should be used.

7. $\boxed{C}$ Past tense.

8. $\boxed{C}$ Proving himself as a sergeant happened before being promoted to colonel, so the past perfect should be used. Simple past also works but it isn't in the answer choices.

9. $\boxed{A}$ Present tense.

10. $\boxed{A}$ The ghost sightings are continuing into the present, so the present perfect is needed. The keyword *since* is a good indicator that the present perfect tense should be used.

11. $\boxed{A}$ Past tense.

12. $\boxed{C}$ All verbs are in the present perfect: *has invested, has built, has traveled.*

13. $\boxed{D}$ The writer is continuing to look for a job and a place to stay into the present, so the present perfect is needed (in this case it's actually the present perfect progressive, but the concept is the same). The keyword *since* is a good indicator that the present perfect tense should be used.

14. $\boxed{A}$ Present tense.

15. $\boxed{B}$ Present tense.

Exercise 3:

1. $\boxed{D}$ Present tense.

2. $\boxed{A}$ Pluto was considered a planet before scientists deemed it too small. Therefore, the past perfect should be used. Simple past also works but it isn't in the answer choices.

3. $\boxed{B}$ Past tense.

4. $\boxed{D}$ Past tense.

5. $\boxed{D}$ Present tense.

6. $\boxed{B}$ Scientists are continuing to explore the possibility of alien life into the present, so the present perfect is needed. The keyword *for* is a good indicator that the present perfect tense should be used.

7. $\boxed{C}$ Past tense.

8. $\boxed{D}$ Past tense.

9. $\boxed{B}$ The doctor prescribed the medication before he took Mark off them. Therefore, the past perfect should be used. Simple past also works but it isn't in the answer choices.

10. $\boxed{B}$ Past (perfect) tense.

11. $\boxed{C}$ Amazon's expansion started in the past and continues into the present, so the present perfect is needed. The keyword *from* is a good indicator that the present perfect tense should be used.

12. $\boxed{B}$ Past tense. *Called on* is the correct idiom here, meaning to demand that someone do something.

13. $\boxed{C}$ This is more of a parallelism error than a tense error: *After what he said, it will be hard for him **to recover** in the polls, let alone **(to) win** the election.*

14. $\boxed{C}$ The waiters going home happened before we got a seat. Therefore, the past perfect should be used.

15. $\boxed{D}$ Past tense.

Chapter 16: Commas, Dashes, & Colons

Exercise 1:

1. A

2. B

3. A

4. A

5. B

6. D

7. D

8. A

9. D

10. A

11. B

12. C

13. B

14. C

15. C

16. C

17. A

18. B

19. D

20. D

21. C

Exercise 2:

1. D

2. B

3. D

4. C

5. C

6. C — The phrase *or give in* is a nonessential element that helps define *acquiesce*. The preposition *to* must remain outside the nonessential phrase because when the nonessential phrase is removed, the sentence must still make sense on its own: *the chairman could not **acquiesce to** the organization's demand*.

7. B

8. C

9. A

10. B

11. A

12. D

13. C — *referring to* should be kept together.

14. A

15. B

16. B

17. C

18. C — A comma can go before *such as* (to designate a nonessential phrase), but not after it.

19. D

20. B — The quotation must be enclosed by both beginning and ending quotation marks. A colon can be used to direct attention to a supporting quotation.

21. C — This is a tricky question. Answers A and B produce a run-on sentence in different ways.

Exercise 3:

1. A

2. B

3. B

4. C

5. A

6. B

7. C

8. C — Answer D is incorrect because it creates a nonessential clause that, when removed, does not leave a sentence that makes sense: *Very heavy paper is ideal for wet-folding in the early 1900s.* It makes it seem like the statement only pertains to a certain time period when that's obviously not the case.

9. D

10. A

11. B

Chapter 17: Apostrophes

Exercise:

1. B

2. D

3. B

4. A We know the plural *friends* is intended because of the *they* previously in the sentence.

5. B Yes, *whose* can be used for things.

6. A

7. C

8. B

9. C

10. D

11. A

12. C

13. D

14. C

15. B

16. B

17. B

18. A

19. B

20. A

21. D

22. B

Chapter 18: Word Choice

Exercise 1:

1. B	5. C	9. B	13. B
2. C	6. B	10. C	14. D
3. D	7. D	11. B	15. C
4. C	8. D	12. A	

Exercise 2:

1. C	5. A	9. D	13. A
2. B	6. C	10. C	14. B
3. A	7. C	11. C	
4. A	8. D	12. C	

Chapter 19: Transitions

Exercise 1:

1. A	9. C
2. C	10. A
3. D	11. C
4. D	12. D
5. C	13. B
6. D	14. D
7. B	15. B
8. D	

Exercise 2:

1. D	10. D
2. B	11. C — Answer B doesn't work because the crux of the previous sentence is *"The idea ... has been made obsolete by space research."* The supposed example that would follow is a bit awkward because it has nothing to do with space research. In fact, the bottom of the ocean might even be considered the opposite of outer space.
3. D	
4. A	
5. B	
6. C	
7. D	12. C
8. B	13. C
9. A	14. B
	15. D

Chapter 20: Topic, Conclusion, & Transition Sentences

Exercise 1:

1. [B] The sentences following the underlined portion compare teenagers with older drivers (different age groups).

2. [D] The chosen transition must describe *these failed attempts*.

3. [A] A contrast between where the money is expected to come from and where it actually comes from needs to be expressed.

4. [C] A link between the unknown purpose of the masks and staving off invaders is made only with choice C.

5. [D] Choice D leads best into the next sentence, which mentions several sites (temples, sushi joints, mall).

6. [B] From the context, the narrator watches other people on the train on a good day.

7. [B] The chosen transition should reference *the long break*.

8. [C] The chosen transition should clarify *Serena's winnings*.

9. [A] The last sentence elaborates on the wide range of tasks a professor does. Choice A sets that up.

10. [D] The narrator could not follow the doctor's advice. Choice D expresses why.

11. $\boxed{C}$ A connection must be made between the first paragraph (Boston's bustling economy) and the second (high cost of living). Choice C makes that connection.

12. $\boxed{D}$ The last phrase *loses composure when under pressure* means that pilots who can withstand the pressure are sought after.

13. $\boxed{B}$ From the last sentence, we can glean that the main benefit is that the desert approach is much less crowded.

14. $\boxed{D}$ The phrase *extreme pressures found at these depths* is a clear reference to the ocean.

15. $\boxed{C}$ The last sentence expresses an added reward for good work. Therefore, the transition must express what the standard reward is.

Exercise 2:

1. $\boxed{D}$ The examples are in response to a *virus*. Answer D is the one that most directly indicates that.

2. $\boxed{B}$ The entire paragraph discusses cheaper options for textbooks. Only answer B deals with students' finances.

3. $\boxed{C}$ The paragraph discusses the differences between Eastern philosophy and Western philosophy.

4. $\boxed{A}$ The second half of the sentence points out one particular instrument. Therefore, the first half should bring up several instruments.

5. $\boxed{C}$ The paragraph discusses how Carolina's priorities have shifted from helping customers in person to growing her business. As a result, she delegates to her staff. Answer C is the only one that aligns with this main idea. While the other choices are somewhat feasible, answer C is by far the most relevant.

6. $\boxed{B}$ Answer B is the one that best sums up the experience with amnesia. The other choices are all just loosely related.

7. $\boxed{D}$ The rest of the paragraph discusses *protests* and distributing *flyers*, actions taken to raise awareness.

8. $\boxed{D}$ The rest of the paragraph discusses a whole range of possible raw diets.

9. $\boxed{B}$ The paragraph brings up *aggressions* as well as the *brutality and senselessness* on TV that parents are uncomfortable exposing their children to.

10. $\boxed{A}$ The paragraph's main idea is the potential transformative power of hypnosis. Answer A best reflects that.

11. $\boxed{B}$ The paragraph's main idea is that winning sumo wrestlers become stars. Answer B best reflects that.

12. $\boxed{D}$ The paragraph discusses the struggles faced by law school graduates, not law schools.

13. $\boxed{C}$ The paragraph discusses the burden of student loans on parents.

14. $\boxed{B}$ The information that follows discusses clothing. Only answer B brings up clothing.

15. $\boxed{B}$ The paragraph's main idea is the rise of virtual employees and working remotely from home, which the writer views favorably. Answer B best sums that up.

Chapter 21: Supporting Evidence & Examples

Exercise 1:

1. $\boxed{A}$ The key word here is *carnivorous*. Answer A is the only example with a plant that feeds on other animals.

2. $\boxed{C}$ Answer C is the only one that directly states why food should not be eaten off the floor, even if it's picked up shortly after.

3. $\boxed{B}$ Answer B explains why spreading out study time is a good thing, even at the risk of forgetting.

4. $\boxed{D}$ Answer D is the only one that brings up a household appliance like the dishwasher.

5. $\boxed{C}$ Answer C shows in detail the poor state of Mongolia's economy.

6. $\boxed{D}$ Answer D mentions a specific work of art that reflects Van Gogh's mental state. Answer B is not specific. The other answers do not support the underlined portion.

7. $\boxed{B}$ Answer B is the only one that elaborates on a difference between dark energy and dark matter.

8. $\boxed{B}$ Answer B gives more reasons why Zermatt is a popular tourist destination—skiing and hiking.

9. $\boxed{C}$ The key word is *smell*. Answer C further establishes the bond between humans and dogs through smell.

10. $\boxed{D}$ Answer D is the only one that gives specific examples of the *procedures*.

11. $\boxed{A}$ Answer A gives emphasis to *high volume* by using big numbers that reflect the size of Wal-Mart's business.

12. $\boxed{D}$ The purpose of a microloan is to help ambitious people who currently don't have the means. While the other answers may be true, answer D is the one that most directly relates to the topic of the paragraph.

Exercise 2:

1. $\boxed{C}$ Answer C has the only example of *organic* architecture.

2. $\boxed{B}$ Answer B further gives examples of initiation that happen in different places.

3. $\boxed{C}$ Answer C explains how the Andean people used the coca leaf and what it meant to them. The other answers do not show why it was significant.

4. $\boxed{D}$ We're looking for a second example of *ballet-blanc*. Answer D is the only one that brings up white costuming, which is the defining characteristic.

5. $\boxed{A}$ Answer A details the danger of having different standards. There is no danger in the other answer choices.

6. [C] Answer C directly links honeybees to the agricultural industry through the amount of crops they help grow. The other answer choices ignore either honeybees or the agricultural industry.

7. [C] The example is Aralsk-7, which involved testing biological weapons on innocent people. Answer C further describes what happened and does not shift the focus to something less important.

8. [D] Answer A shows how the genus is different, but not how snow leopards, in particular, are different. Answer D is the one that does so.

9. [B] The key word is *impermanence*. Things do not last forever.

10. [C] Answer C is the only one that presents a legitimate obstacle to a man landing on Mars.

11. [B] Answer B is the only one that brings up specific animals (e.g. *seabirds, seals, penguins*). The other answers are vague.

12. [B] Answers A and C are only tangentially relevant. Yes, Santa Claus is based on Odin, but we can do better than just state that. The key words here are *modern portrayal*. Answer B gives a common image of Santa Claus and effectively links it back to Odin. Answer D doesn't mention Santa Claus at all and is completely irrelevant.

Chapter 22: Relevance & Purpose

Exercise 1:

1. C	4. D	7. B	10. C	13. D
2. C	5. A	8. C	11. D	
3. C	6. C	9. C	12. D	

Exercise 2:

1. A	3. B	5. B	7. D	9. B
2. D	4. C	6. C	8. C	10. C

Exercise 3:

1. B
2. C
3. C
4. A
5. D
6. C

7. C — The answer is not D because the fact that spears sprout from asparagus has already been established in the previous paragraph. The answer is C because the underlined portion is giving a condition that must be met before asparagus can be harvested. They should only be harvested when the spears are a few inches apart. This point is definitely important and relevant in the context of the passage.

8. A

9. C

Chapter 23: Placement

Exercise 1:

1. $\boxed{B}$ Notice the pronoun *they* in sentence 6. For that pronoun to be defined by the context, sentence 6 should be placed after sentence 1 or sentence 2 so that *they* refers to *machines* (sentence 2 contains *they*, which also refers back to *machines*, so it's possible to continue from sentence 2). However, sentences 2 and 3 should stick together because they contrast with each other, *they usually win* vs. *intended to lose*. Furthermore, sentence 6 is a good supporting sentence for sentence 1.

2. $\boxed{A}$ It's only after both sentences 4 and 5 does Chloe confirm with certainty that Erik is gone.

3. $\boxed{D}$ The pronoun *it* in sentence 5 is best defined by sentence 3, *a weighty piece of machinery*. Sentence 4 talks about what happens if the machinery could be lifted, so it's logical it follows a statement that the machinery is too heavy to lift in the first place. So sentence 5 is best placed between sentences 3 and 4.

4. $\boxed{C}$ Sentence 5 needs to be placed right before sentence 3, which discusses pursuing the duke after he escaped the attack on his province.

5. $\boxed{A}$ Sentence 5 serves as a contrast to sentence 4, what we can't know vs. what we do know.

6. $\boxed{C}$ Sentence 1 should be placed after sentence 4, which defines *the city* as Los Angeles. Sentences 2, 3, and 4 need to stick together uninterrupted because they continue from the question posed in sentence 2.

7. $\boxed{B}$ Sentence 5 should be placed right before sentence 3 so that it better defines *the renewed taste for coffee elsewhere*.

8. $\boxed{B}$ Sentence 5 elaborates on sentence 1 and also provides a statement that Ramos can disagree with in sentence 2. Otherwise, it's a bit unclear what Ramos is disagreeing with.

9. $\boxed{D}$ Sentence 5 should be placed right before sentence 4, so that *this vital physical clue* is defined as the *magnetized rock*.

10. $\boxed{D}$ Notice that sentence 4 mentions *staying in the same place*, which is the only logical reference for *this lack of movement* in the given sentence.

11. $\boxed{C}$ The given sentence logically follows after sentence 3, which talks about the rewards for delivering cargo the fastest. The given sentence also contains the word *merchants*, which is important to sentence 4, which makes a reference to *one such merchant*.

12. $\boxed{A}$ Sentence 6 contains the pronoun *they*, which is in need of a clarifying reference. Sentence 5, which discusses *hydrocarbons*, provides that reference.

13. $\boxed{A}$ The given sentence should be placed after sentence 1 because its purpose is to describe a *drug*, namely Chlorphenamine Maleate.

14. $\boxed{D}$ Sentence 4 serves as a response to the question in sentence 8.

15. $\boxed{B}$ The phrase *the project* references the tomb of Lorenzo brought up in sentence 2. Therefore, the given sentence should be placed after sentence 2. Note that sentences 3 and 4 must stick together since sentence 4 builds off of sentence 3.

Exercise 2:

1. [D] Sentence 5 follows up on *the dark side* mentioned in sentence 3. It also clarifies the statement that *the people have not surrendered so easily* in sentence 4. Otherwise, readers would be asking, "Surrendering to who?"

2. [B] Sentence 5 needs to be placed between sentences 1 and 2 to act as a transition between sugar and molasses.

3. [C] Sentence 5 needs to be placed before sentence 3 to introduce Narcissus. Otherwise, sentence 3 comes off too abruptly.

4. [A] After sentence 1, readers are curious what the *sea creature* is. The given sentence answers that. It also transitions to the following sentences that talk about males and females. It would be odd to jump into those sentences without knowing what animal is being talked about.

5. [C] The given sentence describes one of Charles's childhood experiences. Since his childhood is brought up in sentence 4, the given sentence should be placed after that. It also serves as a reference for *those times* mentioned in sentence 5.

6. [B] Sentence 2 talks about the rest of the world building faster ships. The given sentence is logically placed after that since it brings up the fall of British ships. The given sentence also serves as reference for sentence 3 by defining the pronoun *they*.

7. [A] Sentence 5 is the perfect topic sentence for this paragraph because it mentions what activity is being discussed—kettlebell training. If sentence 1 were left at the start, readers would be left scratching their heads.

8. [D] Sentence 3 brings up tree farming in general. It would awkward to place sentence 5 before that. Sentence 5 discusses Belen's famed trees, which is the perfect lead sentence for sentence 4, which talks about how Belen lost its fame for trees.

9. [C] The given sentence should be placed before sentence 4, which discusses *catching mice and other countryside rodents*.

10. [A] Sentence 5 is a good conclusion sentence. It must come after the name *Louis Pasteur* is brought up and after *this process* is described.

11. [A] The given sentence should come before sentence 2, which contains the phrases *compared to the latest designs* and *those older models*. These phrases need to be clarified by the given sentence, which discusses *early versions* of the tank.

12. [B] The given sentence should be inserted before sentence 3 since it would clarify what *both instruments* refers to. Also note that sentence 3 mentions *the pipe* brought up in the given sentence.

13. [C] Sentence 2 brings up *rock*. Sentence 3 mentions *these particles*. Sentence 5 should be placed in between to build off of sentence 2 and give a reference to *these particles* in sentence 3.

14. [B] Sentence 5 brings up *its unscientific character*, the *its* referring to *numerology* in sentence 1. Furthermore, sentence 5 should be placed before sentence 2 to define the time mentioned there, *around that time*.

15. [B] The given sentence should be placed before sentence 5 in order to define *this division process*.

Chapter 24: Singular Plural Noun Inconsistency

Exercise:

1. The football players put on their **helmets** and grabbed their **water bottles**.

2. The two students put their **minds** to the test by participating in the state chess competition.

3. Revered as **a talented magician** who can do much more than card tricks, David Blaine surprises audiences with superhuman feats of endurance.

4. The caterpillars that emerged from their **cocoons** will soon turn into **butterflies**.

5. Environmental scientists are currently promoting ethanol, natural gas, and chemically stored electricity as **alternatives** to fossil fuels.

6. Mary and Ann dreamed of blossoming into **princesses** and being rescued by **princes**.

7. We competed in many exciting baseball games this year, but our win against last year's champions is by far the most memorable **victory**.

8. Curiosity, diligence, and the willingness to think on one's feet are **strong prerequisites** for a successful career in any industry.

9. **Experts** in the federal tax code, the bank's financial advisors can tell you where to put your investments to maximize your deductions.

10. You will not be able to pass the preliminary background check unless the document you provide is a driver's license, passport, or other valid **form** of identification.

11. The two teams from Pittsburgh won the first and second place **prizes** in the international robotics competition.

12. Two out of every fifteen college students who major in computer science will go on to become **small business owners** at some point in their lives.

Chapter 25: Who vs. Whom

Exercise:

1. The agency recruited overseas teachers **who** would be able to demonstrate a native fluency in English.

2. At Kim's birthday party were millionaires and celebrities, some of **whom** had flown in from New York to attend.

3. Julie's math teacher was a graduate student **who**, after completing his finance degree, decided to get into teaching instead.

4. The police officers, **who** were eating donuts at the time, didn't hear the cries for help.

5. The girl **whom** Dave was matched with was unimpressed by his sense of humor.

6. Anyone **who** has read the book will say that it's much better than the movie.

7. Reflecting on all her past accomplishments, the winner thanked everyone with **whom** she had been associated.

8. Can you tell the boys **who** are at the door to go away?

9. The girls with **whom** I'm going shopping need to borrow money.

10. I want to hire those chefs **who** cooked the perfect pasta at the restaurant we ate at last week.

Chapter 26: Combining Sentences

Exercise 1:

1. $\boxed{C}$ Answer C is not only the shortest way but also the one that doesn't use any unnecessary pronouns like *they*.

2. $\boxed{A}$ Answer A is not only the shortest way but also the one that doesn't use any unnecessary pronouns like *they*.

3. $\boxed{B}$ Answer B keeps the parallelism by maintaining the *-ing* ending. Answer C is in the passive voice, which is wordy and awkward.

4. $\boxed{C}$ Answer C uses a conjunction that expresses the intended meaning. The other answer choices change the intended meaning.

5. $\boxed{A}$ Answer A is the only one that expresses the intended meaning.

6. $\boxed{C}$ Answer C is the only one that expresses the intended meaning and avoids the use of unnecessary pronouns.

7. $\boxed{D}$ Answer D is the only one that expresses the intended meaning and avoids redundant words like *location* and *place*.

8. $\boxed{B}$ Answer B is the only one that expresses the intended meaning and avoids the use of unnecessary pronouns.

9. $\boxed{C}$ Answer C is not only the shortest way but also the one that doesn't use any redundant words. Answer B is wrong because *which* is not just unnecessary, it alters the intended meaning of the sentence. The sentence's intent is to say that Debbie's speeches are long, not her performances. It's a minor but important distinction. If you use *which*, it seems like you are now describing her performances as *so long*. Answer C is correct because *so long*, when used by itself, emphasizes the thing that was already called *long*: her speeches.

10. $\boxed{A}$ Answer A is not only the shortest way but also the one that doesn't use any redundant words.

11. $\boxed{A}$ Answer A is the most concise. No extra words are necessary.

12. $\boxed{B}$ Answer A does not use *such as* correctly. Answers C and D are unnecessarily wordy. Answer B correctly uses a colon to introduce a list.

Exercise 2:

1. [A] Answer B is a weird run-on in which two independent clauses are connected by *which*. Answer C is awkward because it puts two relative clauses in a row. Answer D uses the unnecessary pronoun *it* doesn't connect the two sentences in a meaningful way.

2. [C] Answer A makes it sound like the financial advisor is the one who possesses the old house. Answer B is an inverted sentence, which can work sometimes but is awkward in this case because it's passive. Answer D changes the intended meaning—the suggestion isn't to sell a house before it's evaluated.

3. [D] The relative clause *which is transmitted through the air and called influenza* is awkward in answer A because it pairs up a less important element (*transmitted through the air*) with a very important one (*influenza*). The name of the virus shouldn't be left this way in a relative clause. Answer B is wrong because it starts off with the unnecessary pronoun *it*. Answer C is wrong because it changes the meaning of the sentence. Answer D correctly uses a modifier to combine the sentences.

4. [D] The phrase *which is contradicting* in answer A is awkward; there's no need to use the present progressive tense. Furthermore, the entire relative clause would be more logically placed at the end of the sentence. In answer B, the phrase *in contradiction to* is awkward and wordy. Similarly, the phrase *what's contradicted by* in answer C is awkward and passive. Answer D gives the simplest way of combining the two sentences.

5. [B] Answer A changes the meaning of the sentence. It makes it seem like other hotels chains are *often advertised as the most luxurious hotel in the world*. The same logic applies to answer C. Answer D is wordy— it repeats *the Four Seasons* twice.

6. [A] Answer B is redundant because it uses two elements that signal cause and effect: *the reason* and *is because*. The second half of answer C is very wordy and uses the unnecessary pronoun *he*. Answer D changes the intended meaning.

7. [C] Answer A uses the unnecessary pronoun *these*. Answer B changes the meaning—we don't *make* mental processes. Answer D uses unnecessary dashes and changes the meaning—it's not the *questions* that govern our judgments.

8. [C] In answer A, the phrase *the start of the Civil Rights movement* interrupts the sentence in the wrong place. The words *fight for* should be together. Answer B is passive. Answer D unnecessarily repeats the pronoun *it* and doesn't connect the two sentences in a meaningful way.

9. [B] Answer A is passive and the phrase *despite the low wages* interrupts the sentence in an inappropriate place. Answer C suffers from a modifier error. In answer D, the phrase *working long hours at menial jobs and having low wages* feels disjointed and awkward.

10. [D] Answer A doesn't join the two sentences in a meaningful way. What's *them*? Pronoun reference error. Furthermore, the second half is passive. The phrase *in the accommodation of* in answer B is awkward. Answer B also does not join the two sentences in a very meaningful way. Answer C is inverted and passive.

Chapter 27: Data Interpretation

Exercise 1:

1. [C] Two players both with four years of training had different average speeds of serve.

2. [B] For every state, the percentage of adults who eat vegetables less than one time daily (i.e. none at all) is lower than the corresponding percentage for fruits. That means the percentage who actually eat vegetables at least one time a day is higher.

3. [A] Answer A supports the context of the sentence and accurately follows from the data. For example, the percentage for adults in Alabama was 28.3%, which is smaller than the 45.7% for adolescents in the same state.

4. [C] Keep in mind the percentages in the chart refer to those who eat less than one time daily. So the lower those percentages, the more fruits and vegetables people eat. The adults in Texas have the lowest percentages for fruits and vegetables.

5. [C] Keep in mind the percentages in the chart refer to those who eat less than one time daily. So the lower those percentages, the more fruits and vegetables people eat. The percentages drop much more significantly for vegetables than for fruits going from the adolescent table to the adult table. It can be reasonably inferred that people are eating more and more vegetables relative to fruits as they get older.

6. [B] The percentages for high school boys for fruit juice, soda, and sports drinks are all higher than those for high school girls.

7. [A] The percentages for water, 71.8% and 72.9%, are the closest for any beverage in the table.

8. [D] More females (15.7%) than males (12.1%) drank coffee.

9. [D] The percentage of high school students who drank milk (54.2%) was greater than 50%.

10. [B] For every year in the chart, the darker bar (those with arthritis) is about 10% bigger than the lighter bar (those without arthritis). That means those with arthritis are 10 percent more likely to be obese. Answer A is incorrect because it doesn't read the chart correctly. The chart measures obesity rates among people with/without arthritis, NOT arthritis rates among people who are/aren't obese. They're not the same thing.

11. [C] The dark bars go up over the years, and so do the light bars, which means obesity rates are on the rise regardless of the presence of arthritis.

12. [C] The 15-19 year olds clearly spent more time on leisure (the middle bar) than work and household activities combined (the left and right bars).

13. [B] The white bars go up, which means time spent on household activities rises. The light gray bars go down, which means time spent on leisure falls.

14. [B] In every age range, people spent more time on leisure than on work. This statement is also the one that best supports the context.

15. [C] People in the age ranges above 25 worked at least an average of 25 hours per week (the dark gray bars).

16. [C] There is a greater proportion of sci-fi and horror movies (25% and 20%, respectively) in Korea than in America (both 10%).

17. [B] Sci-fi is the most common genre in Korea (25%) and one of the least common in America (10%).

18. [D] In Korea, no two percentages in the pie chart add up to at least 50%.

Exercise 2:

1. [C] Over the years, both populations increased, but the oxpecker population grew at a slower rate (the slope of the line is not as steep).

2. [D] The two lines cross in the third year, meaning the populations were the same.

3. [B] The density of listeria drops significantly with the third dose.

4. [C] Clostridia density (the light gray bar) decreases the same amount with each additional dose.

5. [D] The vaccine reduces clostridia density with each dose and listeria density with at least three doses.

6. [B] The line is above 10 from month 4 to month 8—that's 4 months.

7. [A] Pollution levels reached a peak at month 6. They were at their lowest at the start.

8. [B] Germany is the line on the bottom, so it has the lowest overall participation rates. The line in the middle is the U.S. and the line on top is Sweden. Therefore, the order from lowest to highest is Germany, the U.S., and Sweden.

9. [D] After 1995, the U.S. and Sweden have participation rates that are roughly in the same place on the chart.

10. [D] Germany, represented by the line on the bottom, always had the lowest participation rates of women in the labor force.

11. [C] Equipment accidents in Boston number 4. Equipment accidents in New York City number 18, which is more than triple. Answer D is accurate but does not support the context of the sentence.

12. [C] Transportation incidents were the leading cause, as shown by the longer bars in both New York City and Boston.

13. [D] As a percentage of GDP, the banking system of the U.S. is the smallest (all commercial banks are ~120% of GDP).

14. [B] On the x-axis, we can see that Belgium's four largest banks own assets totaling 300% of GDP. On the y-axis, all of Belgium's commercial banks represent 300% of GDP. Because they're equivalent, Belgium's four largest banks are essentially all the banks they have. Therefore, the four largest banks control all the banking assets in the country.

15. [A] The point representing France has a y-coordinate of 500%, which means that the commercial banks in France have assets totaling five times its GDP.

Chapter 28: Odds and Ends You Must Know for the Perfect Score

Exercise 1:

1. ☐A☐ The reported question is not an exact quote so a question mark is not needed (indirect speech).

2. ☐D☐ To *take in* means to absorb or learn. To *abide by* means to accept or act in accordance with.

3. ☐C☐ The sentence is in the third-person point of view (*a tourist*), so *he or she* is needed. Keep the point of view the same.

4. ☐B☐ Since the phrase "*(an antioxidant related to . . .)*" defines *lutein* and NOT *lutein-containing foods*, it should be placed next to *lutein*. Answer B is the only one that accomplishes that.

5. ☐D☐ The sentence has two main verbs (*is* and *must be*). Only choice D resolves this issue correctly.

6. ☐D☐ The reported question is not an exact quote so a question mark is not needed (indirect speech).

7. ☐D☐ The sentence is in the third-person point of view (*they*), so the answer is C or D. Between the two, only D gives a noun (*Customers*) that the pronoun *they* can refer to.

8. ☐C☐ The correct idiom is *concern for*. In this sentence, *respect* does not need a preposition after it.

9. ☐C☐ The reported question is not an exact quote so a question mark is not needed (indirect speech). The adverbs *quietly and efficiently* should be placed next to *circulate* since that's the verb they modify.

10. ☐B☐ The sentence has two main verbs (*cut* and *laid*). Only choice B resolves this issue correctly. Choice C is incorrect because the meaning of the sentence gets twisted: the publisher did not cut costs *in order to* lay off staff writers, as choice C would imply. Choice D does not use a colon correctly.

Exercise 2:

1. ☐B☐ The sentence is in the first-person point of view (*we*), so *us* is needed. Keep the point of view the same.

2. ☐B☐ The correct idioms are *comply with . . . deviate from*.

3. ☐C☐ The sentence has two main verbs (*was published* and *shows*). Only choice C resolves this issue correctly. Note that choice D is incorrect because a comma is needed to pair with the one after *Medicine*.

4. ☐C☐ The reported question is not an exact quote so a question mark is not needed (indirect speech).

5. ☐D☐ Choices B and C are wrong because they don't keep the point of view consistent. Because *the tulip orchid* is singular, the pronoun *its* should be used.

6. ☐C☐ Since the phrase "*the practice of distributing audio files to users over the Internet*" defines *podcasting* and NOT *podcasting's popularity*, it should be placed next to *podcasting*. Answer C is the only one that accomplishes that correctly.

7. $\boxed{A}$ The correct idioms are *disregard for* and *distaste for*. Since they both use the preposition *for*, it does not need to be repeated.

8. $\boxed{D}$ The reported question is a quote so we need a question mark after it (direct speech). No question mark is needed after *wondered* since only the quote is a question, not the entire sentence.

9. $\boxed{C}$ The sentence is in the third-person point of view (*software engineers*), so the answer is B or C. Answer C is correct because the plural pronoun *they* should be used to refer to the plural noun *software engineers*.

10. $\boxed{D}$ Since the phrase *"the study of chemicals derived from plants"* defines *phytochemistry* and NOT *phytochemistry research*, it should be placed next to *phytochemistry*. Answer D is the only one that accomplishes that correctly. A dash is needed to pair up with the dash after *plants*.

31

Practice Test 1

The History of Comic Books

Faster than a speeding **1** bullet; able to leap tall buildings in a single bound, Superman was the first comic book superhero. Prior to 1938, when Superman made his debut, early comic books consisted of multiple stories about different characters, many of them humorous. With the arrival of the superhero archetype, publishers began devoting whole issues to single characters. **2** Readers enjoyed the illustrations more than the dialogue.

1

A) NO CHANGE
B) bullet
C) bullet,
D) bullet—

2

Which choice provides the most appropriate introduction to the rest of the passage?

A) NO CHANGE
B) The Golden Age of Comics had dawned.
C) Bookstores didn't have enough space to carry all the new comics that were being issued.
D) These original issues would be worth a lot today.

Over the next few years, Detective Comics, 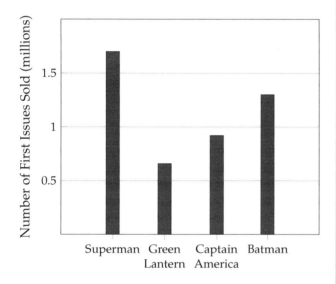 becoming DC Comics later on, introduced a slew of superheroes. Batman, Wonder Woman, Aquaman, and Green Lantern all debuted during the early years of World War II. The need for cheap entertainment for soldiers combined with the wartime imaginations of American youths fueled **4** an insatiable market for comic books. Captain America, introduced in 1941, became one of the most popular heroes as a fighter of Nazis. The first issue alone **5** outsold the first issue of Batman.

3

A) NO CHANGE
B) it later became DC Comics,
C) DC Comics it later became,
D) which later became DC Comics,

4

A) NO CHANGE
B) a discontent
C) a desirable
D) an uncontrollable

5

Which choice most accurately and effectively represents the information in the graph?

A) NO CHANGE
B) sold nearly one million copies.
C) grossed almost a million dollars in sales.
D) sold twice as many copies as the first issue of the Green Lantern.

After the war, demand for superhero comics began to decline, and growing concerns about the corrupting influence of comic books nearly devastated the industry. The 1954 publication of *Seduction of the Innocent* by psychiatrist Fredric Wertham led to Senate hearings investigating the [6] effects of comics to juvenile delinquency. In response, publishers developed a Comics Code to self-regulate the content of comics, effectively [7] exiling comic artists and writers.

The 1960s, [8] similarly, saw a revival as Spider Man, the X-Men, the Fantastic Four, and other characters debuted. These new heroes were more obviously flawed and more human than most previous heroes. The character of Wolverine became the prototype for the antiheroes popularized in the 1980s and 1990s as comics grew darker and more violent. Gritty comics became the norm, and by 2011 all publishers had ceased to operate under the Code.

6

A) NO CHANGE
B) effects of comics on
C) affects of comics on
D) affects of comics by

7

A) NO CHANGE
B) banning
C) propagandizing
D) censoring

8

A) NO CHANGE
B) therefore,
C) however,
D) for instance,

In the world of comics, the issue of creators' rights has been ▣9 constant sources of conflict. In the early days, writers and artists worked long hours for ▣10 publishers. These were the ones that paid them relatively little and claimed the rights to the characters. With the recent popularity of films centered on classic comic characters, a number of lawsuits over copyrights ▣11 have been waged by the children of these creators to secure the royalties their parents never enjoyed.

9

A) NO CHANGE
B) constant conflicting sources.
C) a conflict of constant source.
D) a constant source of conflict.

10

Which choice most effectively combined the two sentences at the underlined portion?

A) publishers; they were those that
B) publishers, and these companies
C) publishers that
D) publishers to get

11

A) NO CHANGE
B) has been waged
C) was waged
D) waged

The Mona Lisa

With her knowing, self-satisfied smile and her eyes that [12] followed viewers around the room, the Mona Lisa has become the most famous and iconic image in the art world. But what is the story behind this Renaissance masterpiece? Who was the woman Leonardo Da Vinci so compellingly captured with paint?

[13] It is known that the portrait depicts the wife of a Florentine cloth merchant named Francesco del Giocondo. At the Louvre in Paris, where the painting has hung since 1797, the title is given as "Portrait of Lisa Gherardini, wife of Francesco del Giocondo." Leonardo most likely completed the portrait sometime between 1503 and 1506, when he lived in Florence. [14]

12
A) NO CHANGE
B) follow
C) had followed
D) follows

13
At this point, the writer would like to emphasize that the identity of the person in the portrait is uncertain. Which choice most effectively accomplishes this goal?

A) NO CHANGE
B) The fact is
C) The best conjecture is
D) It has been established

14
At this point, the writer is considering adding the following sentence.

At the time, Florence was a republic under the powerful influence of the Medici family.

Should the writer make this addition here?

A) Yes, because it explains why Da Vinci moved to Florence.
B) Yes, because it provides important background information related to the Mona Lisa.
C) No, because it blurs the focus of the paragraph with a loosely related detail.
D) No, because Leonardo Da Vinci did not spend most of his life in Florence.

In 2013, Researchers failed **15** in the proof of the subject's identity by creating an image from DNA extracted from Lisa del Giocondo's tomb. Even if she were the woman in the painting, its occasion would remain a mystery. Two events in the Giocondo family history have been suggested as possibilities. One is the birth of a son in **16** 1502; the other is the opening of a new home in 1503. But if Francesco del Giocondo had commissioned the painting, why did Leonardo never give it to him? The artist apparently kept it, and it later became part of the French royal collection.

Other theories of the woman's identity have included both Leonardo's mother and the artist **17** himself, he was disguised as a woman. The truth remains unknown, but **18** some researchers are still determined to find it. The Mona Lisa introduced a new approach to portraiture that set the template for many years afterward. Unlike the rigid portraits of the day, **19** Leonardo's masterpiece depicts a relaxed posture with soft lines. He presents the subject from the front instead of in profile. **20** Nevertheless, the harmony between the woman and the landscape behind her reach a new level of excellence.

15

A) NO CHANGE
B) in the attempt to prove
C) to produce proof of
D) to prove

16

A) NO CHANGE
B) 1502,
C) 1502:
D) 1502

17

A) NO CHANGE
B) himself; cleverly
C) himself cleverly,
D) himself, cleverly

18

Which choice most effectively sets up the information that follows?

A) NO CHANGE
B) the influence of the portrait is indisputable.
C) it still manages to attract millions of tourists each year.
D) its dollar value continues to climb.

19

A) NO CHANGE
B) Leonardo depicts
C) which depict
D) having depicted

20

A) NO CHANGE
B) On the other hand,
C) Moreover,
D) Alternatively,

The monetary value of the painting, estimated in 2015 to be nearly $800 [21] million cannot do justice to its intrinsic worth. No price will ever capture the genius of this beautiful, [22] mystical, and ground-breaking portrait that after 500 years still captures both the eye and the heart.

[21]

A) NO CHANGE
B) million;
C) million,
D) million—

[22]

A) NO CHANGE
B) full of mystery,
C) mysterious,
D) mystified,

Biking to Work

The daily commute to work [23] can suck the life out of a person. My commute, however, actually energizes me and keeps me in shape. I ride a bike, and except for days when the weather is too wet or too cold, I glide to work along beautiful, forested roads.

[1] Several people recommended buying a hybrid designed for commuting. [2] Others suggested I buy a mountain bike and then install road tires on [24] it. [3] Mountain bikes have heavier frames than [25] people with road bikes and can more easily be used to carry bags containing work items. [4] [26] Thus, I was able to buy a mountain bike that was already prepared for the daily commute. [5] It came outfitted with all the commuting [27] essentials; a flashing headlamp, a flashing red tail-light, a rearview mirror, and a small rack for attaching gear. [28]

23

Which choice is most appropriate for the tone of this passage?

A) NO CHANGE
B) can be stressful and exhausting.
C) drives some people crazy.
D) is vexing for many.

24

A) NO CHANGE
B) them
C) these
D) this

25

A) NO CHANGE
B) those who have road bikes
C) road bikes
D) road bike's

26

A) NO CHANGE
B) In addition,
C) To illustrate,
D) Fortunately,

27

A) NO CHANGE
B) essentials,
C) essentials:
D) essentials

28

To improve the coherence of this paragraph, the writer wants to add the following sentence.

When I first started, I knew how to ride a bike, but I didn't know what kind of bike would be best for commuting.

The best placement for the sentence is immediately

A) before sentence 1.
B) after sentence 1.
C) after sentence 2.
D) after sentence 3.

Anyone who wants to commute by bike must learn some basic maintenance and [29] repair–most importantly, how to change a flat tire. I remember going to a bike shop to buy some spare inner tubes for my tires, and the owner immediately recognized me as a novice. He handed me a couple of tire levers and explained that these would prove to be very helpful. [30] I was thankful for them a couple of years later when I had a flat.

On my bike I have enjoyed beautiful weather, endured freezing cold, and [31] have been caught in sudden cloudbursts. I learned the importance of finding a facemask and a pair of thick but functional gloves, because the face and fingers get the coldest during winter. I also learned [32] how important it is to watch the weather carefully and remembering to place all electronics inside a plastic bag in my backpack in case of rain. Those 3.5 miles to and from work on my bike are not only [33] delightful and also enlightening.

[29]
A) NO CHANGE
B) repair;
C) repair, which
D) repair,

[30]
At this point, the writer is considering adding the following sentence.

These small, flat tools unlock the edges of the tire from one side of the wheel in order to gain access to the tube inside that needs to be replaced.

Should the writer make this addition here?

A) Yes, because it presents knowledge that only experienced bikers are aware of.
B) Yes, because it expands on a previous statement by providing relevant details.
C) No, because it distracts from the focus of the paragraph by introducing irrelevant material.
D) No, because it should be placed earlier in the passage.

[31]
A) NO CHANGE
B) caught
C) been caught
D) have caught

[32]
A) NO CHANGE
B) the importance of watching
C) to importantly watch
D) the important nature of watching

[33]
A) NO CHANGE
B) a delightful experience but also enlightening.
C) delightful but also enlightening.
D) delightful but also an enlightenment.

The Architecture of Castles

The castles of fairy tales, with their high, narrow towers, gargoyles, and spires, are more the reflections of nineteenth-century ideas than of the great stone fortresses of the middle ages. [34] Regardless, the architecture of medieval castles centered on one main [35] principle defense.

A wealthy lord would typically build a castle on a defensible [36] site, such as a hill or large rock or even a high crag. A deep ditch called a moat would be dug around the perimeter. Drawbridges typically would provide the only way across the moat so that it could easily be pulled up to prevent enemy access.

[1] The strongest castles were made with stone walls around eight to twelve feet thick. [2] An outer wall of about twenty feet in height would surround an inner [37] wall; where the castle occupants actually lived. [3] Keeping it lower than the inner wall allowed archers to shoot from the inner wall over the men on the outside. [4] The outer wall was the next line of defense after the moat and drawbridge. [5] Archers aimed through vertical slits in the walls called arrow loops, which [38] were often cut in the shape of a cross. [39]

34

A) NO CHANGE
B) Furthermore,
C) Hence,
D) In reality,

35

A) NO CHANGE
B) principle,
C) principle:
D) principle;

36

A) NO CHANGE
B) site such as:
C) site such as,
D) site, such as,

37

A) NO CHANGE
B) wall, which
C) wall, during which
D) wall, within which

38

Which choice results in a sentence that best supports the point developed in this paragraph?

A) NO CHANGE
B) were not introduced until 212 BC.
C) allowed them to fire upon enemies while remaining protected.
D) were invented by Archimedes and popularized by the Greeks and Romans.

39

To make this paragraph most logical, sentence 3 should be

A) placed where it is now.
B) placed after sentence 1.
C) placed after sentence 4.
D) placed after sentence 5.

The gates of castles **40** constituted the greatest weak points. To compensate, a heavy sliding grate called a portcullis would be installed to close vertically over the **41** gateway. What followed next were heavy doors barred from behind with a thick wooden beam. In the tunnel-like space between the portcullis and the **42** doors, and openings in the arched ceiling called "murder holes" enabled defending soldiers to drop heavy objects onto attackers.

Large windows in residential housing were necessary to allow enough light. Apartments and large rooms for gathering, like the great hall and the chapel, were built on the upper levels of the inner walls because **43** the threat presented by their large windows was too perilous.

The farmers and tradesmen who lived in the town surrounding a castle provided food and goods for the wealthy lord, his family and staff, and his militia. They in turn received shelter and sustenance. But ultimately, the castle existed more for his defense than **44** they're protection.

40

A) NO CHANGE
B) composed
C) comprehended
D) circumscribed

41

A) NO CHANGE
B) gateway, followed by
C) gateway follow
D) gateway by following

42

A) NO CHANGE
B) doors,
C) doors with
D) doors were

43

A) NO CHANGE
B) a danger to safety was caused by their large windows.
C) their large windows endangered people to harm.
D) their large windows posed a security risk.

44

A) NO CHANGE
B) for their
C) for there
D) to their

Answers to Practice Test 1

Score your test using the Score Calculator at thecollegepanda.com

1. $\boxed{C}$ The phrase *able to leap tall buildings...* is a modifer, which is a nonessential phrase. These phrases should be separated off by commas.

2. $\boxed{B}$ The next paragraph discusses the rise in popularity of comic books. The answer that best leads into that discussion is B.

3. $\boxed{D}$ Answers B and D put a complete sentence within the complete sentence. You can think of it as a weird run-on. Answer A uses the progressive tense *becoming*, which is awkward because it makes it seem like Detective Comics is still in the process of becoming DC Comics. Answer D, which uses the simple past tense, is correct.

4. $\boxed{A}$ *Insatiable*, which means "cannot be satisfied," is the most appropriate word to describe "market." The meaning is that supply could not keep up with demand. While *uncontrollable* could mean the same thing, the word also implies a lot of other things, like the market couldn't be regulated, for example.

5. $\boxed{B}$ The bar above *Captain America* almost reaches 1 million.

6. $\boxed{B}$ *Affect* is a verb, whereas *effect* is a noun. In this case, we want the noun. The correct idiom is *on*. For example, *this had an effect on that.*

7. $\boxed{D}$ In context, to *self-regulate the content of comics* is most equivalent to *censoring* them.

8. $\boxed{C}$ The previous paragraph discusses the decline of comic books. This paragraph discusses the *revival*. This contrast is best expressed through *however*.

9. $\boxed{D}$ Singular-plural noun inconsistency error. Because *"the issue"* is singular, the singular noun *"a constant source"* is needed for consistency.

10. $\boxed{C}$ Answer C is the shortest one that avoids using pronouns. Answer D is incorrect because *to get paid them* is grammatically incorrect.

11. $\boxed{A}$ The subject *a number* is plural (there's more than one). Answer A provides the plural verb *have* that goes with that plural subject. Answer D results in an incomplete sentence.

12. $\boxed{B}$ Because *the eyes* is plural, the verb should be plural. And because the present tense is needed to express a truth, *follow* is correct.

13. $\boxed{C}$ *Conjecture* means guess. The other answer choices sound much too certain.

14. $\boxed{C}$ The given sentence shifts the focus away from Leonardo. It might be okay to add it if the passage continued to talk about Florence, but it doesn't.

15. $\boxed{D}$ The other answer choices are redundant and wordy.

16. $\boxed{A}$ We're connecting two independent clauses so a semicolon is needed.

17. $\boxed{D}$ Answer A is a run-on. *Cleverly disguised as a woman* is a nonessential phrase that needs to be separated by a comma.

18. $\boxed{B}$ The rest of the paragraph talks about the innovative style and technique Da Vinci used to paint the Mona Lisa. In particular, it *introduced a new approach to portraiture.* This discussion speaks to the painting's influence.

19. $\boxed{A}$ Answer B results in a modifier error. We cannot compare *rigid portraits* with a person, *Leonardo.* Answers C and D result in sentence fragments.

20. $\boxed{C}$ The sentence continues to discuss the artistic merits of the Mona Lisa.

21. $\boxed{C}$ The nonessential phrase starting with *estimated in 2015...* must be closed off by a comma.

22. $\boxed{C}$ Answer C is parallel and expresses the intended meaning. In answering this question, you have to consider the overall passage and its main question: who is the person depicted in the Mona Lisa? What's the story behind it? That's why the answer is "mysterious" and not "mystical". *Mystical* implies a spiritual or religious aspect, which isn't applicable in this particular context.

23. $\boxed{B}$ Answers A, C, and D are vague because of words like *people* and *many.* Answers A and C are too informal while answer D uses inflated language.

24. $\boxed{A}$ The singular noun *mountain bike* should be referred to by the singular pronoun *it.*

25. $\boxed{C}$ Compare *mountain bikes* with *road bikes*, not *people with road bikes.*

26. $\boxed{D}$ The previous sentences mention that mountain bikes would require road tires to be installed. The writer, *fortunately*, didn't have to do that.

27. $\boxed{C}$ What follows is a list, which is best punctuated by a colon.

28. $\boxed{A}$ The given sentence serves as a good topic sentence, before the suggestions of what bike to get.

29. $\boxed{A}$ The phrase *"most importantly, how to change a flat tire"* is an interrupting thought that is best led into by a dash. The other choices lead to grammatically incorrect sentences. For instance, consider answer D, which puts two commas around *"most importantly"*. These commas indicate that *"most importantly"* is a nonessential phrase in the sentence. That means we should be able to take it out and the remaining sentence should still make sense. However, when we do that, we get *"...learn some basic maintenance and repair how to change a flat tire."* The phrase *"repair how to change a flat tire"* doesn't make sense. Therefore, it would be incorrect to put a comma after *repair.*

30. $\boxed{B}$ The previous sentence brings up *tire levers* and says that they would prove to be *helpful.* The given sentence explains why.

31. $\boxed{C}$ Parallelism. The *have* carries over to each element in the list so there is no need to repeat the *have* again.

32. $\boxed{B}$ Parallelism. We need an *-ing* ending to pair up with *remembering.* That leaves us with answers A and D. Answer D is wordy.

33. $\boxed{C}$ *Not only* should be paired with *but also.* That leaves us with C and D. Answer D is not parallel, whereas answer C smoothly uses two adjectives.

34. [D] The first sentence brings up *fairy tale* depictions of castles. The second sentence describes what they're like *in reality*.

35. [C] The sentence leads into *defense* being the main principle. The other answer choices lead to grammatically incorrect sentences.

36. [A] There is no punctuation needed after *such as*.

37. [D] Answers A and B are grammatically incorrect. Answer C is nonsensical because *during* refers to a time. Here, we're discussing a wall.

38. [C] The paragraph's main purpose is to support the point that a castle's design is based on defense. Answer C best supports that point.

39. [C] Sentence 3 should be placed after sentence 4 because it explains how the outer wall was the *next line of defense*. Furthermore, the discussion of archers would then continue nicely into sentence 5. While it may seem like sentence 3 is fine after sentence 2, that placement would make sentence 4 seem misplaced and break up the discussion about archers.

40. [A] *Constitute* means to *make up* or *form*. The other answer choices are nonsensical.

41. [B] Answer A is passive and wordy. Answer C introduces a double-verb, which is nonsensical. Answer D changes the meaning of the sentence to something nonsensical.

42. [B] The first part of the sentence is a nonessential phrase that should be set off by just commas and nothing more. Answer C leads to a long sentence fragment. Answer D results in a double-verb.

43. [D] Answer D is the most concise. The other answer choices are wordy and redundant.

44. [B] We need the plural possessive *their* to refer to the farmers and tradesmen. The correct preposition is *for* to maintain the parallelism (*for his defense than for their protection*).

32

Practice Test 2

35 Minutes—44 Questions

The Lewis and Clark Expedition

In 1803, the western border of the United States of America was the Mississippi River. Then, with one stroke of his pen, **1** President Thomas Jefferson, expanded the young nation's borders west to the Rocky Mountains in what would become known as the Louisiana Purchase. Jefferson **2** manufactured an expedition to explore and map these unknown lands and to seek passage by water to the Pacific Ocean for the purposes of trade and future expansion.

1

A) NO CHANGE
B) President, Thomas Jefferson,
C) President Thomas Jefferson
D) President, Thomas Jefferson

2

A) NO CHANGE
B) fabricated
C) represented
D) commissioned

In May of the following year, thirty-three soldiers led by Meriwether Lewis and William Clark headed west along the Missouri River. Two small rowboats took the lead followed by a fifty-five-foot keel boat that carried most of the supplies and men. Resembling a Viking war ship, **3** the keel boat's twenty-two oars propelled it up the river.

[1] This great adventure brought exciting discoveries and harrowing experiences. [2] Clark **4** reported that it took ten musket balls to bring down the giant grizzly. [3] They recorded over 300 previously unknown animal and plant species, including the mule deer, **5** pronghorn antelopes, and the sea otter. [4] They once encountered a brown bear even more massive than the black bears of the east. **6**

3
A) NO CHANGE
B) the keel boat had twenty-two oars that
C) the twenty-two oars of the keel boat
D) the keel boats' twenty-two oars

4
A) NO CHANGE
B) reported, that
C) reported—that
D) reported that,

5
A) NO CHANGE
B) the pronghorn antelope
C) the pronghorn antelope,
D) a pronghorn antelope,

6
To make this paragraph most logical, sentence 4 should be placed
A) where it is now.
B) after sentence 1.
C) after sentence 2.
D) after sentence 3.

The quiet and intense Lewis was the leader of the expedition, while his co-captain, the red-haired and [7] jovial Clark, was the chief mapmaker. [8] Subsequently, the expedition wound into the Rocky Mountains toward the source of the Missouri, the river grew swift and shallow, and they had to abandon the keel boat, along with some gear. The brutal winters left them tired and with few rations. [9] They might have starved to death had it not been for help from some of the Native Americans they encountered along the way.

Particularly helpful was a young Shoshone woman named Sacajawea, the wife of a French trader named Toussaint Charbonneau. The couple served as interpreters for Lewis and Clark as they encountered new Indian tribes. The sight of Sacajawea with her baby son [10] brought insurance that this group of explorers meant no harm. In the end, the expedition successfully crossed the Rockies and reached the Pacific Ocean. Their maps of previously unknown territories [11] set the stage for future U.S. expansion after their return in the September of 1806.

7

A) NO CHANGE
B) jovial, Clark,
C) jovial Clark
D) jovial Clark—

8

A) NO CHANGE
B) However,
C) As
D) DELETE the underlined portion, and capitalize the start of the sentence.

9

The writer is considering deleting the underlined sentence. Should the writer do this?

A) Yes, because it exaggerates the difficulties faced by Lewis and Clark.
B) Yes, because it blurs the focus of the paragraph with irrelevant details.
C) No, because it reinforces the point that the expedition was largely unsuccessful.
D) No, because it helps set up the main topic of the next paragraph.

10

A) NO CHANGE
B) brings insurance
C) brought assurance
D) brings assurance

11

A) NO CHANGE
B) set up
C) made the preparations
D) got things into shape

The Igbo People of West Africa

The Igbo people constitute one of the largest ethnic groups in Africa, residing mostly in eastern Nigeria. In postcolonial times, they have worked hard to unite themselves culturally and to rebuild and maintain many of their traditions and ethnic **12** deviations.

The Igbo were traditionally an agricultural **13** people who's way of life centered **14** towards the yam. Most meals in some way involved yams, and a man was judged by his yam crop each growing season. Other agricultural products **15** included cassava, coco-yams, and palm wine.

Before the arrival of British colonists in the 1800s, the Igbo dwelled as loosely associated tribes **16** united together by a common language. Each tribe comprised several villages linked by a common market. Each village consisted of a network of family compounds, with houses typically made of mud walls and thatched roofs. One man could have multiple wives, and each wife would have her own dwelling for herself and her children. **17** As a man's stature in the village was judged by the yield of his yam crop, a woman's honor depended on the size and prosperity of her family.

12
A) NO CHANGE
B) discrepancies
C) divisions
D) distinctions

13
A) NO CHANGE
B) people's
C) people whose
D) people whom

14
A) NO CHANGE
B) about
C) on
D) at

15
A) NO CHANGE
B) included,
C) included;
D) included:

16
A) NO CHANGE
B) united
C) united as a group
D) united as one

17
A) NO CHANGE
B) Since
C) Just as
D) Until

18 Christianity has been converted to now by most Igbo people. Their traditional religion was polytheistic. They believed in a creator god but did not relate directly to him, focusing **19** their worship instead on a number of deities associated with nature-related forces like the weather and fertility.   Oracles, priests, and priestesses spoke for the gods and acted as **20** doctors, and these used various concoctions and incantations to address illnesses and other troubles. Many Igbo people today practice a blend of Christianity and traditional rituals.

At the time of colonization, Europeans assumed that African tribes were thoroughly uncivilized. **21** Only after much conflict and negotiation with the Igbo did the colonists begin to understand them. Even ceremonial objects had a role in resolving disputes and of maintaining justice. For example, the fierce-looking masks that now sit in museums as works of art **22** were crafted from padauk wood and painted with milk-based ochre pigment.

18

Which choice most effectively combines the underlined sentences?

A) NO CHANGE

B) While most Igbo people have now converted to Christianity, their traditional religion was polytheistic.

C) Their traditional religion being polytheistic, most Igbo people have now converted to Christianity.

D) Most Igbo people have now converted to Christianity; furthermore, their traditional religion was polytheistic.

19

A) NO CHANGE

B) there

C) they're

D) its

20

A) NO CHANGE

B) doctors, with the use of

C) doctors for using

D) doctors, using

21

Which choice most effectively sets up the information that follows?

A) NO CHANGE

B) They didn't wear shoes and relied on hunting for food.

C) The laws and traditions of the Igbo people, however, bound them together and brought order.

D) Europe had developed an infrastructure that supported clean water and organized government.

22

Which choice provides the most relevant detail?

A) NO CHANGE

B) held an essential function in their society.

C) attract many historians curious about the Igbo.

D) allowed the tribal elders to ask the ancestral spirits for wisdom concerning important issues.

Head Wounds

As a kid, my brother was a magnet for injury. He broke his leg when he was a year old trying to climb off of [23] our parent's bed. When he was two, he tipped a pot of hot water over and burned his arm. When he was three, he [24] spilled an entire carton of milk on the floor. But it was the head wounds that I remember the most.

Our dad is a doctor, so the first time James cracked his head open, Dad didn't seem worried at all. A toddler at the time, [25] the back of James's scalp had been punctured by falling backwards onto a doorstep. Dad calmly applied a gauze compress and then cleaned the wound. He didn't have his stitching kit with him, so he just twirled hairs [26] together. These hairs were on either side of the wound. He tied them together tightly over the cut, putting a tiny dab of superglue just under the knot to hold it in place. [27]

23

A) NO CHANGE
B) our parents'
C) their parents'
D) their parent's

24

Which choice provides the most relevant detail?

A) NO CHANGE
B) learned the counting system and the names of different colors.
C) slept with a night light to fend off imaginary monsters under the bed.
D) stepped on a fallen nest and was swarmed by hornets.

25

A) NO CHANGE
B) James had punctured the back of his scalp
C) a puncture to the back of James's scalp was made
D) James's scalp was punctured in the back

26

Which choice most effectively combines the two sentences at the underlined portion?

A) together so these hairs were
B) together
C) together, being
D) together; those were

27

At this point, the writer is considering adding the following sentence.

The wound healed nicely after just one week.

Should the writer make this addition?

A) Yes, because it provides an important result that concludes the paragraph.
B) Yes, because it gives a sense of how long wounds typically take to heal.
C) No, because it interrupts the discussion of the medical treatment James received.
D) No, because it should be placed earlier in the passage.

The next time it happened, my mom and I were the only ones at home. James was about **28** four, and he and I were riding bikes down the hill in front of our house. He fell off his bike and hit his forehead on a sharp rock. The blood kept coming, running down his face as I got him inside and yelled for our mom. It pooled on the floor next to him as we tried to stanch it with a **29** dishcloth, and it made me almost faint.

We got him to the emergency room, but no one there seemed that worried. Dad showed up, and he wasn't worried either. It turns out that head wounds **30** which tend to bleed a lot due to the high numbers of blood vessels in that part of the body. A high volume of blood actually **31** help sweep contaminants away from the wound, **32** decreasing the risk of infection by 10%. Cuts to the head may look scary, but they usually are **33** no big deal unless they are accompanied by a concussion.

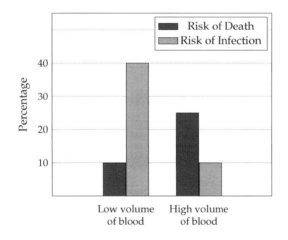

28

A) NO CHANGE
B) four; and
C) four,
D) four as

29

A) NO CHANGE
B) dishcloth, almost fainting.
C) dishcloth—I almost fainted.
D) dishcloth, I almost fainted.

30

A) NO CHANGE
B) that
C) are
D) DELETE the underlined portion.

31

A) NO CHANGE
B) helps
C) helping
D) helped

32

Which choice offers the most accurate interpretation of the data in the chart?

A) NO CHANGE
B) reducing the risk of death by 25%.
C) reducing the risk of infection by 30%.
D) decreasing the risk of death but increasing the risk of infection.

33

A) NO CHANGE
B) not serious
C) trifling matters
D) things of no importance

Nero: Monster or Visionary?

Of all the Roman emperors, none calls forth more disapproval and disgust in the popular mind than Nero. His legendary status as a moral monster [34] bears no resemblance in the history of western civilization. A lunatic who burned Rome to make room for his palaces and a tyrannical persecutor of Christians, [35] for whom he blamed for the fiery disaster, he is known as a bloodthirsty murderer of his mother, wife, and brother. But how much is true, how much is exaggerated, and how much is pure myth?

In recent years, a number of archaeologists, cultural historians, and politicians [36] have sought to rehabilitate Nero's image. The September 2014 issue of *National Geographic* presents a fresh picture of this maligned monarch, [37] and his violent acts take a back seat to his architectural accomplishments, his artistic patronage, and his popular appeal. While it remains true that he did, [38] in other words, murder several family members, including his wife and mother, and that he did oversee the martyrdom of many Christians, he also presided over a cultural renaissance that promoted Greek values throughout Rome. [39]

34

A) NO CHANGE
B) cannot be found an equal
C) is unparalleled
D) is duplicated by nothing

35

A) NO CHANGE
B) who's
C) who he
D) whom he

36

A) NO CHANGE
B) has sought
C) seek
D) seeking

37

A) NO CHANGE
B) which
C) one in which
D) DELETE the underlined portion.

38

A) NO CHANGE
B) however,
C) for example,
D) indeed,

39

At this point, the writer is considering adding the following sentence.

Greece was once the cultural center of the world before the rise of Rome.

Should the writer make this addition here?

A) Yes, because it explains why Nero might have wanted to promote Greek values.
B) Yes, because it reinforces the point that Greek culture was very influential.
C) No, because it blurs the paragraph's main focus with a loosely related detail.
D) No, because it fails to indicate how Rome overcame Greece.

A poet and an artist, Nero established the Neronia, an exposition of poetry, art, and athletic games. **40** Nevertheless, his rule produced some of the most awe-inspiring architectural feats in the history of Rome. He built a sprawling **41** palace, the Domus Aurea, full of hundreds of lavishly decorated rooms with vaulted ceilings. The grounds included an art gallery, a bathhouse, an amphitheater, and **42** even had a man-made lake for boating.

43 Estimates say the construction of these buildings took over 10 years. It's impossible to know for sure; historians can only say that he took advantage of the fire's devastation to put something magnificent in its place. There is no evidence that he played fiddle as the city burned. In the end, Nero may have been no more bloodthirsty than many of the other emperors. Many of them were notorious for their **44** poor decision making and unstable personalities.

40
A) NO CHANGE
B) More notably,
C) Either way,
D) In contrast,

41
A) NO CHANGE
B) palace the Domus Aurea,
C) palace, the Domus Aurea
D) palace the Domus Aurea

42
A) NO CHANGE
B) featured
C) came with
D) DELETE the underlined portion.

43
Which choice provides the most appropriate introduction to the passage?
A) NO CHANGE
B) Did Nero burn the city down in order to install these new buildings?
C) Some believe that Nero used force to restrict the public's access to these attractions.
D) How long did Nero's grand creations last?

44
Which choice best supports the statement made in the previous sentence?
A) NO CHANGE
B) lavish meals and taste for fine wine.
C) ruthless purges of political rivals, religious minorities, and dissidents.
D) arrogance and self-absorption.

Answers to Practice Test 2

Score your test using the Score Calculator at thecollegepanda.com

1. $\boxed{C}$ There is no need for commas because *Thomas Jefferson* is a restrictive element that specifies which President. There is also no need to put a comma after the phrase because that would then incorrectly separate the subject from the verb.

2. $\boxed{D}$ *Commission* means to order or authorize something.

3. $\boxed{B}$ Modifier error. What resembles a Viking war ship? The keel boat. Not the keel boat's oars.

4. $\boxed{A}$ In almost all cases, there is no need to put punctuation around *that*.

5. $\boxed{C}$ Parallelism. Every element in the list starts off with *the* followed by the singular word for the animal.

6. $\boxed{B}$ Sentence 4 describes an encounter with a brown bear. Sentence 2 discusses how Clark shot it. Therefore, sentence 4 belongs after sentence 1.

7. $\boxed{A}$ *Jovial* is an adjective that doesn't need any punctuation after it to describe *Clark*. However, *the red-haired and jovial Clark* is a nonessential phrase that DOES need to be separated off by commas.

8. $\boxed{C}$ The wrong answer choices lead to run-ons. Furthermore, *as* is the only one that results in a logical sentence.

9. $\boxed{D}$ The next paragraph talks about *Sacajawea*. The given sentence is a perfect transition to that topic.

10. $\boxed{C}$ *Assurance*, which means certainty and confidence, is the right word here. *Insurance* means protection against something.

11. $\boxed{A}$ *Set the stage* is the correct idiomatic phrase here. It's the most natural sounding.

12. $\boxed{D}$ *Distinctions*, which refers to the important or unique qualities of something, is the correct word here.

13. $\boxed{C}$ The contraction *who's* means *who is*. We want the possessive *whose*.

14. $\boxed{C}$ The correct idiom is *on*.

15. $\boxed{A}$ There is no punctuation needed after the verb *included*.

16. $\boxed{B}$ The wrong answer choices are all redundant.

17. $\boxed{C}$ The sentence draws a similarity between a man's stature and a woman's honor. The correct word here is *just as*.

18. $\boxed{B}$ The two sentences contrast with each other. The use of the word *while* in answer B best expresses that contrast.

19. $\boxed{A}$ We want the plural possessive *their*, which refers to the Igbo people.

20. ☐D Answer D is the most concise and doesn't change the intended meaning like answer C does.

21. ☐C The following sentence talks about *resolving disputes and maintaining justice* within the Igbo community. Furthermore, the word *even* in the phrase *even ceremonial objects...* implies that the sentence in question should support the following one. Only answer C accomplishes that.

22. ☐D Answer B is too vague. Answer D is the one most relevant to the idea of *resolving disputes and maintaining order* in the previous sentences.

23. ☐B *Parents* is plural so we need the apostrophe after the *s*.

24. ☐D The brother was a *magnet for injury*. Answer D is the only one that involves an injury.

25. ☐B Modifier error. *James* needs to be next to the modifier at the start of the sentence.

26. ☐B Answer B is the most concise. Answers A and D use unnecessary pronouns. Answer C is awkward.

27. ☐A The given sentence tells the reader what eventually happened after the accident.

28. ☐A Use the comma and conjunction *and* to connect two independent clauses.

29. ☐C Answer A is wordy and passive. Answer D is a run-on. Answer C is active and best expresses the dramatic feeling being described.

30. ☐D Answers A and B result in sentence fragments. Answer C leads to an ungrammatical double-verb.

31. ☐B The singular subject, *a high volume*, requires the singular verb *helps*.

32. ☐C For a low volume of blood, the risk of infection is 40%. For a high volume, it's 10%. The risk of infection is decreased by 30%.

33. ☐B Answer B best maintains the tone and style of the passage. Answers A and D are too informal. Answer C uses inflated language.

34. ☐C The wrong answer choices are wordy and unnatural.

35. ☐D We don't need the *for* in front of *whom*. For example, you wouldn't say, *I blame for them*. You would just say, *I blame them*. Only use the preposition if you would normally do so when the sentence is restructured. For example, *I asked for the employees*, and *the employees for whom I asked*.

36. ☐A The plural subject, *a number*, requires the plural verb *have*. Answer C is wrong because the tense of the sentence isn't in the present.

37. ☐C The way you should read this is *a fresh picture in which his violent acts....* The other answer choices lead to run-ons or sentence fragments.

38. ☐D The writer is making a concession here by reinforcing the fact that Nero murdered family members. The correction transition word to express that is *indeed*.

39. ☐C The focus of the paragraph is Nero, not Greece.

40. $\boxed{B}$ The sentence continues to present a positive view of Nero, building off of the previous sentence.

41. $\boxed{A}$ The phrase *the Domus Aurea* is a nonessential phrase that should be set off by commas.

42. $\boxed{D}$ Parallelism. Article-noun, article-noun, article-noun,...

43. $\boxed{B}$ The following sentence discusses *the fire's devastation*. Answer B poses the relevant introductory question.

44. $\boxed{C}$ The previous sentence makes a point about *bloodthirsty* emperors. Answer C is the only one that supports that point.

33

Practice Test 3

35 Minutes—44 Questions

The Bloody Jungle of the Belgian Congo

In 1890, a young writer named Joseph Conrad took a job on a steamship in the Belgian **1** Congo; a European colony in central Africa. In Europe, he had heard of all the wonderful work that was happening there. King Leopold II of Belgium had won the admiration of many in Europe and America for his descriptions of his colony. **2**

1

A) NO CHANGE
B) Congo
C) Congo,
D) Congo, and

2

Which choice most logically follows the previous sentence?

A) Due to his popularity, he had the longest reign of any Belgian monarch.
B) In 1893, he oversaw the first revision of the Belgian constitution, which introduced universal male suffrage.
C) He maintained Belgium's neutrality in times of war by building a strong military defense.
D) He had spoken eloquently of philanthropy, free trade, scientific exploration, and the end of the Arab slave trade in central Africa.

But what Conrad **3** found—immortalized in his short novel *Heart of Darkness*, could in no way be reconciled with the grandiose descriptions of progress **4** toward civilization in what Europeans perceived as an uncivilized part of the world. The novel describes a devastated landscape and an over-worked and underfed African labor force that had essentially been conquered and enslaved. Violent atrocities had become the **5** norm, being all for the sake of ivory and rubber. They were the result of greed and ruthlessness on a massive scale, enabled by European attitudes of racial superiority and abetted by zealous men and women **6** whose belief that colonization would bring a higher quality of life to Africans.

By the time *Heart of Darkness* was published in 1902, a movement was already underway to expose the the large-scale theft and murder occurring in the Congo. **7** Dozens of missionaries had begun sending reports, including photographs, to bear witness to the violence. William Sheppard, an African-American Presbyterian, was one of these missionaries. He sent out shocking testimony of lands being seized by force, of people living under a reign of terror, and **8** soldiers who cut off the hands of women and children.

3
A) NO CHANGE
B) found,
C) found;
D) found:

4
A) NO CHANGE
B) in
C) on
D) forward

5
A) NO CHANGE
B) norm; all
C) norm, all
D) norm, all of this

6
A) NO CHANGE
B) whom believed
C) who believed
D) who's belief

7
The writer is considering deleting the previous sentence. Should the writer make this change?
A) Yes, because it does not take into account the crime happening outside the Congo.
B) Yes, because it repeats information found elsewhere in the passage.
C) No, because it provides a logical introduction to the paragraph.
D) No, because it reinforces how influential Conrad's novel was.

8
A) NO CHANGE
B) of soldiers cutting
C) soldiers cutting
D) the fact that soldiers cut

An Englishman named E.D. Morel gathered the many reports and photographs and [9] published them. He drew crowds to listen to eyewitness accounts of colonial atrocities. He lobbied the British Parliament to denounce the Belgian king's [10] horrifying, even terrifying, practices. This became the first modern humanitarian movement, [11] and they successfully exposed the horrendous violence in the Congo. However, historians estimate that, by that time, between 10 million and 20 million Congolese people had lost their lives.

9

A) NO CHANGE
B) published it.
C) publish them.
D) to publish them.

10

A) NO CHANGE
B) horrifying
C) horrifying, plus terrifying,
D) horrifying and terrifying

11

A) NO CHANGE
B) and it
C) by
D) DELETE the underlined portion.

The Disappearing Panda

The adorable Giant Panda is the rarest breed of bears in the world. With a diet consisting mostly of bamboo trees and a home high in the western mountains of China, these bears **12** <u>don't bother anyone.</u> They don't have any natural predators, so why are they disappearing from the face of the Earth?

Extinction is a natural process that happens over the course of hundreds of thousands of years, sometimes millions of years. **13** The rapid decline in the panda population is evidence that the two main causes are hunting and habitat loss. Only a few pandas **14** <u>fall down</u> to poachers each year, but many are accidentally killed by hunters of other animals. Furthermore, human developments increasingly invade their **15** <u>forests,</u> the natural habitat of the panda gets smaller and smaller, as does the supply of bamboo.

12

Which choice best maintains the style and tone established in the passage?

A) NO CHANGE
B) aren't annoying at all.
C) are harmless.
D) keep it to themselves.

13

The writer is considering deleting the previous sentence. Should this sentence be kept or deleted?

A) Kept, because it helps provide a contrast that supports a later point.
B) Kept, because it clarifies a term that may confuse readers.
C) Deleted, because it is not relevant to the topic of the paragraph.
D) Deleted, because it does not answer the question posed in the preceding paragraph.

14

A) NO CHANGE
B) fall over
C) fall in
D) fall victim

15

A) NO CHANGE
B) forests, but
C) forests, and so
D) forests

The good news is that [16] humans are now working very hard to protect the panda bear and [17] their home in the magnificent forests of the Yangtze Basin. After all, pandas are an important part of these areas. As they forage for food, they spread the seeds of the vegetation, [18] thereby encouraging the forest's continued growth. [19]

They are also an important part of the economy. As the national symbol of China and one of the most unique bears in the world, the panda, as well as its habitat, [20] draw millions of ecotourists to the area every year. But, this activity is also part of the problem. With the increased traffic, more roads and railways are needed, which slices up the beautiful forests, preventing the bears from finding suitable mates.

16

Which choice is most relevant to the information in this sentence?

A) NO CHANGE
B) nature lovers
C) tree huggers
D) conservationists

17

A) NO CHANGE
B) it's
C) its
D) they're

18

A) NO CHANGE
B) which then
C) to
D) and

19

At this point, the writer is considering adding the following sentence.

This area also supports multi-colored pheasants, dwarf blue sheep, and golden monkeys, which are also facing extinction.

Should the writer make this addition here?

A) Yes, because it supports the point that the panda's habitat should be protected.
B) Yes, because it provides specific examples of endangered animals.
C) No, because it distracts from the focus of the paragraph.
D) No, because it gives examples of animals that do not pose a threat to pandas.

20

A) NO CHANGE
B) draws
C) drew
D) drawing

The bears **21** isolated from each other often die without reproducing. Zoologists have had some success with mating bears in captivity, but the real answer is controlling development in its habitat so that the panda bear can live and breed as nature intended. **22** At any moment now, the Giant Panda bear could be extinct in as little as three generations.

21

A) NO CHANGE
B) bears, isolated from each other,
C) bears; isolated from each other,
D) bears isolated from each other,

22

A) As a result,
B) In particular,
C) Admittedly,
D) As it stands now,

Dubai

The city of Dubai, located on the southeast coast of Persian Gulf in the United Arab Emirates, has **23** turned up as one of the globally prominent cities in the world and heavily influences significant issues **24** important in the Arab world. **25** Regarded as the Las Vegas of the Middle East, the city brings in tourists looking for fun, cultural attractions, and luxury.

Dubai's economy **26** flew into the sky with the discovery of oil, which has brought in higher and higher revenues since 1960. This continued boom has fostered the growth of businesses, skyscrapers, roads, and parks. Recently, however, oil reserves have been depleting rapidly; thus, there has been **27** a development of an interest in other areas such as tourism, real estate, financial services, and airlines.

23
A) NO CHANGE
B) emerged
C) unfolded
D) appeared

24
A) NO CHANGE
B) that have impact
C) of great consequence
D) OMIT the underlined portion.

25
The writer is considering deleting the underlined portion (capitalizing the start of the sentence). Should the writer make this deletion?

A) Yes, because it offers irrelevant background information.
B) Yes, because it does not clarify where Dubai is located.
C) No, because it provides a comparison that describes Dubai in a frame of reference that may be more familiar to readers.
D) No, because it supports the point that the West has greatly influenced the city of Dubai.

26
Which choice best maintains the tone established in the passage?
A) NO CHANGE
B) ran wild
C) took off
D) went crazy

27
A) NO CHANGE
B) an interest in developing
C) an interesting developing of
D) an interested development of

Retail has become one the prime strategies of the government to ensure a constant flow of cash into the emirates. With more than 70 shopping centers, [28] the biggest source of local jobs, the city has made retail shopping the biggest attraction to tourists. Luxury brands and local [29] boutiques eager to capitalize on the demand, have opened multiple locations that feature the very latest offerings. Among the most popular items to shop [30] for are designer handbags, jewelry, and shoes.

Another main attraction is the architecture. Architectural innovation and a boom in the construction industry has enabled Dubai to build some of the tallest buildings in the world. The greatest display of the city's technological capability is the Burj Khalifa, or the Khalifa Tower. The tower reflects an Islamic style of architecture and [31] accounts for being the tallest building of the world.

[28]

Which choice results in a sentence that best supports the point developed in this paragraph?

A) NO CHANGE
B) many of which I've bought souvenirs from,
C) which are a great way to get out of the heat,
D) hundreds of stalls and stores at each one,

[29]

A) NO CHANGE
B) boutiques,
C) boutiques that are
D) boutiques which,

[30]

A) NO CHANGE
B) for are:
C) are for
D) are for,

[31]

A) NO CHANGE
B) stands as
C) rises to be
D) measures for

One of the most recent endeavours is the city's Miracle Garden, which covers more than 72,000 square meters. The garden holds 45 million flowers and employs [32] technology to reuse water through the means of drip irrigation.

The airline industry has also surfaced as a fast growing sector. Airlines such as Emirates and Flydubai offer a variety of flights to thousands of passengers every day, and their offerings continue to expand. [33] Given how the city has grown so quickly, it will be exciting to see what the city looks like in a few years.

32

A) NO CHANGE
B) drip irrigation technology to reuse water.
C) reusable water by technology in drip irrigation.
D) drip irrigation to reuse water by technology.

33

At this point, the writer wants to further reinforce the paragraph's claim about the rise of Dubai's airline industry. Which choice most effectively accomplishes this goal?

A) Authentic Middle Eastern meals including falafel and tabouli are served on most flights.
B) Airline employees have lobbied the government for increases in pay and benefits.
C) The International Airport in Dubai is now the fifth busiest airport in the world.
D) Pilots who are trained in Dubai are some of the best in the world.

Sushi

An ancient emperor once enjoyed a special dessert so much that he kept it a royal secret until Marco Polo, who was the first European to record his travels in [34] China and took the dessert to Italy. That delicious dessert was ice cream. This fact may come as a surprise since [35] many people think Chinese food tends to be associated with chop suey rather than [36] the creators of the ice cream. What's ironic is that chop suey didn't even originate in China, but in Chinese restaurants in America that wanted to cater to Western tastes.

Just as ice cream was invented in one place before its rise in popularity elsewhere, the sushi that Japan is famous for was first created in Southeast Asia and then spread to Southern China before it was introduced in Japan. The original type of sushi, called "nigiri," is typically made by hand. The cook takes a small amount of vinegared rice and presses [37] these into a round shape. Sliced raw fish is then placed on top. [38] Tuna is the most widely used fish for sushi among the Japanese, but other kinds of seafood—salmon, lobster, eel, octopus, and squid—are also much appreciated. Despite sushi's [39] simplicity, but it usually takes more than a year to learn how to make sushi with the proper technique.

34

A) NO CHANGE
B) China, took
C) China, taking
D) China, and had taken

35

A) NO CHANGE
B) the common misconception is that
C) it's widely known that
D) OMIT the underlined portion.

36

A) NO CHANGE
B) making ice cream.
C) the invention of ice cream.
D) ice cream.

37

A) NO CHANGE
B) them
C) it
D) OMIT the underlined portion.

38

At this point, the writer is considering adding the following sentence.

Raw fish is an acquired taste and may take a while to get used to.

Should the writer make this addition here?

A) Yes, because it explains why not all people enjoy sushi.
B) Yes, because it encourages readers to keep eating sushi.
C) No, because the focus of paragraph is more about making sushi than eating it.
D) No, because it contradicts sushi's popularity, which is mentioned previously in the essay.

39

A) NO CHANGE
B) simplicity,
C) simplicity, and
D) simplicity in that

In Japan, there are several different types of sushi restaurants competing with each other. Of course, there's the convenient take-out sushi available at most fast food places. Then there are the sushi bar restaurants where diners are served by a chef at the bar or a waiter at a table. *Kaiten* sushi refers to a restaurant in which a revolving conveyer **40** belt that goes round and round, allows a customer to select **41** their own food. There are even restaurants that house large fish tanks where tourists can fish for their soon-to-be meals. The prices of sushi **42** is different depending on the quality of the fish and the experience of the restaurant. For example, **43** salmon may cost $5 per piece at a sushi bar but only $4 per piece at a kaiten sushi restaurant. Some higher-end establishments charge as much as $250 for a set menu consisting of multiple courses. But regardless of the price, eating sushi at a local Japanese restaurant will always be a more illuminating experience than **44** the food at the hotel.

Sushi prices

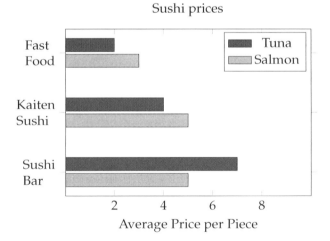

Average Price per Piece

40
A) NO CHANGE
B) belt allows
C) belt, allows
D) belt that spins allows

41
A) NO CHANGE
B) there
C) our
D) his or her

42
A) NO CHANGE
B) are
C) were
D) had been

43
Which choice most accurately and effectively represents the information in the graph?
A) NO CHANGE
B) tuna may be $2 a piece at a fast food stall but $5 at a kaiten sushi restaurant.
C) a piece of salmon may cost $2 at a fast food stall but $5 at a sushi bar.
D) a piece of tuna may be $4 at a kaiten sushi restaurant but $7 at a sushi bar.

44
A) NO CHANGE
B) the restaurant at
C) eating at
D) OMIT the underlined portion.

Answers to Practice Test 3

Score your test using the Score Calculator at thecollegepanda.com

1. $\boxed{C}$ The phrase *a European colony...* is a nonessential phrase that should be set off by a comma.

2. $\boxed{D}$ Given the previous sentence, the one in question should elaborate on his *descriptions of his colony.* Answer D is the one that does that.

3. $\boxed{B}$ The phrase *immortalized in his short novel Heart of Darkness* is nonessential and should be separated off by commas.

4. $\boxed{A}$ *Toward* is the correct idiom here, just like you would work *towards* something.

5. $\boxed{C}$ Answer B uses a semicolon when what's being connected aren't two independent clauses. Answer D uses the unnecessary pronoun *this.* Answer A is awkward. Answer C is the most concise.

6. $\boxed{C}$ Answer A results in an incomplete thought. Answer D has the same problem and uses an incorrect contraction. Answer B uses *whom,* which is incorrect because it doesn't follow a preposition. The answer is C, which results in a complete sentence.

7. $\boxed{C}$ The given sentence makes for a great topic sentence by introducing the *movement* that's further discussed in the paragraph.

8. $\boxed{B}$ Parallelism. *Of lands being, of people living, of soldiers cutting.*

9. $\boxed{A}$ Past tense. The plural pronoun *them* refers to *the many reports and photographs.*

10. $\boxed{B}$ *Horrifying* means the same thing as *terrifying* so there is no need to use both words.

11. $\boxed{B}$ The singular noun *movement* requires the singular pronoun *it.*

12. $\boxed{C}$ The wrong answer choices are too informal.

13. $\boxed{A}$ The slow process of extinction should be placed side by side with the rapid decline of the panda to make the narrator's point that there must be human factors at play: hunting and habitat loss.

14. $\boxed{D}$ The narrator would like to say that pandas die from poachers who hunt them, meaning pandas *fall victim* to poachers.

15. $\boxed{C}$ The run-on needs to be corrected with the correct conjunction: *and* followed by *so* to signal cause and effect.

16. $\boxed{D}$ *Conservationists* is the most specific word and fits perfectly within the context of protecting nature and animals.

17. $\boxed{C}$ The singular noun *the panda bear* needs to be referred to by the singular pronoun *its.*

18. $\boxed{A}$ *Thereby* means *as a result.* The other answer choices result in ungrammatical sentences.

19. $\boxed{C}$ The focus of the paragraph is the panda, not other animals.

20. $\boxed{B}$ The subject *the panda* is singular so we need the singular verb *draws*. Don't be fooled by the comma phrase *as well as its habitat*. It is separated off by commas and does not count towards the subject.

21. $\boxed{B}$ The phrase *isolated from each other* is a nonessential phrase that should be set off by a pair of commas.

22. $\boxed{D}$ *As it stands now* is a phrase that means *in the current situation*. The other choices are illogical.

23. $\boxed{B}$ No easy explanation. Answer B is the one that most naturally fits.

24. $\boxed{D}$ The incorrect answer choices are repetitive because the sentence already mentions that the issues were *significant*.

25. $\boxed{C}$ The phrase compares *Dubai* with *Las Vegas* to help the reader understand Dubai as a city in the context of the Middle East.

26. $\boxed{C}$ The incorrect choices are too informal.

27. $\boxed{B}$ Answer B is the most natural phrasing. Answer D, for example, makes it sound like *development* is *interested* in something, as if *development* were a person.

28. $\boxed{D}$ The paragraph emphasizes how big shopping is in Dubai. The choice that supports that point is D.

29. $\boxed{B}$ A comma is necessary to pair up with the comma later on in the sentence. Answer D produces a sentence fragment (remove the nonessential phrase starting with *eager* to see this more clearly).

30. $\boxed{A}$ *Shop for* is the idiomatic phrase—you shop **for** something. That's why the *for* should come before *are*. No colon is necessary after the main verb. Remember that a colon must be preceded by an independent clause.

31. $\boxed{B}$ Answer B is the most natural phrasing.

32. $\boxed{B}$ The incorrect answer choices are too wordy. The phrase *by technology* is especially awkward.

33. $\boxed{C}$ The paragraph mentions how Dubai's airline industry is a *fast growing sector*. Answer C, which states just how busy Dubai's airport is, best supports the paragraph's main point.

34. $\boxed{B}$ The *who* clause after *Marco Polo* must be set off by a pair of commas. What remains must still be a sentence.

35. $\boxed{D}$ The incorrect answer choices are redundant.

36. $\boxed{D}$ The comparison must make sense: **chop suey** *rather than* **ice cream**. Compare food with food.

37. $\boxed{C}$ Because *vinegared rice* is a singular noun, we need a singular pronoun to refer to it.

38. $\boxed{C}$ Nowhere in the paragraph is eating sushi ever brought up.

39. $\boxed{B}$ We're not connecting two independent clauses so there is no need for a conjunction. Answer D produces a long sentence fragment.

40. $\boxed{B}$ Answers A and D have redundant words since the belt is already described as a *revolving* one. Answer C has an unnecessary comma—don't separate the subject (*belt*) and verb (*allows*) of a clause with a comma.

41. $\boxed{D}$ The pronoun must refer to the singular noun *customer*. Remember that *his or her* is a singular pronoun.

42. $\boxed{B}$ The plural subject *prices* must be paired with the plural verb *are*. Furthermore, the sentence is in the present tense.

43. $\boxed{D}$ The prices of tuna are represented by the darker bars. At a kaiten sushi restaurant, the price per piece of tuna is $4. At a sushi bar, the price is $7. This makes answer D correct. The other answer choices do not accurately reflect the graph.

44. $\boxed{C}$ Answers A, B, and D create faulty comparisons. *Eating sushi* (an activity) should not be compared with *food* (not an activity), nor should it be compared with *the hotel* or *the restaurant at the hotel* (both places, not activities). Instead, *eating sushi at a local Japanese restaurant* should be compared with *eating at the hotel*. Note the parallelism.

Thank You!

Thank you for purchasing and reading this book. If you enjoyed it, I ask that you please leave a review on amazon. It really helps support my work.

If you haven't already, make sure to sign up for The College Panda newsletter at https://thecollegepanda.com

You'll also receive exclusive tips, updates, college admissions advice, inspirational stories, and resources that go far beyond the useless College Board information packets. This information is not found on the blog or anywhere else.

Don't miss out on tips that could make the difference on the SAT and in college admissions. Sign up now.

Made in the USA
Middletown, DE
09 July 2019